The Rambam and the Rav on the 54 Portions of the Torah

An Analysis of the Writings of Rabbi Moshe ben Maimon (Maimonides) and Rabbi Joseph B. Soloveitchik (the Rav) on the 54 Portions of the Torah

by Rabbi Richard Borah

In memory of my parents Harry and Judith Borah zt'l

With thanks & appreciation to my wife Andrea for her support and encouragement.

In Honor & appreciation to my Rebbeim who have given me the Torah – life's most precious gift.

With appreciation to Caryn Liebman for her assistance.

Your words were found and I ate them; and Your word was to me the joy and rejoicing of my heart, for I am called by Your Name. (Yermiyahu 15:16)

Table of Contents

Sefer Bereisheit

Sefer Shemot

Vayikra

Bamidbar

Devarim

Introduction

Maimonides ("the Rambam") and Rabbi Joseph B. Soloveitchik ("the Rav") are widely acknowledged as scholars of the highest level who have profoundly impacted the Jewish communities of their generations. Maimonides' 3 major works- his Commentary on the Mishneh, the Mishneh Torah and the Guide for the Perplexed (*Moreh Nevukim*)-are still at the heart of Jewish learning and remain fresh and vital in providing insights and challenges to those who learn them with determination and intensity. Rabbi Soloveitchik has had a profound impact on contemporary Orthodox Judaism by combining an unparalleled mastery of the Talmud and Jewish law with deep philosophical insights on the broadest range of topics. Although the Rav did not publish widely in his lifetime, what he did print has become central to the Orthodox communities' quest to understand Orthodoxy in a manner that is in absolute compliance with the authentic Jewish tradition, but which also addresses and analyzes contemporary positions in areas including science, philosophy and psychology. Since his passing in 1993, much of his vast trove of writings have been published through Yeshiva University and his students, many who themselves are now among the Jewish community's leading scholars. Neither the Rambam nor the Rav wrote a commentary on the Torah. But in what both have communicated in their writings they have commented widely on the Chumash and the events and ideas contained within in. The objective of the current volume is to provide the reader with easier access to these writings as they relate to each of the 54 Torah portions. I have provided brief analyses of some of their statements and, on occasion, compared the differing perspective of the Rambam and the Rav on a particular issue. But in most cases, although there is a statement or statements by the Rambam and the Rav on each of the Torah *parshiot*, they are not always statements relating the same issue in a particular *parsha.*

The intellectual relationship of the Rav with the Rambam is a rich and complex one. In general, there is no greater modern commentator than the Rav on the Rambam's scholarship, in both the halakhic and philosophical areas. The awe and reverence with which the Rav held the Rambam is profound and undeniable. But, as is proper with true Torah scholars, the Rav did not refrain from expressing his disagreement with the Rambam in many important areas. These differences are quite apparent in the Rav's early works, such as Halakhic Man as well as in many of the Rav's writings which have emerged in the years since his death. Much of these differences center around the Rav rejection of the Rambam's rationalism which is expressed in its purest form in the Guide for the Perplexed. In the Rav's recently published text "From There You Shall Seek", he clarifies his own position that knowledge can have its source in a broader spectrum of human experience. This, the Rav explains, is in contrast to Maimonides position that knowledge is acquired through the rational mind alone. However this discussion and the distinction between the position of the Rambam and the Rav in this area require their own thorough analyses so as not to be overly simplified or completely misunderstood. A certain amount of contemporary scholarship has been devoted to understanding and clarifying these differences. This is not the purpose of the current text, although in some of the 54 essays presented, these differing philosophical underpinnings between the Rambam and the Rav have been briefly addressed.

BEREISHEIT

IN THE BEGINNING OF GOD'S CREATING THE HEAVENS AND THE EARTH. (BEREISHEIT 1:1)

BEREISHEIT

Adam and Chava-Before and After the Sin

Maimonides (the Rambam) and Rabbi Joseph B. Soloveitchik's (the Rav's) comment on the creation and development of Adam and Chava and the sin of eating from the Tree of Knowledge (Beresheit 1:27). The Rambam in his philosophy text, "The Guide for the Perplexed", responds to an inquiry from "the objector" as to how man could have been punished for disobedience with regard to eating from the Tree of Knowledge. The Rambam states:

It would at first sight," said the objector, " appear from Scripture that man was originally intended to be perfectly equal to the rest of the animal creation, which is not endowed with intellect, reason, or power or distinguishing between good and evil; but that Adam's disobedience to the command of God procured him that great perfection which is the peculiarity of man, viz., the power of distinguishing between good and evil-the noblest of all faculties of our nature, the essential characteristic of the human race. It thus appears strange that the punishment for rebelliousness should be the means of elevating man to a pinnacle of perfection to which he had not attained previously. This is equivalent to saying that a certain man was rebellious and extremely wicked, wherefore his nature was changed for the better, and he was made to shine as a star in the heavens.

The Rambam rejects this idea that man was some type of primitive child-like being before the sin and that the sin endowed him and Chava with intellect and the ability to choose between good and evil. This capacity, the Rambam explains, was endowed to man with his initial creation by God through his being made "in His (God's) own image". The Rambam continues:

With reference to this gift the Bible states that "man was created in the form and likeness of God." On account of this gift of intellect man was addressed by God, and received His commandments, as it is said: "And the Lord God commanded Adam" (Gen. 2:16)- for no commandments are given to the brute creation or to those who are devoid of understanding. Through the intellect man distinguishes between the true and the false. This faculty Adam possessed perfectly and completely. "

The Rambam continues by describing a different faculty from that of the intellect which "distinguishes between the true and the false." This distinct faculty distinguishes instead between the "right and wrong". He states:

"The right and the wrong are terms employed in the science of apparent truths (morals) not in that of necessary truths, as, e.g., it is not correct to say, in reference to the proposition "the heavens are spherical" it is "good" or to declare the assertion that "the earth is flat" to be "bad"; but we say of the one it

is true, of the other it is false. Similarly, our (Hebrew) language expresses the idea of true and false by the terms *emet* and *sheker,* (and) of the morally right and the morally wrong, by *tov* and *ra.* Thus it is the function of the intellect - to discriminate between the true and the false-a distinction which is applicable to all objects of intellectual perception. When Adam was yet in a state of innocence (before the sin), and was guided solely by reflection and reason - on account of which it is said: "Thus has made him (man) a little lower than the angels" (Psalm 8:6), he was not at all able to follow or to understand the principles of apparent truths; the most manifest impropriety, viz., to appear in a state of nudity, was nothing unbecoming according to his idea. He could not comprehend why it should be so. After man's disobedience however, when he began to give way to desires which had their source in his imagination and to the gratification of his bodily appetites, as it is said, "And the wife saw that the tree was good for food and delightful to the eyes" (Gen, 3:6), he was punished by the loss of part of that intellectual faculty which he had previously possessed. He therefore transgressed a command with which he had been charged on the score of his reason; and having obtained knowledge of the apparent truths, he was wholly absorbed in the study of what is proper and what is improper." (Guide: Book 1, Chapter 11 –Page 14-15-Friedlander translation)

The Rambam is explaining that man, before his punishment for eating from the Tree of Knowledge of Good and Evil, possessed an intellect which viewed things as "true or false" but not as "proper or improper". Man's thought processes were more objective and of greater clarity in the "pre-sin" period. After the sin, concern for what was "proper or improper" became part of man's thought process, he sensed the impropriety of his nakedness, and his ability to discern truth and falsehood were impeded by this additional dimension of his personality. Therefore, the Rambam explains, man's punishment makes sense as it is a diminishment of his clarity of mind, and his sin makes sense, as he was, from the beginning of his existence, a person of intelligence with the capacity to choose and was therefore, culpable for his choices.

The Rav provides very different approach to these events in his essay "Family Redeemed". Man, according to the Rav, actually seems to progress, transforming into a higher being through the awakening of his imagination and his confrontation with God's command to restrain from partaking of the forbidden tree. At first man, although endowed with the *tzelem Elokim* (image of God) lacks reflection and a sense of individual personality. The Rav states:

"In the first chapter of Genesis, the Torah tells us about creation of male and female…Man as he emerges on that mysterious Friday at the end of the

first chapter, is not an outsider to the cosmos, not alien to nature; he is not a foreigner and intruder. Man is a child of Mother Nature, as is the brute and the beast. The narratives about the creation of plant (Gen: 1:11-12), animal (1:20-26) and man (1:27) are almost identical; all three take account of the common origin of life, namely the earth. Death is the common destiny of all three exponents of living matter that emerged out of Mother Earth, founded upon the affinity of the biological occurrences in man, animal and plant.... Of course there is a distinctive element in man, the *Imago Dei*, the *tzelem Elokim*, the image of God. Judaism considered the *imago* element to be not a gratuitous grant bestowed upon man but rather a challenge to be met by man; not as an endowment fashioned by God but rather as a mission to be implemented, as a *hyle,* a formless matter to be molded by man. Perhaps the central norm in our ethical system is related to *Imago Dei*, to be like God, reflect His image, become a Divine being, live like a creature who bears resemblance to its Maker. It is up to man to either realize or shake off the *Imago Dei.*"

The Rav continues to describe the process of man and woman's development from a being that lives in harmony with the natural world to one that becomes a reflective and unique personality which is outside of nature. This is described as a step forward in human development. The Rav states:

Man and woman make their entry into the universe as natural cosmic beings. They are endowed with talent and exceptional ability. However, man and woman of whom chapter one speaks, have not made as yet the momentous decision to turn a non-reflective, instinctive existence into a self-conscious one… The question that then arises is: Where is the critical boundary to be found, the line which separates cosmic man from persona, natural uniformity from existential complexity, a non-reflective life from a meditative existence? At which point did Adam make the leap into the new ontological dimension, this new dimension of being? I believe that the Biblical story has singled out two turning points… Only by breaking out from his natural immediacy and instinctive uniformity, by discovering his unique identity, can man reject boundaries and long for vastness and boundlessness. Man-persona has an imagination, a fantasy which revels against limitations and weaves a beautiful halo around him, crowning him with an enchanting vision of infinity. Man-natura is a realist, man-persona a dreamer-I might say, a bold dreamer; a visionary. He is an adventurer and a very daring one. He yearns for beauty and pleasure, for true happiness, He creates a civilization, a culture. Man-persona wants to accomplish more and more; man-natura is happy with the little he achieves. Judaism approves of fantasy-aroused man-persona. Indeed, God purposely planted the Paradise for man, who was called upon to

cultivate and guard it. Man is encouraged to build, to plant, to beautify his life, to enjoy his life as much as he can.....But two horrible fears haunt man steadily, trailing him like an everlasting shadow: the fear of nihility, of nonbeing-death-and the fear of ignorance. Man wants to live and to know. He is eager to lead an intelligent enlightened, inextinguishable existence. His greatest aspiration, his most fascinating dream, is to defeat death and to grasp the mysterium magnum, the great mystery of creation. God did plant the garden with trees pleasant to look at and delightful as far as taste is concerned. And in the middle of the garden grew the two mysterious trees representing two basic aspirations of man: to live and to know. Yes, God planted the garden in Eden in order to place there the man whom He formed, for man is entitled to desire, to quest, to long for and be fascinated by something great and wonderful-immortality omniscience.

The Rav explains that although man's ability to imagine and dream is key to his becoming a reflective being, it was still not the most significant aspect of the transformation that took place. He continues:

The most significant turning point, however, is not the birth of human fantasy but the confrontation with God's moral will, which resulted in the birth of a moral awareness of man's own. After man had been placed

in the Paradise in Eden, his fantasy began to aspire to an unlimited existence which knows only of forward marching, of surging towards the boundless, of victorious advance and conquest. Adam met suddenly with God's moral will, with the moral law which challenges man in numerous cases to do just the opposite, to refrain from advancing and to withdraw, to defy the very fantasy that made him man, to stop at times even if the fantasy tells him to move on, to give up when fantasy is about to grasp. This meeting between man and the infinite moral will of God brought the metamorphosis that was initiated with the birth of human fantasy that aspires to a paradisiacal existence. The final liberation of man from his environment, the transformation from natural into metaphysical man, occurred at his first confrontation with *Hashem*, at his first rendezvous with God Who tells him of a Divine imperative, reveals the concept of duty and burdens him with the moral load. Man turns into a metaphysical personality the very moment he realizes that to be human means to carry a load and that a human existence is not all *hedone*, not all pleasure. In a word, the critical boundary is to be detected in verses 16 and 17, in "*Va-yetzav Hashem Elokim al ha-adam*" in God commanding man to refrain from eating from the tree of knowledge." (Family Redeemed, pgs. 6-12)

The Rav's explanation here does not explain the punishment and changes that occurred to man after the sin as the Rambam does. His focus is on the development of man's personality that takes place from his creation as a thinking but natural being to one that develops a life of fantasy and bold visions of his future. This man-dreamer, with his boundless goals and desires for a majestic future, is then confronted with God's command and, it seems, the moral load and inherent conflict that is part of human existence. These two dimensions of man- the bold conqueror/builder and the humble, obedient servant of God, are described in depth and form the core of the Rav's great essay "The Lonely Man of Faith" in which the Rav uses the terms "Adam the first" and "Adam the second" to describe these two inherently conflicting dimensions of the core human personality. The Rav states in this essay:

Adam the first is dynamic and creative, transforming sensory data into thought constructs...Adam the second explores not the scientific abstract universe but the irresistibly fascinating qualitative world where he establishes an intimate relation with God.

NOACH

The Descent of man Before The flood

Maimonides and Rabbi Joseph B. Soloveitchik both comment on the specific qualities of the generation of the flood which we read about in the Parsha of Noach. This parsha describes the rapid descent of man into a hedonistic and idolatrous state. The Rambam, in his great work the Mishnah Torah, provides an analysis of the progressive stages of the world's transition from the worship of God to the worship of idols. He states:

"During the times of Enosh, mankind made a great mistake, and the wise men of that time gave great counsel. Enosh himself was one of those who erred. Their mistake was as follows: They said God created stars and spheres with which to control the world. He placed them on high and treated them with honor. (They perceived this) to be the will of God, blessed be He, that they magnify those who He magnified and honored, just as a king desires those who stand before him to be honored. Indeed doing so is an expression of honor to the king. After conceiving of this notion, they began to construct temples to the stars and offer sacrifices to them. They would praise and glorify them with words, and prostrate themselves before them, because by doing so, they would, according to their false conception- be fulfilling the word of God. This was the essence of the worship of false gods, and this

was the rationale of those who worshipped them. They would not say that there is no other god except for this star. After many years passed, there arose people –false prophets –who told the people that God has commanded them to say: Serve this star-or all the stars-sacrifice to it, offer libations to it, build a temple for it and make an image of it so that people, all people-including the women, the children and the common people – could bow to it. He would inform them of a form that he had conceived, claiming that this is the image of a particular star, claiming that this was revealed to him in a particular vision. In this manner people began making images in temples, under trees, and on the tops of mountains and hills...Subsequently other deceivers arose and declared that a specific star, sphere or angel had spoken to them and commanded them: Serve me in this manner. He would then relate a mode of service (telling them) Do this, do not do this. Thus these practices spread throughout the world, one more distorted than the other. As the years passed, God's glorious and awesome name was forgotten by the entire population. It was no longer part of their speech and they no longer knew Him... The world continued in this way until the pillar of the world –the Patriarch Abraham – was born. (Mishneh Torah, Laws of Idolatry (Chapter 1: Laws 1-2)

It is informative that the Rambam describes the first step in this descent as "the essence of idolatry" (the words in the Rambam's commentary which I have underlined above.) This essential error was the conception by the "wise" of Enosh's time that it was proper to make the comparison between a human king and his sub-rulers with God and the stars. This, they reasoned, was similar to a human king, where the honoring of their counselors and the making of requests to them, makes sense, as the king is human and the counselors are human as well. They (the king and the counselors) share the same qualities and nature, both being human, though the king has the ultimate authority and power in the kingdom. So why was this analogy between the human king and God so essentially false and why does it constitute the "essence of idolatry", which is the most fundamental sin in the Torah's system of laws?

I would suggest that the error of applying this analogy of the king and his counselors to God and the stars is that with regard to God and the stars you have the Creator (God) and the created (stars) which is a unique distinction. The quality of being the Creator, who is the cause and maintenance of all existence is unique in his greatness, while the stars, though at the "top" of the created pantheon, are creations nonetheless and therefore cannot be paralleled to the ministers of a king. To conceive the two as differing only by degree, as is the case with the human king and his counselors is a profound error. The stars do not share the essential character of being creators. There is only one creator - God. Everything else is simply a type of creation. Therefore the stars cannot be "stand-in" or "representatives" of that with which they have nothing truly in common. An analogy would be a painter and a painting. No matter how great the painting we would not treat it as a painter, requesting art lessons from it or asking the painting its opinion on the meaning of modern art. The painting is an object created by its creator and does not share the painter's essential nature as a human being and independent, creative force.

Equally important is the distinction between God as the Transcendent Being who is not part of the universe and the stars which are, once again, still only a part of the creation. There is an absolute distinction here between God and everything else. The acknowledgement of this distinction is what removes Judaism from having pagan elements. From a pagan perspective, God exists within the world as a part of it, though as an exalted, powerful part. Judaism absolutely rejects this idea, with God being "holy, holy, holy" as we state in the *Kedusha* portion of the *Shemoneh Esrei.* God is completely and absolutely "holy" or separate and exists outside of the universe that he has created. This distinction is, of course, not true of the human king and his counselors, both of which reside within the universe.

Once this distinction was overlooked by the people in Enosh's generation, and they distinguished between God and the creation only by degree, the pagan perspective was introduced into the world. God was conceived as being at the top of a pantheon of powerful, eternal beings.

Rabbi Soloveitchik (the Rav) describes the psychological dimension of man's descent into idolatry which occurred in the generation of Enosh. In doing so, he relates this error to society today, in which actual idolatry is rare. What follows in from a transcription of one of Rabbi Soloveitchik's classes found in a recent text: "The Rav Thinking Out Loud on Parsha Beresheit " by Rabbi Holzer:

"Basically, paganism preaches a way of life. Not just paganism: It teaches not just idolatrous cultic services: it is a way of life as well....Apparently, mankind is still pagan. Not as far as the ceremonials are concerned, he doesn't observe anything. He is skeptic. It is a generation of skeptics. I would say materialists, skeptics and atheists- *avodah zarah* plays no role as idolatry, yes. But the way of life of man is pagan, completely pagan. What does paganism preach as a way of life? ... You know very well that a person who is not aware of morals is not as bad as a person who is aware but reverses the moral norm, and converts the immoral norm into a moral command. Paganism actually preaches two systems of morality. One system of morality that paganism preaches is, as a way of life, is based on an oversensitivity to an unredeemed, carnal beauty....And the *pasuk* says: "And the *bnei ha-elokeem* saw that the daughters of man were good and

they took for themselves wives" (Beresheit, 6:2). What do they preach here in American society, Western society? What do they preach in Eretz Yisrael, *rabbosi*, if you read the articles in *Haaretz*? There is only one thing, one topic: Permissiveness. That nothing should interfere if man wants to enjoy life. No norms, no commands, no responsibilities, no restrictions. If a man thinks that this is way to enjoy life, and he wants to derive pleasure, he has the right. This is part of his freedom. He has the right to gratify all his carnal needs." (pages 90-92)

I would conclude from the Rav's analysis that, in his view, the idolatrous drive of man is not based on an uncontrolled, perverse attempt to come close to God. Instead, the rituals and cultic activities of the idolaters, though translated in a religious context, served as a means of obtaining personal license for the fulfillment of unrestricted carnal pleasure and power. Once the instinctual drives have been disguised as religious ritual they lose all restraint, as the rebellion against God is disguised as a form of worship. The idolatrous cult was, as the Rav explains, the transformation of the immoral into a distorted, false form of morality which freed man from his fear of challenging the rule of God and left him unbounded in the pursuit of his own carnal lusts. In this format, the idolatrous drives remains potent in contemporary society as the instinctual drives for sex, food and power are couched in modern moral dressings such as "cultural diversity", "the individual's right to self-expression" and "sexual liberation". These contemporary "moral positions" are just a few of the disguises the instincts have taken in contemporary society.

LECH-LECHA

Avraham- The Covenantal Man

The Rambam, in his great work, the Mishnah Torah, provides an account of the development of Avraham from childhood to his full emergence as prophet and father of the Jewish people. It was with Avraham that the covenant was established between God and his chosen people. The Rambam states:

"After this mighty man was weaned, he began to explore and think. Though he was a child, he began to think (incessantly) throughout the day and night, wondering: How is it possible for the sphere to continue to revolve without having anyone controlling it? Who is causing it to revolve? Surely, it does not cause itself to revolve. He had no teacher, nor was there anyone to inform him. Rather, he was mired in Ur Kasdim among the foolish idolaters. His father, mother, and all the people (around him) were idol worshipers, and he would worship with them. (However) his heart was exploring and (gaining) understanding." (Laws of Idolaters Chapter 1: Law 2)

This introduction is relevant to the Rambam's position on the capacity of a person's free will, in stating that Avraham, of his own free choosing and without any positive influence from teachers or parents, took these decisive steps towards the truth of transcendental monotheism. All Avraham had to guide him was the creation (nature) ,which he observed with his senses, and his mind with which to interpret these experiences. That was all, it seems, that was required. This depiction of Avraham expresses the Rambam's position on the complete freedom of the human being's will. As the Rambam states in the Laws of Repentance:

"Free will is granted to all men. If one desires to turn himself to the path of good and be righteous, the choice is his. Should he desire to turn to the path of evil and be wicked, the choice is his... There is no one who compels him, sentences him, or leads him towards either of these two paths. Rather he, on his own initiative and decision tends to the path he chooses." (Laws of Repentance: Chapter 5: Laws 1-2)

The Jewish people's root cause was this great act of free will of Avraham, as the Rambam states:

He (Avraham) had no teacher, nor was there anyone to inform him. Rather, he was mired in Ur Kasdim among the foolish idolaters. His father, mother, and all the people (around him) were idol worshipers, and he would worship with them.

The Rambam continues with the description of Avraham's development. He states:

"Avraham was forty years old when he became aware of his Creator. (*hee-keer et Boray*). When he

recognized and knew Him, he began to formulate replies to the inhabitants of Ur Kasdim and debate with them, telling them that they were not following a proper path.... When he overcame them through the strength of his arguments, the king desired to kill him. He was saved through a miracle and left for Charan. There he began to call in a loud voice to all people and to inform them that there is one God in the entire world and it is proper to serve Him....He (Avraham) planted in their hearts this great fundamental principle, composed texts about it, and taught it to Isaac, his son." (Laws of Idolaters: Chapter 1: Law 3).

The Rambam describes here, an intense intellectual journey as Avraham developed from a small child to his full development as the brilliant expounder of transcendental monotheism. But he also describes Avraham's exceptionally courageous and dangerous undertaking as he struggles to bring this monotheistic idea to a world that was entrenched in the darkness and ignorance of idol worship.

Rabbi Joseph B. Soloveitchik ("The Rav") in his essay "Family Redeemed" explores the character of Avraham as well. But instead of focusing on Avraham's profound intellectual development, the Rambam gives insight into the development and quality of his faith in God. This faith, in the Rav's view, is based on the covenantal relationship between God and the Jewish people by which man connection to God includes an element beyond the solely intellectual dimension. At the core of the relationship is a "mutual possession" between God and the Jewish people, in which each possesses the other. The Rav explains this concept:

When God reached the covenant with His chosen community, He was concerned not only with the worldly goods He placed at its disposal, but with the people as people themselves. He claims not only our material but our spiritual possessions as well. He lays claim to body and soul, to perception and thought to experience and idea. God owns our very lives, our very essence and existence as selves. The covenant was many times sealed with blood....Hence, the chosen community lays existential claims to God as its God. The community belongs to God, and at the same time God belongs to the community." ("The Family Redeemed" page 43-44)

There is a dimension of the Jewish community's connection to God which is beyond that of the awe-struck observer. We are an actual possession of God and, astoundingly, He is also our possession, so to speak, due to a freely entered agreement of the Covenant. This covenantal relationship is the determining factor of our destiny and, as the Rav explains, results in a complete binding of the Jewish people to this destiny, regardless of circumstance:

"The covenant introduces into the historical ever-changing reality an element of persistence or

constancy. Through the covenant the God-man drama becomes protected from the arbitrariness of destiny. Something permanent is brought into the historical occurrence. Within the covenant community relationship retain their identity no matter how powerful and how staggering the forces of historical change are…Abraham, the Knight of Faith, knew the secret of this kind of loyalty. Countless generations after him have demonstrated the same ability to believe, to be attached and dedicated to an old covenant which many a time has weighed heavily on our frail shoulders and which quite often has appeared to the human eye to be out of context with historical realities. This kind of loyalty and faith is anomalous; it is, to use the Platonic-Kierkegaardian term, a 'Divine madness', a passion from which our people cannot liberate itself. Of course, this loyalty is nurtured by a great all-enveloping, all-overwhelming and all-consuming love between God and His charismatic community. ("The Family Redeemed"-page 45)

The Rav's insight clarifies that the Covenant consists of more than the knowledge and wisdom the Jewish people have acquired through the receiving of Torah. It is also more than the obligations that the Jewish people have taken upon themselves through accepting the "yoke of the King of Heaven". The Covenant is, at its core, an eternally enduring relationship that has been formed between God and the Jewish people in which both are bound and, in the case of the Jewish people is a relationship that defines its essence and its destiny.

VAYERA

Avraham and the Angels

The parsha of VaYera begins with God appearing to Avraham, who is sitting at the entrance of his tent after having his *bris milah.*

And the Lord appeared unto him by the terbinths of Mamre as he sat in the door of the tent in the heat of the day" (Beresheit, 18: 1). We are then told that Avraham "lifts up his eyes" and sees three men in his presence and that "he ran to meet them from the door of the tent" after which he invites them to rest with him and receive his hospitality:

Let now be fetched a little water and wash your feet, and recline yourselves under the tree. And I will fetch a morsel of bread, and rest, after which you will pass on, as you have come to your servant." (Bereisheit, 18: 4-5).

Avraham then proceeds to inform and instruct Sarah and Yismael in the preparing of food for the three guests. After this, the men inform Avraham that Sarah will give birth to a son. Sarah, we are told, laughed about this and later, denied doing so. Avraham corrects her, stating "No, you did laugh". Then God "decides" to inform Avraham about the impending destruction of Sodom. Avraham asks God about whether the presence of 50, 45, 40, 30, 20 or even 10 righteous people will save Sodom from destruction and then "Avraham returned to his place"

This event is the source of a well-known statement by Maimonides in the Guide for the Perplexed in which he makes clear that this meeting is a "*ma-areh nevuah*" –"a vision of prophecy". Maimonides explains that whenever an angel is mentioned in the Torah, this always refers to a visionary experience and not one that takes place in the world outside the mind. This position was vigorously rebutted by Nachmanides (the Ramban) and has been a point of contention throughout traditional Jewish scholarship. The Rambam states in the Guide: "

"We have explained that whenever it is mentioned that an angel was seen or had spoken, this has happened only in a vision of prophecy (*ma-areh navuah*) or in a dream whether this is explicitly stated or not, as has been said before. Know this and understand it thoroughly. And there is no difference between a statement in which the prophet literally affirms from the first that he saw the angel and a statement according to whose external sense the prophet at first thought that a human individual had appeared to him, whereas at the end it became clear to him that it was an angel. For inasmuch as you find in the course of the event that he who was seen and had spoken was an angel, you ought to know and to establish as true that the event was from the first, a vision of prophecy or a

dream of prophecy....One of the Sages, may their memory be blessed, in fact a great man among those of them who were great, arrived at this capital principle. It was Rabbi Hiyya the Great, when speaking of the text of the Torah: *And the Lord appeared unto him by the terebinths of Mamre, and so on.* For after he had first propounded the proposition that God manifested Himself to him, he began to explain what the form of this manifestation was; and he said that at first he saw *three men* and ran; whereupon they spoke and were spoken to..." (Book 2, Chapter 42).

So the Rambam is unequivocal in his position that the three visitors to Avraham were angels (*malachim*) and that these 3 angels, appeared to Avraham in a vision of prophecy (*ma-areh nevuah*). The Rambam also makes clear, it seems to me, that an angel does not ever manifest itself in physical form and that whenever an angel is "met" by a person, it takes place in a vision or a dream. As mentioned earlier, Nachmanides (the Ramban) takes exception to this position and points to difficulties with this view including the details of the food prepared, which seems unnecessary, as well as the lameness that resulted when Yaakov wrestled the angel. Nachmanides states in his commentary on Beretsheit:

Now if in the vision there appeared to Abraham only men partaking of food, how then does Scripture say, *And the Eternal appeared to him,* as God did not

appear to him in vision or in thought? Such is not found with respect to all the prophecies. And according to his words, Sarah did not knead cakes, nor did Abraham prepare a bullock, and also, Sarah did not laugh. It was all a vision! If so, this dream came *through a multitude of business,* like dreams of falsehood, for what is the purpose of showing him all this! Similarly did the author of the Moreh Nebuchim say in the case of the verse, *And a man wrestled with him,* that it was all a prophetic vision. But if this be the case, I do not know why Jacob limped on his thigh when he awoke! And why did Jacob say, *For I have seen an angel face* to *face,* and my *life is preserved*? The prophets did not fear that they might die on account of having experienced prophetic visions. Jacob, moreover, had already seen a greater and more distinguished vision than this since many times, in prophetic visions, he had also seen the Revered Divinity. Now according to this author's opinion, he will find it necessary for the sake of consistency to say similarly in the affair of Lot that the angels did not come to his house, nor did he bake for them *unleavened bread and they did eat.* Rather, it was all a vision! But if Lot could ascend to the height of a prophetic vision, how did the wicked and sinful people of Sodom become prophets? Who told them that men had come into Lot's house? And if all these [i.e., the actions of the inhabitants of Sodom], were part of prophetic visions, then it follows that the account

related in the verses, *And the angels hastened Lot, .saying: Arise take thy wife ...And he said, Escape for thy life... See, I have accepted thee,* as well as the entire chapter is but a vision, and if so, Lot could have remained in Sodom! But the author of the Moreh Nebuchim thinks that the events took place of themselves, but the conversations relating to all matters were in a vision! But such words contradict Scripture. It is forbidden to *listen to* them, all the more to believe in them!... (Commentary on Bereisheit 18:1)

It is important to make clear that Maimonides, in attributing the event of Avraham's meeting with the three men to a vision of prophecy, does not mean to imply that it lacked reality or actual occurrence. A vision of prophecy is not simply an internal, mental activity that results from an individual's own imagination and creative thinking. According to Maimonides, angels (*malachim*) are real existents, separate from the mind of an individual. He describes their qualities and the ten levels of the angels in some detail in the Mishnah Torah's volume "*Yesoday Haora*"-("Fundamentals of the Torah") after which he states:

All these forms are alive. They recognize and know the Creator with very immense knowledge, each of the forms according to its level and not according to its greatness. (Chapter 2: Law 8).

The Rambam's position of the meeting of Avraham and the angels being a vision of prophecy does not detract from it being a true meeting between four different living, intelligent beings (3 angels and 1 human). Angels, though, having no physical body, and, according to the Rambam, never take physical form, do exist and communicate with humans through the human being's non-physical element- the mind. Rabbi Joseph B. Soloveitchik ("The Rav") clarifies this point in a discussion brought down in the text "The Rav Thinking Aloud on the Parsha Sefer Bereishis" compiled from tapes of actual conversations with the Rav by Rabbi David Holzer. The Rav states:

The Rambam interprets *va'yeira l'Avraham, va'yeira eilav Hashem,* (God appeared to Avraham) is *bi'nvuos* (through prophecy). The *sh'loshah anashim* (three men) were part of the *mar'ah,* not three travelers. What did he see? *Ribbono Shel Olam* does not reveal Himself through the medium of vision. Man cannot see *Ribbono Shel Olam-lo yir'ani adam va' chai.* ("man cannot see God and live"). When he sees something, Ribbono Shel Olam shows him something. He beholds a vision. What vision did Avraham behold? *Sh'loshah anashim* (three men). *Va'yaratz likrasam-* everything is *b'mar'ei ha'n'vuah....*"

Rabbi Holzer concludes that the Rav not only holds that the vision of prophecy is a real meeting but that, at least in the case of Avraham's meeting, there were actually physical

3 men in the physical world that occurred in a parallel manner to the vision of prophecy. This conclusion is unclear to me from the words of the Rav, but Rabbi Holzer was present with the Rav having this discussion of the Rav, so it is certainly a significant point to consider. Rabbi Holzer states:

The Rav now explains that there is a type of reality where the two areas merge. In *mar'os ha'n'vuah* there is a physical reality that coincides with a spiritual reality. Sarah saw the *mal'achim* as an event, guests coming to visit. Avraham experienced their arrival as a *n'vuah* from Hashem, as well. To Avraham there is a higher level of reality. These are not simple guests to Avraham, for Avraham perceives the guest as *mal-achei Hashem* bringing a message. Whereas for the average person the events are standard physical events, the navi can experience them as a *gilui Hashem* at the same time. (p. 182 - The Rav Speaking Out Loud on the Parsha-Sefer Bereishis)

The difficulty with interpreting the Rav's position on Maimonides in this way is that the Rambam states clearly that an angel (*malach*) never takes a physical form. So if Rabbi Holzer is saying that the men are physical but that only Avraham saw them as angels, you have contradicted the Rambam's restriction on angels taking physical form. On the other hand, if you say that there are physical men who are used in some way by the angels to "act out" the angels' mission with the angels providing a mental "overlay" for the prophet, you are posing, what seems to me to be a cumbersome structure, though one not in direct contradiction to Maimonides position that *malachim* (angels) do not take physical form.

CHAYA SARA

When Avraham Buried Sara

At the beginning of the parsha of Chaya Sara, Avraham buries his wife and we are told:

And the life of Sarah was a hundred and twenty and seven years; (these were) the years of the life of Sarah. And Sarah died in Kiriat-arba the same is Hevron in the land of Canaan; and Abraham came to mourn for Sarah, and to weep for her. (Bereisheit, 23:1-2)

"The Rav", (Rabbi Joseph B. Soloveitchik) clarifies the definitions and differences between Abraham's mourning for Sarah and his weeping for her. The Rav states:

Weeping and mourning are two different stages in bereavement. Weeping is a primeval, instinctive reaction to a tragedy, especially one that strikes without warning. It is not a deliberate performance; it bursts forth spontaneously. Weeping is a release of unbearable tension when the whole world seems to be crumbling. Mourning *hesped*, in contrast, is a rational and planned performance. It is an act of appraisal, an attempt to evaluate the repercussions of what has transpired. *A hesped* is formulated not in emotional terms, but in logical analysis. With the death of Sarah, Abraham had suffered a double loss. First was his personal sorrow, the death of his wife, his partner and

comrade. No one can understand the bleak loneliness and painful nostalgia of a surviving mate. One's whole world seems dislocated. Abraham was a great human being, and he felt profoundly disoriented; his beloved Sarah was gone. Another tragic and distressful experience was his dilemma to what would now become of the covenant which was the *raison d'etre* of all his strivings. He knew the secret that it was not entrusted to him alone. What would happen now? The mother of the covenant was missing. Would God have confidence in him alone, or was life's work now coming to an end? The first thing he did was to appraise Sarah's contribution, *lispod et Sarah*, to review the formation and successful growth of the covenantal community, the role she had played and what she had accomplished. He mourned her departure together with many thousands of other adherents of the covenant who had adopted the faith. He mourned the passing of a great woman in objective categories. Only after the evaluative presentation did Abraham break down in tears and cry." (Man of Faith in the Modern World: Reflections of the Rav-Vol. 2: The Covenantal Role of Sarah: pages 87-88).

The hesped (eulogy), the Rav clarifies, is carried out by praising the deceased "in objective categories", reviewing the accomplishments and qualities of the person. This, as opposed to a personal expression of one grief, is the core of the *hesped.* As the Rav states "*hesped…* is a rational and planned performance." Abraham's "weeping for Sarah" was a separate act of personal distress and one which was lonely and incommunicable in its nature. The Rav explains: "No one can understand the bleak loneliness and painful nostalgia of a surviving mate." The personal outpouring and the public, objective assessment are both required, separate elements of the mourner's response to the loss of a close member of family.

In Maimonides' (Rambam's) great work, the Mishnah Torah, he states regarding the eulogy (*hesped)*:

A eulogy is an honor for the deceased. Therefore we compel the heirs to pay the wages of the men and women who recite laments and they eulogize him. If the deceased directed that he not be eulogized, we do not eulogize him. If, however, he directed that he not be buried, we do not heed him, for burial is a mitzvah, as (Devarim 21:12) states. "And you shall certainly bury him". (Laws of Mourning: 12:1)

It seems that the mourner has an obligation to honor the deceased, but the deceased can dispel with that honor, if they choose to. The Rambam then continues in the next halachah, bringing down the statements from the Gemora Shabbos. He states:

Anyone who is sluggish (*ha-meet-hatzale*) with regard to the eulogy for a sage will not live long. Anyone who is sluggish with regards to the eulogy of an upright

person (*adam kasher*) is fit to be buried in his lifetime. Anyone who shed tears for an upright person will have his reward for this guarded by the Holy One, blessed be He." (Laws of Mourning: 12:2)

From the Rambam's statements here we can see that there is a core defect in the character of a person who "is sluggish" with regards to a eulogy for sage or for a regular, decent person. For sluggishness with a sage the punishment is a shortening of one's life and for an "*adam kasher*" the one who is "sluggish" is "fit to be buried in his lifetime". These punishments are described in the *Gemora Shabbos* as being punishment "measure for measure". The *Maharsha* provides an interpretation that the mourner is treating the buried as if they were alive (not giving the honor to the deceased "*kavood hamase*") so therefore the mourner, who is punished "measure for measure" is treated as dead and buried while they are alive ("buried in his lifetime").

These punishments deserved by one whose wrong is being "sluggish" with the eulogy, seem unusually harsh for a "victimless crime". The mourner perhaps has some lack of focus in his attending to the eulogy. There are many emotional or psychological reasons why a mourner could be reluctant or conflicted with regard to this emotionally wrenching activity. The eulogy is a public acceptance of the death, and it seems understandable that the mourner might be uneasy with a situation of such an emotionally charged experience, acknowledging his catastrophe. But the Torah is quite demanding of the eulogy being done with alacrity. Why is this so essential in the case of even an "*adam kasher*", let alone for a scholar?

Perhaps the Maharsha's explanation that the deceased is being treated as one who is "alive" can open up the area up for us. One way of understanding the Maharsha is to distinguish between the living and the deceased. A living person can fend for him or herself. They can advocate for themselves. If we are "sluggish" is providing a living person with that which he or she is entitled to, the person can step in and demand justice. But the deceased, who in the act of honoring the dead, is treated as a personage, is helpless to act and cannot take any initiative on his own. To be sluggish and delay with regard to the dead is a unique form of injustice as the deceased is without any power of his own and completely dependent upon the mourner to provide the deceased with what he/she is entitled to (a proper eulogy). Of course, the deceased does not personally suffer, but the act shows a profound injustice on the part of the mourner. This mourner, who is so deficient in justice, is therefore deserving of harsh punishment. Perhaps this can be seen as the "flip side" of the idea that when a person attends to the needs of the deceased it is called "*chesed shel emes*", ("true kindness"). Kindness and justice performed for the deceased, who cannot respond to unkindness and injustice, are a reflection of the true nature of the one performing the kind act, as there is no benefit that the deceased can bestow, nor any reprisal the deceased can carry out against those who do not act towards him or her in a just and kind manner.

TOLDOS

Deceiving Yitzchak

In the parsha of Toldot, Rifka takes the pivotal step of planning and executing the deception of her husband Yitzchak in securing Esau's blessing for Yaakov. The parsha quotes Rivkah:

And now my son, hearken to my voice, to what I am commanding you. Go now to the flock, and take for me from there two choice kids, and I will make them tasty foods for your father, as he likes. And you shall bring [them] to your father that he may eat, in order that he bless you before his death." And Jacob said to Rebecca his mother, "Behold, my brother Esau is a hairy man, whereas I am a smooth man. Perhaps my father will touch me, and I will appear to him as a deceiver, and I will bring upon myself a curse and not a blessing." And his mother said to him, "On me is your curse, my son. Only hearken to my voice and go, take [them] for me.

Rivkah's action of deceiving Yitzchak is one that requires explanation, to say the least. According to the Maimonides (the Rambam), Yitzchak and the other Patriarchs had achieved a level of knowledge and prophecy only exceeded by Moshe. The Rambam states in the "Guide for the Perplexed":

"The Patriarchs likewise attained this degree of perfection; they approached God in such a manner that with them the name of God became known in the world. Thus we read in the Scripture; "The God of Abraham, the God of Isaac, and the God of Jacob... 'This is my name for ever'. (Exod. Iii, 15). Their mind was so identified with the knowledge of God, that He made a lasting covenant with each of them: "Then will I remember my covenant with Jacob" etc. (Lev. Xxvi,42). For it is known from statements made in Scripture that these four, viz, the Patriarchs and Moses, had their minds exclusively filled with the name of God, that is, with His knowledge and love; and that in the same measure was Divine Providence attached to them and their descendants." (Book 3, Chapter 51).

One would wonder:

1- What was the special and superior insight Rivkah had into this situation?

2- Why wasn't she able or willing to discuss the issue with Yitzchak, in a manner similar to the way that Sarah advised Avraham to send away Yismael?

Rabbi Soloveitchik ("The Rav") in his essay, "The Family Redeemed" provides a brilliant clarification into the different roles the matriarch and patriarch and, similarly, the mother and the father, in the progression of the Jewish people (known as the covenantal community). He states:

There is a distinction between mother's and father's mission within the covenantal community, since they represent two different personalistic approaches. Father's teaching is basically of an intellectual nature. Judaism is to a great extent an intellectual discipline, a method, system of thought, hierarchy of values. In order to be acquainted with all these aspects, one must study, comprehend, acquire knowledge and be familiar at least with its basic principles. Let me confide: it is not too easy a task. The teaching must be strict, exact and conscientious. If the father cannot accomplish it all himself, he must see to it that his child obtains the necessary instruction..... However, Judaism is not only an intellectual tradition but an experiential one as well. The Jew not only observed but *experienced* the Shabbat, the Jew *experienced* Rosh Hashanah and Yom Kippur. He does not only recite prayers on those days. The seder was not just a ceremonial, but a great *experiential* event. There is beauty, grandeur, warmth, and tenderness to Judaism. All these qualities cannot be described in cognitive terms. One may behold them, feel them, sense them. It is impossible to provide one with a formal training in the experiential realm....All this is to be found in the maternal domain. The mother creates the mood; she is the artist who is

responsible for the magnificence, solemnity and beauty.

The Rav continues that in times of crisis the maternal dimension of the covenant comes to the fore:

While intellectual involvement is important, in times of crisis and distress the experiential commitment is indispensable. Were it not for the mother, the Jews would not have been able to defy and to survive so many crises which threatened to annihilate our people... The mother in times of crisis assumes the role of her husband's keeper, his guardian and teacher. In the covenantal community, motherhood is a more powerful spiritual force than fatherhood. The shy, modest, reserved mother turns into an active personality whenever critical action is called for. Man's mind roams about in a world of abstractions and twisted ideas. He is at times too critical, too skeptical to realize the simple truth which brooks no interference from the oversophisticated intellect. This is why the Bible has always portrayed the woman as the determining influence, saving the male from committing grave errors. She quite often changed the course of destiny.... Rebecca (Rivkah) is responsible for the covenant being transmitted to Jacob instead of Esau (Gen. 27). Isaac had contemplated entrusting the spiritual heritage to his oldest son. At the hour of

crisis Rebecca intervened and thereby determined the historical destiny of the covenantal community.

A distinction of Judaism's women is their ability to view with great clarity, certain situations due, in part, to their not being focused on the "world of abstractions and twisted ideas" which is at the core of the Jewish man's life of studying the written and oral Torah. A woman's intense involvement in these abstract ideas to an intense level may be destructive to the perceptive clarity that is unique to women.

Women, according to the Rambam, can be as brilliant and spiritually developed as men, (the Rambam cites in his "Guide for the Perplexed" that Miriam, along with Moshe and Aaron was one of the 3 people in human history to achieve the level of development required for death by "the divine kiss". The Rambam explains:

This kind of death, which in truth is deliverance from death, has been ascribed by our sages to none but to Moses, Aaron and Miriam. The other prophets are pious people beneath that degree; but their knowledge of God is strengthened when death approaches. The intellect of these people remains then constantly in the same condition, since the obstacle is removed that at times has intervened between the intellect and the object of its action; it continues for ever in that great delight, which is not like bodily pleasure. We have explained this in our work, and others have explained

it before us." (Book 3: Chapter 51 –Guide for the Perplexed, Page 390-391 in Friedlander translation)

However, in an effort to provide "full disclosure" we must state the famous and troublesome statement the Rambam writes in the Mishnah Torah about the teaching of Torah to women. He states in the Laws of Teaching Torah ("*Hilchos Talmid Torah*"):

A woman who has studied Torah has a reward, but it is not like the reward of a man. For she was not commanded, and the reward of anyone who does a thing concerning which he is not commanded is not like the reward of him who is commanded and has done it, but is less than it (cf. BT *Kiddushin* 31a). Yet even though she has a reward, the Sages commanded (Mishnah, *Sotah* 3:4) that a man not teach his daughter Torah, for the mind of the majority of women is not adapted to be taught, rather they turn the words of the Torah into words of nonsense according to the poorness of their mind. The Sages said: "Anyone who teaches his daughter Torah is as if he taught her lasciviousness!" [ibid.] With reference to what are these words said? With reference to the Oral Torah. But with reference to the Written Torah, he ought not to teach her before the fact, though if he has taught her he is not as if he teaches her lasciviousness.

The Rambam's perspective may be that there <u>are</u> exceptional women who can master abstract knowledge at the deepest level - Miriam being at the pinnacle of this group. But it would appear from his statement quoted above from the Mishneh Torah, that this type of woman is more exceptional than the man who is capable of such mastery. It is certainly true that with both man and woman, the great scholar is a highly exceptional group. Perhaps with men, the Torah learning is a halachkic requirement, because the man's personality is more naturally acclimated to it. An additional reason may be that he needs Torah more intensely due to his lack of the intuitive sense of truth which the woman inherently possesses. Also, the male aggressive drive is such that unbounded, it often leads to a life of vulgar brutality. In the case of the woman who is not of the highly exceptional type that can develop abstract study to a high degree, the involvement in an in-depth learning of Torah or philosophy may skew or distort an inherent quality of insight and clarity of vision which she possesses by virtue of her character, personality and particular way of understanding the world.

VAYEITZE

A Place of Holiness

In the parsha of VaYeitze when Ya'akov awakes from his dream of the angels going up and down the ladder he states: **"God is truly in this place (*b-makom hazeh*), and I didn't realize it."**

The concept of **place** *("makom")* is explored by Maimonides (the Rambam) in the "Guide for the Perplexed" in the first book where he clarifies the meaning of key words in the Torah. He states here regarding the word "*makom*": (Book 1: Chapter 9)

"Place (*makom*)-Originally this term was given the meaning of a particular and general place. Subsequently, language extended its meaning and made it a term denoting an individual's rank and situation; I mean to say with reference to his perfection is some matter so that it is said that 'A certain man has a certain place' with regard to a certain matter. You know how often the people of our language use this meaning when they say: 'Occupying the place of his ancestors in wisdom or piety' or when they say: 'The difference of opinion still subsists in its place', which mean, in its station. It is this figurative manner that it is said: "Blessed be the glory of the Lord from His place" (Ezekiel 3:12), meaning according to His rank and the greatness of His portion in existence.

Similarly in every mention of "place" referring to God, the sole intention is to signify the rank of His existence, may He be exalted; there being nothing like or similar to that existence, as shall be demonstrated. "

The Rambam is clarifying the term "place" to be understood not only as a physical location, but also to mean a level of accomplishment or perfection. As the Rambam is very clear that to conceive of God as being located in a particular place would be a profound error, whenever we refer to God as "HaMakom" or the "place of God" it refers to His exalted level of perfection which is superior and unlike any other.

The Rambam also discusses in the 3rd book of the "Guide for the Perplexed", the nature of there being specific physical locations on Earth that have been designated for holy activities.

"It is known that idolaters sought to build their temples and to set their idols in the highest places they could find there: "Upon the high mountains" (Devarim: 12:2). Therefore Abraham our Father singled out Mount Moriah, because of its being the highest mountain there, proclaimed upon it the unity of God…In my opinion there is also no doubt that the place singled out by Abraham in virtue of prophetic inspiration was known to Moses our Master and to many others. For Abraham had recommended to them that that place should be a house of worship, just as

Onqelos, the translator sets forth when he says "Abraham worshiped and prayed in that place and said before the Lord; Here will worship the generation, etc. (Onqelos translation of Genesis 22:14) (Book 3: Chapter 45)."

Although, in the Guide, the Rambam does not explain the particular significance of Mount Moriah, (except for its height), in the Mishneh Torah: (Laws of the Temple) he clearly indicates the unique nature of this place as central to the development of mankind and the Jewish people:

The Altar is [to be constructed] in a very precise location, which may never be changed, as it is said (II Chronicles 22:1): "This is the Altar for the burnt offerings of Israel." Isaac was prepared as a sacrifice on the Temple's [future] site, as it is said (Genesis 22:2): "Go to the land of Moriah," and in Chronicles (II 3:1), it is said: "Then, Solomon began to build the House of the Lord in Jerusalem, on Mt. Moriah, where [the Lord] appeared to David, his father, in the place that David had prepared, in the threshing floor of Ornan, the Jebusite." It is universally accepted that the place on which David and Solomon built the Altar, the threshing floor of Ornan, is the location where Abraham built the Altar on which he prepared Isaac for sacrifice. Noah built [an altar] on that location when he left the ark. It was also [the place] of the Altar on which Cain and Abel brought sacrifices.

[Similarly,] Adam, the first man, offered a sacrifice there and was created at that very spot, as our Sages said: "Man was created from the place where he [would find] atonement. "(Laws of the Temple: Chapter 2: Laws 1-2)

From this explanation it is clear that the place of the Holy Temple is the earth's designated location for man's offerings to God. One would not at first think that one place differs from another in this regard. However, this does seem to be the case. Why is this so? In Rabbi Soloveitchik's text, "The Emergence of Ethical Man" we see clearly that he does not ascribe to the view that the physical holiness of the land is due to some unique quality of its substance, but instead attributes it to the place's historical role in the formation of the Jewish people and how the awareness of this history impacts the mind and soul of the individual. He states:

***Kedushah (holiness)*, under halakhic aspect, is man-made; more accurately, it is a historical category. A soil is sanctified by historical deeds performed by a sacred people, never by any primordial superiority. The halakhic term *kedusha-ha-aretz*, the sanctity of the land, denotes the consequence of a human act, either conquest (heroic deeds) or the mere presence of the people in that land (intimacy of man and nature). *Kedushah* is identical with man's association with Mother earth. Nothing should be attributed a priori to**

dead matter. Objective kedusha smacks of fetishism. (pg. 151)

For the Rav, the holiness of the land of Israel is due to the cluster of events by which God and man interacted meaningfully in that place. The offering of Isaac on the Mount Moriah was also the place where Jacob had laid his head and dreamed. It would become the sight of the Temple in the future. The holiness is bestowed upon the place, according to the Rav, because of its history of consequential events, not due to any inherent spiritual power within the physical land itself.

The Rav also explains in this essay the concept of "place" as being central to understanding of man's nature and his place in the creation. He states:

"What is important to emphasize now is the fact that man is confined to a specific area in the cosmos and his task is to live in full harmony with his environment. Nor is this environment total static. At times, it is determined by certain historical events. Like man, it emerges through the historical process. The Bible usually defined this unique environment, and God, in His voluntary exile, meet at certain crossroads. God chances upon and surprises man. By virtue of this sudden encounter, man takes root in this mystical place. Jacob met God in Beit-El, and a new bond between him and that place formed. "I am the God of

Beit-El, where you did anoint a pillar, and where you did vow a vow to Me: now arise, get out of this land, and return to the land of your birth (Gen. 31:13). The union of God-man-place is expressed here. Jacob was imprisoned within a geographic area, but together with him, God confined Himself to that place. This paradigm is crucial to understanding Judaism: as a natural being, man is arrested within concreteness and, as such, can never reach a transcendent God. In order to meet man (i.e., revelation), God descends from transcendental infinity into concrete finitude and confines Himself to the identical area in which man was placed. Man discovers God within finitude, within man's own realm, and this discovery determines man's belonging to a determinate environment. *Kedusha* (holiness) bespeaks God's and man's entirety, a definite segment of the cosmos and their encounter there. When man frees himself from such natural bonds, he loses contact with his God. (The Emergence of Ethical Man: 61-62).

According to the Rav, the connecting of man to the Earth through a specific place or "makom" where he has historically encountered God, is essential for his spiritual fulfillment or redemption. Man as a physically bound being must experience his relationship with God in a concrete, Earth-bound manner or this relationship will not reach fruition. Exile is not only the loss of the Temple and its exalted, uplifting activities; it is the removal of the Jewish people from their place on Earth where they encounter God. In exile the religious experience becomes too abstract to be fully realized by man who is both spiritual and physical and so fundamentally connected to the Earth. In exile the Earthly, physical dimension of his encounter with the Creator is severed.

VAYISHLACH

Yaakov, the Limping Hero

In the parsha of VaYishlach, on the evening before meeting with his brother Esav, Yaakov crosses back over the River Yabbok. He returns to the camp where he and his family were living. While there, Yaakov has an encounter with "a man" with whom he wrestles until daybreak. The pasha states: (Bereisheit 32:25-29)

And Jacob was left alone, and a man wrestled with him until the break of dawn.

When he saw that he could not prevail against him, he touched the socket of his hip, and the socket of Jacob's hip became dislocated as he wrestled with him.

And he (the angel) said, "Let me go, for dawn is breaking," but he (Jacob) said, "I will not let you go unless you have blessed me."

So he said to him, "What is your name?" and he said, "Jacob."

And he said, "Your name shall no longer be called Jacob, but Israel, because you have commanding power with [an angel of] God and with men, and you have prevailed."

Rabbi Joseph B. Soloveitchik ("The Rav"), in the essay

"Worship of the Heart" explains Yaakov's transformation:

Jacob on his way to meet Esau (Gen. 32), wrestled with the mysterious antagonist throughout the dark night, lonely and abandoned by everybody. Did he win the battle? Yes and no. The adversary could not prevail against him; he could not destroy Jacob. But at the hour of triumph, when he held his antagonist convulsively fast, felt also defeated; his thigh was out of joint and he therefore limped. Jacob understood that only the Divine blessing could assure him success and victory, could disperse the gloom of the haunted night of conflict and anguish. Jacob prayed for this, unwilling to let the adversary go without his blessing. ("Worship of the Heart" pgs. 34-35)

The Rav explains here, and as well as in his essay "Halakhic Man" that due to man's inherently conflicting nature, his greatest triumphs always reveal to him his inherent limitations and are therefore accompanied by an element of defeat.

"Man desires infinity itself yet must be satisfied with a restricted, bounded existence. When he reaches out he anticipates the endless and boundless, enrapturing himself with the vision of unlimited opportunities. At the hour of achievement, however, he finds himself hemmed in by finitude." ("Worship of the Heart" p. 34)

I understand this to mean that a human being, possessing a soul that partakes of infinity and the "*tzelem Elokeem*" longs for this infinite aspect in his earthy accomplishments. When someone achieves his greatest triumphs, he seems on the verge of incorporating this infinite quality within his physical life. But at these times of significant triumph man senses his greatness but is also struck with his mortality, fragility and that he is a small insignificant being in a vast universe. So, when Yaakov triumphs over the angel in his struggle, he realizes too, that without God's blessing his victory is a hollow one, and immediately asks for the blessing. The Rav in his essay, "The Rise of Ethical Man" describes another aspect of Yaakov's triumph over the angel and how this is represented by the name of Israel ("Yisrael") bestowed upon him by the defeated *malach*.

Driven to utter absurdity and self-negation, entangled in a night-long conflict with a hostile transcendental being, at dawn he emerges a hero, winning the battle by reforming himself and changing the aspect. God becomes a comrade-king, a fellow-participant in the social drama, a member of political society, whose unity was primarily forged by the realization of the covenant. *Elokei Yisrael* conveys political rule; in such a social milieu man frees himself from the primordial horror instilled in him by the original sin, bridges the gap separating him from God, and establishes friendly communion with Him.... God rules as comrade-king. Man does not retreat before him. ("Worship of the

Heart, p. 200)

The victory of Yaakov included a change in his relationship with God. When Yaakov is confronted by God he is filled with the realization of his (Yaakov's) own nothingness beside the Absolute Existence. But with the change of his name from Yaakov to Yisrael, he obtains a structured and positive relationship with God as a servant to a King for whom he can perform meaningful actions through the halachah (the covenant). This is the essence of his new self of Yaakov. This is his triumph. As the Torah states regarding the angel bestowing Yaakov's new name of Yisrael (Genesis 32:28-29):

And he (the angel) said, "Let me go, for dawn is breaking," but he (Jacob) said, "I will not let you go unless you have blessed me."	**כז.** וַיֹּאמֶר שַׁלְּחֵנִי כִּי עָלָה הַשָּׁחַר וַיֹּאמֶר לֹא אֲשַׁלֵּחֲךָ כִּי אִם בֵּרַכְתָּנִי׃
28. So he said to him, "What is your name?" and he said, "Jacob."	**כח.** וַיֹּאמֶר אֵלָיו מַה שְּׁמֶךָ וַיֹּאמֶר יַעֲקֹב׃
29. And he said, "Your name shall no longer be called Jacob, but Israel, because you have commanding power with [an angel of] God and	**כט.** וַיֹּאמֶר לֹא יַעֲקֹב יֵאָמֵר עוֹד שִׁמְךָ כִּי אִם יִשְׂרָאֵל כִּי שָׂרִיתָ עִם אֱלֹהִים וְעִם אֲנָשִׁים וַתּוּכָל׃

with men, and you have prevailed."

To shift gears quite a bit now, Maimonides (the Rambam), as we have discussed previously, makes clear in his "Guide for the Perplexed" that the wrestling between Yaakov and the *malach* was a prophetic vision. The Rav, we mentioned previously, is interpreted by Rabbi Holzer in his text "The Rav Thinking Aloud on the Parsha Sefer Bereishis" that although the *malach*, according to the Rambam does not take physical form, the *malach* is certainly a very real being that man encounters through the mind. In other words, the malach which a prophet encounters in his vision is not an imaginative creation of the prophet's mind, but a separate existing being. The Rambam describes in his work The Mishnah Torah, the ten levels of malachim, with lowest level being *ishim*, that interact with the prophet.

The tenth (and lowest) level is that of the form called *ishim*. They are the angels who communicate with the prophets and are perceived by them in prophetic visions. Therefore, they are called *ishim*, because their level is close to the level of human knowledge. (Mishneh Torah: Fundamentals of Torah: Chapter 2: Law 7)

The Ramban (Nachmanides) objected to the Rambam's view that the *malachim* do not take physical form. One of the particular objections of the Ramban to the Rambam's view addresses the damage that Yaakov sustained due to his struggle with the *malach*.

The Ramban questions how a prophetic vision could cause a physical injury. But perhaps we can address this objection. Maimonides states in the Mishnah Torah regarding these *malachim*, the *ishim*, that they are responsible for the form of the physical world as God as given them this role. He states:
"God gives each body the form appropriate to it through the angels of the tenth level, which is the form called *ishim*." (Fundamentals of Torah: Chapter 4: Law 6). So, although the angel does not take physical form, it does impact the physical world in a most fundamental way, by giving form to the physical world. With this approach it is understandable how this *malach* who, although according to the Rambam, does not take physical form, could still impact the body of Yaakov and cause the dislocation of his hip, if this was part of his angelic mission.

VAYAYSHEV

Joseph's Dreams of Grandeur

In his essay, "Joseph and Chanukah" Rabbi Joseph B. Soloveitchik ("The Rav") explains that the holiday of Chanukah celebrates the Jewish maintenance of holiness in the midst of the exile. The most difficult times for the exiled Jewish people to remain faithful to their ideals and obligations is not during times of hardship, but during times of prosperity. The Rav states:

Historically the Jew has proven his ability to remain loyal and devoted to his tradition in poverty, in oppression, in distress. However; he failed miserably to prove his loyalty when his destiny was one of success and glorious achievements. We met the challenge of poverty and oppression and persecution with courage and determination, and we emerged victorious. However, with few exceptions, we have failed the challenge of affluence, of prominence in society. (Days of Deliverance, Page 164)

The Rav continues, explaining that Joseph's vision, as expressed through his coat of many colors (*ketonet passim*) and his two dreams, envisioned the ability to achieve prosperity and power, while at the same time maintaining his commitment to the holiness of the Jewish people's destiny. The Rav states:

In aristocracy, each family has a coat of arms, an emblem. What was the emblem of Joseph? It was the *ketonet passim*, of course, the multicolored coat, a coat composed of stripes that his father made for him. When Joseph came to Dothan, the brothers immediately stripped him of the *ketonet passim*, the banner that Joseph carried. Without the ketonet ha-passim, Joseph's power dissipated and disappeared. I believe the *ketonet ha-passim* is the symbol of the Jewish people as well, of the Hasmoneans and of every generation of Jews. Joseph beheld two visions. He dreamt of his *alumroot*, sheaves, which rose and stood up high while the sheaves of his brothers came and bowed down to his. When he told that dream to his brothers, they were not envious of that dream. True, their hatred was deepened and strengthened, but their envy was not aroused. Then he dreamt another dream. He dreamt of the sun and the moon and the stars bowing to him. When he told this dream to his father, "*va-yekan'u bo ehav*", his brother envied him (Genesis. 37:11)-not only did they hate him, but they were envious of him as well. I am not a dream interpreter, but the prima facie interpretation is that Joseph had two visions. One was of material economic power, of prosperity and opulence, and that vision came true one hundred percent. The other dream apparently revolved around spiritual greatness, heavenly sweep and heavenly grandeur. Joseph wanted to be powerful in the political sense, to attain

wealth and prosperity, to be respected by people because of his power, feared by people because of his might; but he also wanted to be great spiritually, to be loved by people, to be revered by people because of the greatness of his wisdom and kindness....Apparently, Joseph thought that he could combine both. This is the meaning of the *ketonet ha-passim*-multicolored, not monochromatic, not one monotonous color. If there are many colors, there are many contradictions. Colors clash with one another, and Joseph was the synthesis of *alumot* and the heavenly bodies.... That synthesis is exactly what the Hasmoneans stood for. They were excellent warriors, but the very moment they laid down their swords, their interests centered around *kedushah*, holiness, around the oil for the menorah which burned in the Temple, of "purification of the entire Temple and dedication of the altar" (II Macc.2:19). Here is the link between Joseph and the Hasmoneans and the visions of Jewish history." (page 165-166)

Maimonides (The Rambam), in the third book of the "Guide for the Perplexed" in describing the structure of the different animal sacrifices related the use of a goat for the sin offerings "*seirim*" to the idea that a goat was used in the sin carried out by the brother of Joseph when they killed a goat and put its blood on Joseph coat and brought it to Jacob. He states:

Our Sages, however, explained the fact that goats were always the sin-offerings of the congregation, as an allusion to the sin of the whole congregation of Israel; for in the account of the selling of the pious Joseph we read "And they killed a kid of the goats: (Genesis 37:31). Do not consider this as a weak argument; for it is the object of all these ceremonies to impress on the mind of every sinner and transgressor the necessity of continually remembering and mentioning his sins. Thus the Psalmist says, "And my sin is ever before me" (Ps. 51:3) The above-mentioned sin-offerings further show us that when we commit a sin, we, our children, and the children of our children, require atonement for that sin by some kind of service analogous to the sin committed. (Guide, Book 3)

The use of the goat offering to remind the Jewish people of the sin of the brothers is understandable in that sins that are done at the establishment of a people have impact on the society that results from those root individuals. They "set the tone" so to speak for all that follows. For this reason the sin of the golden calf is mentioned often as limiting our development and closeness to God from that point on. But what is truly astounding about the Rambam's statement here, is the need for atonement for sins committed by our parents or ancestors. I can understand the need to reflect on these sins as they have influenced our development, but they are certainly not our sins. The Rambam also states in the Misneh Torah, (Laws of Repentance) that a person needs to continue to do *teshuvah* on sins that he or she has previously done *teshuvah.* But this can be explained, as the person who commits a sin and does *teshuvah-* although he may achieve pardon (*kapara*) is not the same as someone who did not commit the sin. This person can still benefit from reflection and recognition of their violation. Similarly, a person who is pardoned for a crime by a government can still benefit from reflecting on the crime they committed and continue to repair the effects the committing of the crime had on them.

I do not think that the Rambam's position is that a person needs actual pardon for sins committed by his or her ancestors but that one must repent and "return" from the impact sins committed by one's ancestors can have on the path of the nation of which the person is a part. If you were brought up by many generations of uncharitable or unkind people, it may "creep into" your attitudes and actions although you make a strong conscious effort to live charitably and kindly. This person must reflect on these sins and guard against them more than one descended from kind and generous people. Similarly the sins that impacted the initial formation of the Jewish people (the golden calf, the selling of Joseph) became part of the "spiritual DNA" and must be continually reflected upon by the Jewish people to minimize or eliminate the expression of these qualities by the individual, the congregation and the nation.

MIKEITZ

Yehuda and Joseph: King vs. King

Rabbi Soloveitchik ("The Rav"), in a lecture given on January 6, 1979, comments on fact that Yehuda's name is not mentioned in the initial meetings between the brothers and Joseph:

When the brothers come to Mitzraim for the first time to buy food and presented themselves before Joseph, they were accused of espionage and denied the charges, Judah's name is not mentioned. No matter where you look, he isn't mentioned. We find in the conversation between the brothers and the Viceroy the word, "*Vayomru*" - ("and they said") but it doesn't mention "who said?" "Vayomru" is mentioned in fact several times but not specifically who.

The Rav continues, explaining that Yehuda emerges from the group and takes a lead role only after his conversation with his father in which he convinces Yaakov to let the brother go back to Egypt a second time. The Rav states:

At first, it is Reuven - the oldest brother who intervenes right away and is rejected by the father. Much later, it is Yehuda. Scripture tells us there was no food and then Yehuda repeated basically what his brother spoke before him. Suddenly, he emerges from the shadows to the forefront. Apparently, his appeal was irresistible

and was accepted. He could have said it before the food was consumed but waited till the point of starvation. When they come to Joseph's house Yehuda again disappears in the background. When they were caught with the silver chalice in Benjamin's possession, again, Yehuda is not mentioned. The turning point is where Yehuda is singled out in a solemn manner. Yehuda took over the leadership.

The Rav explains that Yehuda is called to the fore in times of crisis in fulfillment of his role as the tribe with kingship ("*malchos*") over Bnei Yisroel. The Rav continues by explaining that Maimonides in the Mishneh Torah: Laws of Kings, describes the role of the king as being two-fold: 1) to enforce justice 2) to fight "*milchamah*". The Rav explains that "*milchamah*", which is often translated as "war", has a broader definition, meaning any time of crisis – military, economic or spiritual. He states:

When times are normal there is no need for such unity. In times of war, we need unified, collected leadership. He is responsible for the well-being of the people and their continued existence. Secondly, the king is responsible for the principles of justice. The courts were composed of three, twenty three, or seventy one justices and found in all the cities. But the king is necessary when justice is being trampled in time of crisis and is in danger of disappearing. When the principles of justice are being desecrated, where the

people make mockery, the Bes Din (court) is not sufficient. For example, the Hashmonayim lived in critical times. They fought against the "mishyavnim" — the revisionists in combat and the power were seized by Yehuda Hamaccabee. He had the courage and ability of a king. These are the two objectives which a melech (a king) should pursue: general crises and justice."

The Rav explains, the distinction between the original situation of meeting with Yoseph and the later crisis that develops. It is only in the crisis situation that Yehuda stepped forward.

When the brothers first come to Joseph and he accused them of espionage, they thought he was irritated but not critical. After all, he acted like a gentleman, was handsome and in general conducted himself exemplarily. When they finished the food, <u>Yehuda smelled danger</u>. His conscience was affected. "<u>I must come forward at once, it is a crisis!</u>" Later, he withdraws because again there is no crisis. He becomes humble, modest, withdrawn. When he comes before Joseph, they exchange gifts etc. Again he withdraws and his name is not mentioned. When the goblet is discovered and they tear their clothes in despair, now he must emerge. <u>It is a critical time</u>. They all come to Joseph's house and Joseph understands very well that he'll have to deal with them, but he

thought it would be collective bargaining. However, "Vayigash Yehuda" —Yehuda stepped forth.... The possibility that the house of Jacob will be destroyed aroused the "Lion of Judah".

The Rav then clarifies elements of the narrative of Joseph and the brothers by explaining that Joseph's complex deception of the brothers had an objective beyond that of bringing about their repentance. Joseph wanted to have "*malchus*" (kingship) in both the physical realm (which he had already accomplished as viceroy of Egypt) and the spiritual realm (i.e. - being the source of the messiah). The Rav states:

In order to have all this he had to have one condition. When Joseph beheld the second vision, this is the one which he revealed to Jacob. Jacob declared, "Do you expect me to bow to you?" Jacob is the sun! In order to recognize fulfillment of the second condition, Jacob must bow. Jacob had the key - the control. Jacob will never accept and Joseph can never lay claim to "malchus". His problem was, "How can he make Jacob prostrate himself?" Thus, he contrived the following plan. He will contain or retain Benjamin — fully knowing that Jacob will not remain in Canaan if Benjamin doesn't return. He will come to Egypt, bow just once to the "Egyptian Viceroy" as a matter or protocol and the "malchus" will come to him. Judah did not understand all this but he felt that the strange

Egyptian leader had an interest in making Jacob leave Canaan and come to Egypt. "Jacob will come without knowing the identity." Should he know, he surely will not bow and Joseph cannot take over "malchus".

The Rav concludes this portion of his lecture by explaining that Yehuda, on some level, sensed this desire of Joseph, even though he did not know it was Joseph! Yehuda defeated Joseph's plan by clarifying to him that Yaakov would die if Joseph kept Benjamin and this clarification ended Joseph's attempt for the malchus which rightfully was Yehuda's portion. The Rav concludes:

What did Judah tell Joseph? "You are making a mistake. Jacob will never come. You cannot achieve you objective. If you keep Benjamin, Jacob will die but not in Mitzraim. You have lost your game! You'll never force Jacob to come! "This is when Joseph broke down and realized that "*hashgocha*" (providence) has different plans. Now he no longer could control his own emotions.

http://www.613.org/rav/ravnotes2.html#jan0679

Although many understand Yaakov as preparing Joseph for leadership and attribute to this the bestowing on him of the *ketonet passim* (coat of colors) and his giving Joseph the role of "watcher" of his brothers, it seems that both Yaakov and Yehuda were aware on some level that the kingship and source of the Messiah belonged to Yehuda. The final blessing Yaakov gives to Yehuda states: **"The staff shall not depart from Yehuda, nor a ruler from between his feet, until the coming of Shilo, and the peoples shall obey him."** An interesting question is whether Yaakov was aware of this role for Yehuda from an earlier point or whether it was revealed to him later, perhaps at the time of the giving of the blessings.

In this parsha, Yoseph deceived his brothers, pretending to not know them and suspect them of spying. He puts them through tremendous anguish and frightens them greatly until he reveals himself as their brother Yoseph. Interestingly, Yoseph is never criticized for this behavior either by the brothers, his father or the classic commentators. This requires an explanation as we know that the deceive someone is prohibited in Judaism, certainly if it causes fear and anguish as it did here. Maimonides describes this prohibition against deception in the Mishneh Torah, *Hilchot Deot* ("Laws of Personality Traits") where he states:

It is forbidden to deceive people, even a non-Jew. For example, one should not sell a gentile the meat of an animal which has not been ritually slaughtered as if it were ritually slaughtered meat, nor a shoe made from the hide of an animal which has died of natural causes as if it were made of the hide of a slaughtered animal. One should not press his colleague to share a meal

with him when he knows that his colleague will not accept the invitation, nor should he press presents upon him when he knows that his colleague will not accept them. He should not open casks supposedly for his colleague which he must open for sale, in order to deceive him into thinking that they have been opened in his honor. The same applies with all matters of this sort. It is forbidden to utter a single word of deception or fraud. Rather, one should have only truthful speech, a proper spirit and a heart pure from all deceit and trickery. (Mishneh Torah: Laws of Character Traits 2:6)

It also goes without say that one is not allowed to take revenge and therefore give "payback" to someone who has wronged him. This violates a Torah prohibition as Maimonides states:

A person who takes revenge against a colleague transgresses a Torah prohibition, as [Leviticus 19:18] states: "Do not take revenge." Even though [revenge] is not punished by lashes, it is a very bad trait. Instead, a person should [train himself] to rise above his feelings about all worldly things, for men of understanding consider all these things as vanity and emptiness which are not worth seeking revenge for. (Mishneh Torah, Laws of Character Traits: 7:7)

Yoseph is known by our tradition as "Yoseph the Tsaddik" distinguished for his righteousness. How does this align with these actions? The dreams are often pointed to as the motivation and what provides the right for Yoseph to take the course that he did. Yoseph was not one of the 48 male prophets of Israel, yet the dreams are certainly noteworthy as they are included in the Torah. Also, in this parsha, upon meeting his brothers in Egypt, the Torah states in (Bereisheit 41:9) regarding Yoseph, that he remembered the dreams he had:

And Joseph remembered the dreams that he had dreamed about them, and he said to them, "You are spies; you have come to see the nakedness of the land."

ט. וַיִּזְכֹּר יוֹסֵף אֵת הַחֲלֹמוֹת אֲשֶׁר חָלַם לָהֶם וַיֹּאמֶר אֲלֵהֶם מְרַגְּלִים אַתֶּם לִרְאוֹת אֶת עֶרְוַת הָאָרֶץ בָּאתֶם:

Rashi: that he had dreamed about them: Heb. לָהֶם, lit., to them, [but here it means] about them (Targum Jonathan). He knew that they (his dreams) had been fulfilled, for they (his brothers) had prostrated themselves to him. [from Zohar, vol. 1, p. 199b]

אשר חלם להם: עליהם, וידע שנתקיימו, שהרי השתחוו לו:

Yoseph concluded, according to the Rav, that the brothers bowing down to him was Yoseph's confirmation that he was to be the root of the Jewish people's *malchus* (kingship) and that the through this lineage, be the one who the messiah would descend from. Only when Yehuda clarified for him that he was wrong in this assessment, did Yoseph realize that he had made an error and the deception which he was carrying out in order to get his father Yaakov to bow down to him and fulfill the vision of the dream. At this point Yoseph immediately ends the deception and reveals his true identity to the brothers. As the Rav stated:

What did Judah tell Joseph? "You are making a mistake. Jacob <u>will never</u> come. You cannot achieve you objective. If you keep Benjamin, <u>Jacob will die</u> but <u>not in Mitzraim</u>. You have lost your game! You'll never force Jacob to come! "This is when Joseph broke down and realized that "*hashgocha*" (providence) has different plans. Now he no longer could control his emotions!"

So what can we conclude regarding Yoseph's deception? Yoseph did not desire to deceive his brothers or his father or to cause them anguish. However, from his perspective of what the dreams were revealing about the establishment of the Jewish people, he judged it to be God's will and command that he carry out this deception in order to have his father bow down to him. Although not a prophet, Yoseph realized that in his role as viceroy, providence had placed him in a pivotal role in the survival and establishment of the Jewish people, as they journeyed down to Egypt to live. Once Yehuda made clear to Yoseph that he was not to be the root of the kingship of the Jewish people, Yoseph immediately ended the deception and assumed the role of a truthful, compassionate brother and fellow Jews in accordance with the qualities of a righteous person (a "tsaddik") as described by Maimonides.

VAYIGASH

The Role of the Charismatic Personality

In Rabbi Soloveitchik's ("The Rav's") essay, "The Emergence of Ethical Man" he identifies Yaakov as one of the four "charismatic personalities" of the Jewish people, the others being Avraham, Yitzchak and Moshe. The essay is a description of the ethical development of the human being and his role in the creation. The Rav states:

God regretted the creation of man. The orgiastic, esthetic type dominated mankind: *hamas* (violence was the guiding motif of human activities and the demonic superseded the divine personality. The catastrophe by which God punished man-the deluge-did not solve the problem completely. It improved man; yet it did not heal the breach in his personality. Through devious ways and zigzag channels providence began to realize a new human personality; the charismatic. Abraham was selected to rehabilitate man and to reinstate him to the ideal position which he was destined to occupy. *Kivyakhol*, God needed charismatic man to appear on the human stage. (" The Emergence of Ethical Man" Page 144-145)

The Rav describes a number of dimensions of this charismatic person. We will focus on one that relates to a pasuk in parsha VaYigash. When Yaakov is about to leave

Canaan to go to Egypt and live with Yoseph and his other sons there, God appears to him. The Torah states: (Vayigash, 46:2-4)

And God said to Israel in visions of the night, and He said, "Jacob, Jacob!" And he said, "Here I am."

וַיֹּאמֶר אֱ־לֹהִים לְיִשְׂרָאֵל
בְּמַרְאֹת הַלַּיְלָה וַיֹּאמֶר
יַעֲקֹב יַעֲקֹב וַיֹּאמֶר הִנֵּנִי׃

And He said, "I am God, the God of your father. Do not be afraid of going down to Egypt, for there I will make you into a great nation.

וַיֹּאמֶר אָנֹכִי הָאֵל אֱלֹהֵי
אָבִיךָ אַל תִּירָא מֵרְדָה
מִצְרַיְמָה כִּי לְגוֹי גָּדוֹל
אֲשִׂימְךָ שָׁם׃

I will go down with you to Egypt, and I will also bring you up, and Joseph will place his hand on your eyes.

אָנֹכִי אֵרֵד עִמְּךָ מִצְרַיְמָה
וְאָנֹכִי אַעַלְךָ גַם עָלֹה
וְיוֹסֵף יָשִׁית יָדוֹ עַל עֵינֶיךָ׃

The Rav comments on the pasuk 46:4, to explain an aspect of the charismatic personality of Yaakov.

We understand the first half of the prophecy: " I will go down with you into Egypt." Yet the last part of the sentence does not make sense. God left Egypt with the myriads of Children of Israel hundreds of years later. However, Moses exodus is considered as if it were Jacob's personal triumph. – "I will also surely bring you up again." God went out of Egypt with

Jacob, although the latter had been dead for hundreds of years. What is the solution of this mystery?

At this point the Rav describes the "historical personality" which is part of the charismatic personality. This historical personality, the Rav explains, lives as intensely in the past and the future as he does in the present. His people are not just the people of the present time, but all who have died and will be born. The Rav focuses here on the uniqueness of the name "Israel" which is both the name of one of the patriarch's and, at the same time, the name of the Jewish people. He states:

Israel is a people as well as a patriarch. We use it both in plural and in singular: *Bnei Yisrael* ("the Children of Israel") and Israel (both) have an identical connotation: the children of Israel through whom Israel survives the fate of the natural being. The natural ego is assimilated into an individualistic ego who lived at the dawn of history. The nation is as unique and as lonely as their father-shepherd Abraham was. The people relive his life, of course in a different environment yet in identical situations. The uniqueness of such an historical existence consists in projecting a present onto a mystical future, and vice-versa in typing it in with a dim past.... Not only do we remember our past but we relive and re-experience it. Moreover, the past asserts itself in the present. Yet, both past and present manifest themselves in an act of anticipation and expectation of a future....The identity

of Abraham has not been lost throughout the generations. The identity of the Messiah has not been erased from our historical consciousness in spite of its visionary reality." (Page 172)

The Rav is describing the phenomenon of a person whose personality is as much shaped by the Jewish people's historical past and its anticipated future as it is by present day situations. The charismatic personality, of which all Jews are enjoined to cultivate, experiences the whole of Jewish history within their short span of years. So in this way Yaakov did experience "and I will bring you up again" (the redemption from Egypt) as God promised to him, although he experienced it as a future event.

Yaakov and his sons' descent to Egypt exposed them to a dominant culture which was idolatrous with a pantheon of animal-gods. Maimonides ("The Rambam") explains in "The Guide for the Perplexed" that the Torah's use of cattle, sheep and goats for sacrifices was related to their being commonly worshipped by idolaters. He states:

Scripture tells us, according to the Version of Onkelos, that the Egyptians worshipped Aries, and therefore abstained from killing sheep, and held shepherds in contempt. "Behold we shall sacrifice the abomination of the Egyptians," etc. (Exodus, 8:26); "For every shepherd is an abomination to the Egyptians" (Genesis, 46:34). Some sects among the Sabeans

worshipped demons and imagined they took the form of goats and called them therefore, "goats" (*se-irim*). This worship was widespread. "And they shall no more offer their sacrifices unto demons, after whom they have gone whoring" (Leviticus, 17:7). For this reason those sects abstained from eating goat's flesh. Most idolaters objected to killing cattle, holding this species of animals in great estimation. Therefore the people of Hodu (Indians) up to this day do not slaughter cattle even in those countries where other animals are slaughtered. In order to eradicate these false principles, the Law commanded us to offer sacrifices only of these three kinds: Ye shall bring your offering of the cattle, of the herd and of the flock (Leviticus, I, 2). Thus the very act which is considered by the heathen as the greatest crime, is the means of approaching God, and obtaining His pardon for our sins. In this manner, evil principles, the disease of the human soul, are cured by other principles which are diametrically opposite. This is also the reason why we were commanded to kill a lamb on Passover, and to sprinkle the blood thereof outside on the gates. We had to free ourselves of evil doctrines and to proclaim the opposite, that the very act which was then considered as being the cause of death would be the cause of deliverance from death. "And the Lord will pass over the door, and will not suffer the destroyer to come unto your houses to smite you." (Exodus: 12:23). Thus they were rewarded for performing openly a

service every part of which was objected to by the idolaters. (Guide, Book 3: Chapter 46)

The Rambam understands that the removal of any remnant of idolatrous feelings towards these animals will be achieved through their use as the object of sacrifice to God.

VAYACHI

The Burial of Yaakov In The Land of Israel

In parsha Vayachi, Yaakov, after living in Egypt for 17 years, knows he is going to die. Yaakov has Yosef swear to bury him in the land of Israel and not in the land of Egypt. The parsha states: (47:29-31)

29. When the time drew near for Israel to die, he called his son Joseph and said to him, "If I have now found favor in your eyes, now place your hand beneath my thigh, and you shall deal with me with loving kindness and truth; do not bury me now in Egypt.

כט. וַיִּקְרְבוּ יְמֵי יִשְׂרָאֵל
לָמוּת וַיִּקְרָא לִבְנוֹ לְיוֹסֵף
וַיֹּאמֶר לוֹ אִם נָא מָצָאתִי
חֵן בְּעֵינֶיךָ שִׂים נָא יָדְךָ
תַּחַת יְרֵכִי וְעָשִׂיתָ עִמָּדִי
חֶסֶד וֶאֱמֶת אַל נָא
תִקְבְּרֵנִי בְּמִצְרָיִם:

30. I will lie with my forefathers, and you shall carry me out of Egypt, and you shall bury me in their grave." And he said, "I will do as you say."

ל. וְשָׁכַבְתִּי עִם אֲבֹתַי
וּנְשָׂאתַנִי מִמִּצְרַיִם
וּקְבַרְתַּנִי בִּקְבֻרָתָם וַיֹּאמַר
אָנֹכִי אֶעֱשֶׂה כִדְבָרֶךָ:

31. And he said, "Swear to me. " So he swore to him, and Israel prostrated himself on the head of the bed.

לא. וַיֹּאמֶר הִשָּׁבְעָה לִי
וַיִּשָּׁבַע לוֹ וַיִּשְׁתַּחוּ יִשְׂרָאֵל
עַל רֹאשׁ הַמִּטָּה:

Maimonides (the Rambam) in his work the Mishneh Torah, states, within the same halacha in which he discusses living in the land of Israel, the reward and atonement for one's burial in the land of Israel:

The Sages commented: "Whoever dwells in Eretz Yisrael will have his sins forgiven as (Isaiah 33:24) states: "The inhabitants shall not say "I am sick'. The people who dwell there shall be forgiven their sins." Even one who walks four cubits there will merit the world to come and one who is buried there receives atonement as if the place in which he is (buried) is an altar of atonement as (Devarim 32:43) states: "His land will atone for His people." (In contrast the prophet Amos (7:17) used the expression, 'You shall die in an impure land' as a prophecy of retribution. There is no comparison between the merit of a person who lives in Eretz Yisrael (and is buried there) and one whose body is brought there. Nevertheless, our great sages would bring their bodies there. Take an example from our Patriarch, Yaakov, and Yosef the righteous. (Mishneh Torah: Laws of Kings and Their Wars: 6:11)

The Rambam, though making clear the inferior status of one who is buried in Israel without having lived there, does state that even one who is only buried there "receives an atonement". Although there are many, including the Ramban and the Kuzari, that held the physical land itself was of a different quality than that of outside the land, there is no indication that the Rambam, whose approach to mitzvot is one that is focused on their impact on the mind and emotions of the doer, held that this special quality of the physical land itself existed. And even if he did hold this to be true, how would this quality of the soil of Israel be able to atone for ones sins after death?

An approach to this issue can be found in the example the Rambam gives of Yaakov's request to Yosef, in this week's parsha, that he bury him in Eretz Yisrael. In this case, Yaakov burial in the land of Israel is a result of a conscious decision made when Yaakov is alive. The decision of his burial place, reflected the nature of Yaakov's understanding of his core Identity as a Jew and as one whose burial in the land of Israel would express this idea. Similarly, a person who during his or her life was not able to live in Israel, due to practical or emotional issues, indicates by their desire to be buried there, expresses in this act their core identification with the Jewish people and the desire, possessed though unrealized, to live in the land. From this perspective one can see why the Rambam includes burial in the land of Israel with the explanation of living in the land of Israel. Where one arranges one's burial reflects the true nature of the person's beliefs and values. After death, one is not going to be taken to task for their decision, so this decision can be one that most purely reflects the deepest, truest nature of the person's desire. For this reason, the burial "is an atonement".

Rabbi Joseph B Soloveitchik recounts a story of burial in the land of Israel that he relates to Yaakov's request in this week's parsha. The Rav states:

Baron Edmond de Rothschild (1835-1934) was instrumental in developing the wind industry in Eretz Yisrael. He was responsible for the expansion of the settlements of Rishon le-Ziyon and Zikhron Ya'akov and was a focal figure in the development of the Yishuv. He died in Paris, a year before his wife. Years later it was decided to reinter his remains and those of his wife in Eretz Yisrael. Alain de Rothchild related to me that Charles DeGaulle told him: 'I will tell you frankly. I do not understand you Jews. I always thought that the Rothschild family was devoted and loyal to France, that they were real Frenchman and only differed as to their religious commitment. But I would like to ask you to give me the real definition of who is a good Frenchman?...And listen to what I am going to say now. A good Frenchman is one who dies and is buried in French soil. I cannot imagine a good Frenchman whose body is transferred somewhere else.... It is not only a reflection on him but on you and on the rest of the family. Actually, I could forbid the reburial....But I do not want to start a fight with the Jews of France.' (The Rav continues) This is exactly what Pharoh said to Joseph. 'And Pharoh told Joseph: Go up and buy your father as he adjured you' (Beresheit 50:6). In other words, "Of course, I am

disappointed that he will not be interred in Egypt. But what can I do, you took an oath to your father. (From a lecture on Parshat Vayechi given at Yeshiva University on December 23, 1980-quoted in the Book, "The Rav: The World of Yosef Soloveitchik by Aaron Rakeffet-Rothkoff, pages 199-200).

This example is particularly interesting because it explains a case of a person who may not have even requested that his body be buried in Eretz Yisrael, but who can still receive atonement for the burial. For although Baron Edmond de Rothschild may not have made the specific request (it is unclear from the story), the acts of his life reflected his great love of Zion and his core identification with the Jewish people and the holy land. So one can say, in a sense, that the acts of his life made clear his intention and his interest to be buried in the land of Israel. Perhaps for matters of family and prestige he indicated that he should be buried in France. But those who knew him best, understood his inner yearning and truest self was with the land and mission of Israel. Therefore his burial in the land was an atonement.

The idea that the land of a person's burial is a clear indication of his or her truest self in reflected in the deep insult felt by Charles DeGaulle and Pharoh when they saw these great "patriots" decide that, although they achieved fame and fortune in the lands where they died, their core value and deepest inner yearning was for Holy Land and to be bound up with the souls of the Jewish people in the land of Israel.

Shemot

Now these are the names of the sons of Israel, who came into Egypt with Jacob; every man came with his household.
Shemot 1:1

SHEMOT

Moshe Rebbenu-In a Class By Himself

The second book of the Torah, Shemot, moves from the lives of the Patriarchs to the events of Egypt with the Jewish people's enslavement and redemption. The narrative focuses intensely on the development and role of Moshe, the greatest of all prophets. Maimonides (the Rambam) in his great work the Mishneh Torah, describes the absolutely uniqueness and superior nature of Moshe's prophetic status in comparison with all of the other prophets, including Avraham, Yitzchak and Yaakov. He states:

In what ways did Moses differ from the other Prophets? Firstly, whereas the other Prophets received their prophecies in a dream or vision, Moses received his while awake and standing, as it is written, "And when Moses was in the Tent of Meeting to speak with Him, he heard the voice speaking to him, et cetera". Secondly, the other Prophets received their prophecies via an angel. Therefore, what they saw was by way of parable and riddle. Moses, on the other hand, did not receive his prophecies via an angel, as it is written, "With him I speak mouth to mouth", "And the Lord spoke to Moses face to face", "...and the outward appearance of the Lord does he behold", that is to say that what Moses saw was not by way of parable, but he saw each prophecy absolutely clearly without any parables or riddles. The Torah said about him,

"...manifestly, and not in dark speeches", showing that when Moses received a prophecy he did not do so by way of riddles, but did so with clarity, and saw everything absolutely clearly. Thirdly, the other Prophets were scared [of their prophetic visions] and would shy away, but Moses wasn't and didn't. Scripture says, "...as a man speaks with a friend" - just as a man is not scared to listen to his friend, so Moses had the capabilities to understand his prophecies and to stand unafraid. Fourthly, none of the Prophets prophesied whenever they wanted to, but whenever God wanted to He would visit Moses and bestow upon him prophecy. Moses did not have to attune his thoughts or otherwise prepare himself, for the reason that he was always prepared and stood like a ministering angel. Therefore, he would receive prophecies at any time, as it is written, "Stand still and I will hear what the Lord will command concerning you". In this God trusted him, as it is written, "Go say to them, `Return to your tents'. But as for you, stand here by Me, and I will speak to you, et cetera". From here we see that whenever any of the other Prophets had finished prophesizing they would return to their houses [and families] and other bodily needs, like everybody else, so they therefore did not separate themselves from their wives. Moses, on the other hand, did not return to his home, and separated himself from his wife, and all that resembled her, forever. His mind was [always] connected to God, and God's glory never

left him at all; light emanated from his face, and he was holy like an angel. (Mishneh Torah, Foundation of Torah: (7:6)

The uniqueness of Moshe's prophecy in comparison with the other prophets is so profound that the Rambam states in his "Guide for the Perplexed" that the use of the same term 'prophecy' when applied to both the prophecy of Moshe and the other prophets is "equivocal", meaning that the differences regarding Moshe's prophetic actions and all others was a qualitative one and not simply one of degree. The Rambam writes in his 13 Principles of Faith:

Principle VII. The prophetic capacity of Moses our Teacher, peace be upon him: And this is that we accept that he was the father of all prophets that were before him and that will be after him. He was on a qualitatively different level than any other, and he is chosen from all other people before and after him of any that have any knowledge of God; for his was the greatest. And he, peace be upon him, rose to the levels of the angels.

It is clear that, not only was Moshe a uniquely superior human being, but also that it is God's will that there should only be one such being. Understanding that there will never arise another like Moshe confirms that the Torah is eternal and cannot be refined or improved at any later point in time. Moshe was a pivotal part of God's creation of the world and was, by any definition of the word, a miracle.

In spite of this exalted nature of Moshe Rebbenu, the Rambam makes clear that there was a developmental process in Moshe's life. The Rambam states in the Guide for the Perplexed, when describing the levels of prophecy that, with regards to the first degree of prophecy *ruach hakodesh* (the lowest level) that **"such a force did not abandon Moshe our Master from the moment he reached manhood,"** implying that he "started out" at the lower part of the prophetic levels. The Rambam also states in the Guide that **"Even Moshe our Teacher received his first prophecy through an angel, 'And an angel of the Lord appeared to him the flame of fire' (Shemot 3:2)".**

Rabbi Joseph B. Soloveitchik ("The Rav") in his essay "The Emergency of Ethical Man" describes both the uniqueness and the torturous development of Moshe and how both his mission and development differed dramatically from Avraham. He states (pages 182-183):

We are not aware of any personal metamorphosis in Moses due to his bitter experience with his mother civilization. In spite of that episode, he remained an elegant courtier. As the daughters of Jethro tell their father: "An Egyptian man ("*mitzri*") delivered us out of the hand of the shepherds (Shemot, 2:19)." Moses did not renounce his affiliation with the Egyptian society. Not until he was well engrossed in his

mission, which resulted from the majestic scene of the burning bush, did our redeemer realize the change which had come upon him. This is the crux of the matter, and that is why the story of Moses is diametrically opposed to that of Abraham. While the father of the nation voluntarily undertakes a historical mission without experiencing any duress or compulsion, the redeemer is forced by apocalyptic command into a historical situation. He did not discover God; nor did he select Him or the moral law. The apocalyptic revelation surprised him and took him prisoner. He encountered apocalyptic necessity. God commanded, and he tried to resist, without success.

The Rav also clarifies in this essay, how Moshe established a new level of man's relationship with God:

Moses introduces a new motif into the God-man fellowship, namely that of *shelihut*-agency. He becomes the divine angel who acts on behalf of God and represents Him.,, "and sent an angel, and brought us out of Egypt" (Numbers, 20:16). The angelic role-that is to say, the role of agent-of the charismatic personality was assigned for the first time to Moses. Abraham was never charged with such a task. He never represented God as His emissary. No divine power was delegated to him. He discovered God, was quite intimate with Him, yet had no right to act as His spokesman. Whatever he preached he did on his own

behalf. The angelic mission was denied to him…Moses was the first person to receive the word from God: "Come now, therefore, and I will send you to Pharaoh" (Shemot 3:10). The idea of the prophetic speech was introduced into the world: *ko-amar Hashem*-"thus says the Lord." Man appears as an agent of God. ("The Emergence of Ethical Man": pages 183-184)

The Rav distinguishes the essential nature of Avraham and Moshe as being distinct. Whereas Avraham came to God through a period of 40 years of thought and reflection, Moshe's mission as the redeemer of the Jewish people was thrust upon him at the burning bush where his life was instantly transformed to one of an agent of God in the redemption of the Jewish people. Moshe, unlike Avraham, Yitzchak and Yaakov has no family-centered dimension to his life. We learn nothing about his relationship with his wife or child. The only dramatic family event is when his wife Tzipora saves him from destruction for delaying the circumcision of his son. Later we are told, Moshe separated from marital relations. The mission was at the core of the lives of the Patriarchs and Matriarchs. But in the case of Moshe Rebbenu the mission was his life and enveloped his entire being.

VAERA

The Role of the Prophet in Miracles

In the pasha of Vayera Moshe begins to carry out the mission of delivering the Jewish people from servitude in Egypt. Central to this deliverance is God's producing of miracles- the ten *"makos"* (often translated as "plagues") that precede the exodus of the Jewish people. The pasha states:

And I will harden the heart of Pharaoh, and I will multiply My signs and my wonders in the land of Egypt. But Pharaoh will not listen to you, and I will lay My hand on Egypt, and I will bring out my hosts, My people the children of Israel, out of Egypt by great judgments. (Shemot: 7: 3-4)

From this verse it is clear that God is the source of the miracles that occurred in Egypt. But what is the role of Moshe in bringing about these miracles? Did he play a passive role in the occurrence of each miracle- a type of "announcer" - one who merely has foreknowledge of the miracle and it's timing? Or did he play some type of active role, being something of a "miracle worker"? This more active role appears to be the position held by Maimonides. He states in his work the "Guide for the Perplexed":

Scripture, therefore, declares that no prophet will ever, like Moses, do signs publicly in the presence of friend and enemy, of his followers and his opponents; this is the meaning of the words: 'And there arose not a prophet since in Israel like unto Moses, etc., in all the signs and wonders, etc., in the sight of all Israel.' Two thing are here mentioned together; namely, that there will not arise a prophet that will perceive as Moses perceived, or a prophet that will do as he did; then it is pointed out that the signs were made in the presence of Pharoh, all his servants and all his land, the opponents of Moses and also in the presence of all the Israelites, his followers. This is a distinction not possessed by any prophet before Moses; nor, as is correctly foretold, will it ever be possessed by another prophet....Your mind must comprehend the distinction of the prophecy and the wonders of Moses, and understand that his greatness in prophetic perception was the same as his power of producing miracles: (Guide for the Perplexed: Book 2: Chapter 35)

So, for Maimonides, the prophet is more than a passive player in the miracle. Only Moshe, he states here, could "**produce**" the public miracles of the plagues and the Exodus. He did more, it seems, than announce them through foreknowledge. But what was Moshe's active role in the production of the miracles? To explore this passive versus active role of the prophet, I would like to revisit the differing positions of Maimonides and *Chazal* regarding whether the miracles were designed into the initial creation of the world (a position held by *Chazal*) or whether it was produced at the time of its occurrence (Maimonides View). In the Guide for the Perplexed he states:

When I, however, said that no prophet ever announced "a permanent change of any of its properties," I intended to except miracles. For although the rod was turned into a serpent, the water into blood, the pure and noble hand into a leprous one, without the existence of any natural cause that could affect these or similar phenomena, these changes were not permanent, they have not become a physical property. This is my opinion; this should be our belief. Our Sages, however said very strange things as regards miracles; they are found in Bereshit Rabba, and in Midrash Koheleth, namely, that the miracles are to some extent also natural; for they say, when God created the Universe with its present physical properties, He made it part of these properties, that they should produce certain miracles at certain times, and *the sign of a prophet consisted in the fact that God told him to declare when a certain thing will take place*, but the thing itself was effected according to the fixed laws of nature (Guide for the Perplexed, Book 2: Chapter 29)

Upon reflection, the difference of opinion between Maimonides and *Chazal* seems to be a difficult one to understand. It is true that miracles occur at a point in time. There is a timeline for all events that take place from the beginning of the creation of the world up to the present moment. For example the splitting of the sea occurred in the Jewish year of 2448 on the 22nd day of Nissan. This is at a specific time. Both Maimonides and *Chazal*, of course agree on this. So what do they disagree about? It seems, at first, that the disagreement is whether the miracle was designed within the structure of the initial creation (*Chazal's* position) or whether this structure was "disturbed or altered" at the time of the miracle. Here is where it becomes difficult to understand. Maimonides holds, as do *Chazal*, I would assume, that God is outside of time. God created time with the other elements of creation. This concept has always been, as I understand it, a fundamental principle of Judaism.

So, if we accept that God is outside of time, as time is a property of the material creation, how can there be a disagreement between Maimonides and Chazal as to the timing of God's causing of the miracle? There are no "different times" with regard to the act of creation by God The idea of arguing whether a miracle was pre-programmed by God at the initial time of creation or done "on the spot" seems meaningless since God doesn't act within the timeline. If time was created at the moment of 'the Beginning" it would seem that everything that was created was created at that point including all future time and its miracles. Time just keeps "rolling out" for us as we experience it's passing in our existence within the physical world.

So what is Maimonides' position that implies an alteration in the creation at the time of the miracle? He certainly does not hold that God creates within time or creates at different times. But perhaps there is another factor in the production of miracles that does exist within time. This temporal factor (one bound by time and existing on the universes timeline) is the prophet. Perhaps Maimonides agrees with Chazal that all miracles have a non-temporal element- that part of the miracle created by God, who is outside of time at the point of creation. However, there is another element causing the miracle that is in time- this being the role of the prophet in bringing about the miracle. Perhaps it is with this role that Maimonides and Chazal differ. This difference is whether the prophet plays a passive role as a simple announcer, knowing the timing and details of the miracle, but having no causative role (*Chazal's* position) or whether the prophet plays a co-causative role with God in the production of the miracle (Maimonides' view).

Rabbi Soloveitchik ("The Rav") states in his essay "The Emergence of Ethical Man" regarding miracles:

The word "miracle" in Hebrew does not possess the connotation of the supernatural. It has never been

placed on a transcendental level. "Miracle" (*pele, nes*) describes only an outstanding event which causes amazement. A turning point in history is always a miracle, for it commands attention as an event which intervened fatefully in the formation of that group or that individual. As we read the story of the exodus from Egypt, we are impressed by the distinct tendency of the Bible to relate the events in natural terms. The frogs came out of river when the Nile rose, the wind brought the locusts and split the sea. All archeologists agree that the plagues as depicted by the Bible are very closely related to the geographical and climatic conditions that prevail in Egypt. Behind the passages in the Bible we may discern a distinct intention to describe the plagues as naturally as possible....The reason for this is obvious. A philosophy which considers the world-drama as a fixed, mechanical process governed by an unintelligent, indifferent principle, may regard the miracle as a supernatural transcendental phenomenon which does not fit into the causalistic, meaningless monotony. Israel, however, who looked upon the universal occurrence as the continuous realization of a divine ethical will embedded into dead and live matter, could never classify the miracle as something unique and incomprehensible. Both natural monotony and the surprising element in nature express God's word. Both are regular, lawful phenomena; both can be traced to an identical source. (pages 187-188)

I do not believe that Rabbi Soloveitchik is in any way denying the miraculous nature of the events of the exodus from Egypt. He is clarifying in the above passage that Judaism sees the miraculous presence of God within the natural order of the universe with its profound wisdom, beauty and ethical meaning. So from the Jew's perspective the awe that one encounters in a miraculous experience such as the 10 *makkos*, is not a distinct and uncanny event. For the Jew the experiencing of the miracles is on the same continuum of awe and wonder he or she experiences in viewing the world in it "non-miraculous" state, seeing the presence of God as the miraculous Creator and Sustainer of "everyday" existence and as One whose connection with human history is an ongoing and continuous phenomenon. Judaism utilizes the terms "*nase nister*" ("hidden miracle") and "*nase niflah*" ("open miracle") to describe this continuum of God's intervention, which though always miraculous, differs in its apparent departure from the natural order which God has established.

BO

The Korban Pesach & the Birth of The Jewish Community

In the pasha of Bo, Moshe is commanded to inform the Jewish people on the Korban Pesach (the special Passover offering):

Speak to the entire assembly of Israel, saying: On the tenth of this month they shall take for themselves-each man-a lamb or kid for each father's house, a lamb or kid for the household. But if the household will be too small for a lamb or kid, then he and his neighbor who is near his house shall take according to the number of people; everyone according to what he eats shall be counted for the lamb or kid. An unblemished lamb or kid, a male, within its first year shall it be for you; from the sheep or goat you shall take it. (Shemot: 12: 3-5)

Maimonides (the Rambam), in the "Guide for the Perplexed", explains particular details of the Korban Pesach as being necessary to assure the performance of this mitzvah in Egypt. He states:

The particular rules concerning the paschal lamb, namely, that it should only be eaten "roasted by fire and in one house, neither shall you break a bone thereof", have all a manifest reason. For just as unleavened bread is due to haste, roasting the lamb is also due to haste. For there was then no time to cook

various kinds of dishes and to prepare various sorts of food. Even delay in order to break its bones and to extract what is in it was forbidden. For the gist of all this has already been mentioned, namely: 'And you shall eat it in haste' (Shemot:12:11). Now haste does not allow for the delay required for breaking the bones or for lending parts of them from one house to another and for waiting for the return of the messenger. All these are actions indicative of laxity and sluggishness, whereas the purpose was to make a show of haste and hurry, lest someone delay and come too late to leave Egypt with the multitude of the people, whereupon he would be exposed to harm and to being set upon by surprise. These circumstances were then perpetuated in order to commemorate the matter as it really was. As it says: 'And you will keep this statute (chukka) in its season from year to year.': Shemot: 13:10. (Guide, Book 3, Chapter 46)

According to the Rambam, the structure of the Korban Pesach was required in Egypt to address the need for haste in preparation as the exodus was imminent and any delay could prevent someone from leaving with the group. After this first Korban Pesach, all those that followed, the Rambam explains, retain the halachic structure of "haste" to 'commemorate' the original Pesach and its need to be eaten in haste to facilitate the leaving from Egypt. Regarding the limitation of the Korban Pesach only being eaten by those who have been circumcised, the Rambam states:

The prohibition against uncircumcised men partaking of it has been explained by the Sages, may their memory be blessed, for they said that during their long stay in Egypt (the Children of Israel) with a view to assimilating themselves to the Egyptians, had omitted observing the commandment of circumcision. When thereupon the paschal lamb was prescribed by the Law and the condition was posed that it should only be sacrificed by someone after 'he himself, his sons, and the members of his household had been circumcised- for only then could he come near and keep it (Shemot: 12;48) –all of them were circumcised; and the blood of circumcision mingled with the blood of the paschal lamb because of the great number of men who had just undergone circumcision, as the Sages have mentioned.

The restriction of the Pascal lamb participants to only those who have been circumcised, addressed the historical issue of assimilation that was widespread in Egypt. It is interesting to speculate as to whether the Rambam is explaining the specific reason for the mitzvah or a beneficial outcome of the mitzvah. This question, it seems to me, rests on the question of whether the Torah's knowledge is of human dimension and fully understandable by the human mind, or possesses a divine dimension of which we can only understand imperfectly at best due to our limited intellect. Has God given humanity a Torah that is a "on their level" and whose reasons can be discerned or instead one of infinite depth of which the human mind can simply assess benefits.

Rabbi Joseph B. Soloveitchik ("The Rav") states in the essay "The Festival of Freedom" with regards to the Korban Pesach:

The birth of the hesed community-of a nation within which people unite, give things away, care for each other, share what they possess-is symbolized by the paschal sacrifice. God did not need the Pascal lamb; He had no interest in the sacrifice. He simply wanted the people-slaves who had just come out of the house of bondage-to emerge from their isolation and insane self-centeredness into the hesed community, where the little that man has is too much for himself, where whatever he possesses transcends his ability to enjoy. A new fellowship was formed around the Pascal lamb; a new community sprang into existence. Being together, living with each other, sharing something many possess in common was made possible by the ceremonial of the paschal lamb. The halakhah coined the term "*havurah*" with reference to the group gathering together for this ceremonial (e.g. Mishneh, Pesahim 8:7). Eating together is a great medium of communication between individuals. Therefore everything is shared. The slave suddenly realizes that the little he has saved up for himself, a single lamb, is too much for him. The slave spontaneously does

something which he would never have believed that he was capable of doing, namely, he knocks on the door of his neighbor whom he had never noticed, inviting him to share the lamb with him and to eat together. (The Seder Night; The Exalted Evening Hagaddah, page 97).

The Rav considers the transformative impact of the Korban Pesach on the individual who has been a slave. In that condition, when survival is tenuous and life intensely cruel, human selfishness is the natural response. The halachik structure of the Korban Pesach and the creation of the gathering inculcates the quality of chesed within the Jew's sense of self. At this crucial juncture in the formation of the Jewish people, as they are being redeemed and undergoing a dramatic and rapid development, the pivotal event between slavery and freedom, the Korban Pesach, establishes this transformation as not only one of submission to God, but also one of Jews joining with one another in a close identification and concern and a realization that a Jewish person can only function as a Jew when in consonance with one another. The Rav, in his great essay "The Lonely Man of Faith" describes this special and unique "Covenantal Community" and the unique qualities of kindness and compassion of this community. He states:

There, not only hands are joined, but experiences as well; there, one hears not only the rhythmic sound of

the production line, but also the rhythmic beat of hearts starved for existential companionship and all-embracing sympathy and experiencing the grandeur of the faith commitment; there, one lonely soul finds another soul tormented by loneliness and solitude yet unqualifiedly committed. (pages 41-42)

For the Rav, it is only when people join together for the purpose of service to God that this highest form of community can be created. The Rav clarifies in this essay that it is only this community which can successfully quell the inherent loneliness and solitude of the individual human being who experiences his uniqueness and incommunicable inner self.

BESHALLACH

The Song by the Sea and Recognizing God's Power

In the pasha of Beshalach, the Jewish people are saved by God's miraculous splitting of the Sea of Reeds. Egypt's pursuing army is destroyed when the sea closes back on them. Moshe and the people respond with a joyous song of praise:

Then Moshe and the children of Israel sang this song to the Lord, and they spoke, saying: I will sing to the Lord for He is highly exalted; the horse and his rider He has thrown into the sea. My strength and song is the Lord, And He has become my salvation; This is my God, and I will glorify Him; My father's God and I will exalt Him. The Lord is a man of war; The Lord is His name. (Shemot: 14:1-2)

Rabbi Joseph B. Soloveitchik ("The Rav") in his essay, "Appointed Days: Purim and Hanukah" explains:

Spiritual achievements are attributed to man; military achievements are attributed to God: 'The Lord is a man of war; the Lord is His name' (Ex. 15:3). In the *Haggadah*, we search in vain for a reference to Moses. Is this not ingratitude on the part of the Jewish people, to omit mention of the name of Moses, the leader whose agency took the Jews out of Egypt, wo

sacrificed himself for the Jews? However, in Judaism any political achievement, any military victory, must not be attributed to flesh and blood; it must be attributed to God. No matter how much the human being accomplishes as far as political and material achievements are concerned, he cannot attribute them to himself. He must not claim credit, because the worst sin is to say: "My power and the might of my hand has gotten me this wealth" (Deut., 8:17). That is idolatry. ("Days of Deliverance" by Rabbi Joseph B. Soloveitchik, p. 124)

In the case of the redemption of Egypt, the Rav points out, the Jewish people were not participants in the physical struggle. This was a situation where God performed his conquest of Egypt with no assistance from the Jewish people and thereby made clear that He and He alone was the source of physical power. The Rav states in this same essay:

It may seem very strange, but at no point in Egypt did a Jew lift a finger in order to accelerate the Exodus or bring it about. This is the way the Bible has portrayed the events. On the contrary we read: 'And none of you shall go out from the door of his house until morning' (Ex. 12:22). In essence, God is saying to the Jewish people, 'Do not help Me; stay home. I will take care of Pharaoh and the Egyptians'. We learn from this that when the fight is spiritual, God invites the Jew to

participate. When spiritual survival is at stake, man must take the initiative (RB-the Rav is referring to the mentioning of the Hasmonians taking the fight to the Greeks at the time of Hanukah). **Even though man is under the guidance of the Almighty, man takes the initiative, and therefore his role is recorded** (RB-the Rav is referring to the mention of the Hasmonian struggle in the *Shemoneh Esrei* additions on Hanukah). **However when it is only a question of physical struggle, God acts differently. When there is a physical menace or the threat of physical destruction, God uses the human hand as an instrument of His will. He recruits man. He uses human energy and human resources, to implement the plan that He has devised. But Judaism has said that in this case the man who is the messenger of God should not be credited with the salvation. ("Days of Deliverance", p. 124)**

I would explain this distinction in terms of the unique quality of the human being's free will. A principal of Jewish thought is that "all is in the hands of God except for the fear of God". There is only one area in which an individual is fully independent and the determiner of his or her own destiny- this is in the choice to obey or disobey God. This is not within the power of God. So in a spiritual struggle man <u>is</u> the true operator and the one who should be recognized and lauded. But when it comes to power and strength man is an infinitesimal player and has no ability to truly determine the outcome. Here it is God, who controls all physical forces without restriction that is the master of war and the master of destruction and salvation. For man to attribute any power to himself in this regard would be a great error in assessment and, as the Rav relates, would stimulate man's illusion of power and control.

The Rambam in the "Guide for the Perplexed" comments on a statement in Beresheit Rabbah regarding the splitting of the Sea of Reeds:

It is said in the passage (from Beresheit Rabba): "**Rabbi Jonathan said: The Holy One, blessed be He, has posed conditions to the sea: that it should divide before Israel. That is (the meaning of the words) 'And the sea returned to its strength when the morning appeared. (Exodus 14:27) x Rabbi Jeremiah son of Elazar, said: The Holy One, blessed be He, has posed conditions not only to the sea, but to all that has been created in the six day of the Beginning.**

The Rambam, although he respects this position that miracles are not changes in nature, but instead, predetermined aspects of nature that appear as unique and coincide with the historic destiny of the Jewish people, he does not agree with it. Rabbi Jonathan's opinion, it seems to me would be that a miracle is something like a comet or Solar eclipse that may seem to be a departure from nature but is a rare but is, in reality, a natural event that occurs at a particular time. Of course the splitting of the Sea has the additional important element of its timing which coincides with the precise historical need of the Jewish people at that time. The Rambam differs with this opinion holding that there are actual temporary changes in nature that are not "programmed" from the beginning and these are what we call "miracles". The Rambam states:

....that which exists has had a beginning, and at first nothing at all existed except God. His wisdom required that He should bring creation into existence at the time when He did do it, and that what He has brought into existence should not be annihilated nor any of its natures changed except in certain particulars that He willed to change; about some of these we know, whereas about others that will be changed in the future we do not know. This is our opinion and the basis of our Law. (Guide, Book 2, Chapter 29)

An interesting related point is that according Rabbi Jonathan's and *Chazal's* position of a precisely programmed splitting of the sea being set from the beginning of creation, we could explain the haste with which the Jews had to leave Egypt. The splitting of the sea being timed to the minute in the beginning of creation was "due" to occur at a particular point in time as creation unfolded. The Jewish people had to be at the Sea of Reeds at the precise preprogrammed moment to have Jewish destiny perfectly mesh with the unfolding of this unique predestined splitting of the waters. This "catching the train" idea puts the concept of the matza in an interesting light as the Jewish people did not have time for the dough to rise as if they were "late" for the miracle, the waters would have opened and closed too late for the Children of Israel to be save and the Egyptian charioteers to be drowned. It seems from *Chazal's* point of view timing is an absolute requirement for the occurrence of miracles. The Rambam's position would not require this level of exact timing as the Rambam holds that the miracle is made "on the spot".

YISRO

The Sabbath-Not For The Angels

In the parsha of Yisro Moshe and the Jewish people receive the Torah. The commandment to observe the Sabbath is stated in the following verses (Shemot: 20:8-11)

8. Remember the Sabbath day to sanctify it.

ח. זָכוֹר אֶת יוֹם הַשַּׁבָּת לְקַדְּשׁוֹ:

9. Six days may you work and perform all your labor,

ט. שֵׁשֶׁת יָמִים תַּעֲבֹד וְעָשִׂיתָ כָּל מְלַאכְתֶּךָ:

10. but the seventh day is a Sabbath to the Lord, your God; you shall perform no labor, neither you, your son, your daughter, your manservant, your maidservant, your beast, nor your stranger who is in your cities.

י. וְיוֹם הַשְּׁבִיעִי שַׁבָּת לַי־הוָ־ה אֱלֹהֶיךָ לֹא תַעֲשֶׂה כָל מְלָאכָה אַתָּה וּבִנְךָ וּבִתֶּךָ עַבְדְּךָ וַאֲמָתְךָ וּבְהֶמְתֶּךָ וְגֵרְךָ אֲשֶׁר בִּשְׁעָרֶיךָ:

11. For [in] six days the Lord made the heaven and the earth, the sea and all that is in them, and He rested on the seventh day. Therefore, the Lord blessed the Sabbath day and sanctified it.

יא. כִּי שֵׁשֶׁת יָמִים עָשָׂה יְ־הוָ־ה אֶת הַשָּׁמַיִם וְאֶת הָאָרֶץ אֶת הַיָּם וְאֶת כָּל אֲשֶׁר בָּם וַיָּנַח בַּיּוֹם הַשְּׁבִיעִי עַל כֵּן בֵּרַךְ יְ־הוָ־ה אֶת יוֹם הַשַּׁבָּת וַיְקַדְּשֵׁהוּ:

Maimonides describes a two-fold purpose of the command to keep the Sabbath in his "Guide for the Perplexed". He states:

You know already from what I have said that no opinions retain their vitality except those which are confirmed, published, and by certain actions constantly revived among the people. Therefore we are told in the Law to honor this day; in order to confirm thereby the principle of Creation which will spread in the world, when all peoples keep Sabbath on the same day. For when the question is asked, why this is done, the answer is given: "For in six days the Lord has made the heaven and the earth…and He rested on the seventh day." (Shemot. 20:11). Two different reasons are given for this commandment because of two different objects. In the Decalogue in Shemot the following reason is given for distinguishing the Sabbath: "For in six days the Lord has made, etc." But in Devarim (5: 15) the reason is given: "And you shall remember that you were a slave in the land of Egypt, and that the Lord your God took you out from there with a strong hand and with an outstretched arm; therefore, the Lord, your God, commanded you to observe the Sabbath day." This difference can easily be explained. In the former, the cause of the honor and distinction of the day is given "Therefore the Lord has blessed the day of the Sabbath and sanctified it" (Shemot, 20:10) and the cause for this is "For in six

days the Lord has made", etc. But the fact that God has given us the law of the Sabbath and commanded us to keep it, is the consequence of our having been slaves; for then our work did not depend on our will, nor could we choose the time for it; and we could not rest. Therefore God commanded us to abstain from work on the Sabbath and to rest for two purpose; namely (1) That we might confirm the true theory, that of the Creation, which at once and clearly leads to the theory of the existence of God. (2) That we might remember how kind God has been in freeing us from the burden of the Egyptians.-The Sabbath is therefore a double blessing; it gives us correct notions, and also promotes the wellbeing of our bodies. (Guide; Book 2: Chapter 31)

The Rambam explains here the intellectual and emotional/physical benefits of observing the Sabbath. There are also a few interesting "minor" points to note. He states that in the future there will be a time "when all peoples keep Sabbath on the same day". This is curious language and brings to mind that the holy day of the Christians is on Sunday and that of the Moslems is on Friday. The one law that non-Jews are not permitted to keep, on penalty of death, is the Sabbath. So the Rambam's statement requires explanation. Perhaps it does not mean that the other nations will keep the statutes of the Sabbath but that, since recognition of God as the Creator is a universal foundation of belief for Jews and Noachides alike, the other peoples will recognize this idea in some permissible manner, though certainly not through the refraining from the 39 types of work that characterize the Jewish Sabbath observance. A second interesting point in the Rambam is the focus on time and the control of time that the Jews gained when they were redeemed from slavery. Mastery of one's own time is a great boon and blessing to the human being and the Rambam explains the Sabbath rest in more than just "down time" for the body but an expression of one's personal control of time, which allows for the taking of time to rest and serve God on this day without restraint from any man. This is an important part of the "*cheres*" (freedom) of the redemption from Egypt and is reflected in the mitzvah of reclining at the seder. Only a human being who has this freedom can fulfill the human potential of acquiring wisdom and the living of a meaningful life.

Rabbi Soloveitchik, "The Rav" explains in his essay "Halakhic Man" that Moshe and the Jewish people's receiving of the Torah was a combining of man's ascent to God and God's, "descent" so to speak, to man. The Rav states:

Holiness means the holiness of earthly, here and now life. "Rabbi Joshua b. Levi said: When Moses ascended on high, the ministering angels spoke before the Holy One, blessed be He, "Sovereign of the universe! What business has one born of woman

among us? He answered them. 'He has come to receive the Torah.' They said to Him, "That secret treasure....Thou desirest to give to flesh and blood!... The Holy One, blessed be He, said to Moses, 'Return them an answer.'... He then spoke before Him, "Sovereign of the universe! The Torah which Thou givest me, what is written therein? *I am the Lord Thy God, who brought thee out of the land of Egypt* (Exodus 20:8*)*. 'Did you (angels) go down to Egypt? Were you enslaved to Pharoh? Etc. Again what is written therein? *Remember the Sabbath day to keep it holy* (Exodus 20:12). Do you then perform work that you need to rest..." The Rav continues: God does not wish to hand over His Torah to the ministering angels, the denizen of a transcendent world. Rather, he handed over His Torah to Moses, who brought it down to earth and caused it to dwell among human beings, "who reside in darkness and deep gloom" (Psalms 107:10) The earth and bodily life are the very ground of the halakhic reality. Only against the concrete, empirical backdrop of this world can the Torah be implemented; angels, who neither eat nor drink, who neither quarrel with one another nor are envious of one another, are not worthy and fit for receiving the Torah. (Halakhic Man, pages 34-35)

This idea that the life of flesh and blood is one that possesses unique qualities and value is a major motif throughout the Rav's works. Human life with the desires of the body and the emotions and the struggle of the will to master them is unique to human life on earth, as opposed to life in the next world. This struggle and challenge is not a necessarily negative aspect, but can instead be the human being's unique glory as he wills himself to follow God of his own choice and masters the darker forces of self to emerge as a humble and joyous servant of God. This spiritual quest is something that angels who have no body and no free will, cannot accomplish. It is man's struggle and unique nature for which the Torah was given and for which it serves as the greatest joy and what the Talmud calls the "perfect cure" (the *sam tam).*

MISHPATIM

God, Man and The Plant World

In the parsha of Mishpatim, the Torah states the requirement of "*Shmeeta*", (not cultivating the land on the seventh year). The Torah states in Shemot 23:10

10. Six years you may sow your land and gather in its produce.

י. וְשֵׁשׁ שָׁנִים תִּזְרַע אֶת אַרְצֶךָ וְאָסַפְתָּ אֶת תְּבוּאָתָהּ:

11. But in the seventh [year] you shall release it and abandon it; the poor of your people shall eat [it], and what they leave over, the beasts of the field shall eat. So shall you do to your vineyard; to your olive tree[s].

יא. וְהַשְּׁבִיעִת תִּשְׁמְטֶנָּה וּנְטַשְׁתָּהּ וְאָכְלוּ אֶבְיֹנֵי עַמֶּךָ וְיִתְרָם תֹּאכַל חַיַּת הַשָּׂדֶה כֵּן תַּעֲשֶׂה לְכַרְמְךָ לְזֵיתֶךָ:

Rabbi Joseph B. Soloveitchik ("The Rav") in his essay "The Emergence of Ethical Man" cites this commandment in his discussion of how man is part of the continuum of Earthly life which includes the plants, and that there is a close, intimate relationship between men and plants that is expressed in the Torah. The Rav states in this essay:

That all organic existence is on one continuum is a postulate of Judaism....Of course, the Torah has granted man the privilege of using the plant, of destroying its life, only for his own sustenance. Yet it is only tenancy-rights that man holds in regards to vegetative life. It may never be acquired absolutely by him, an idea expressed regularly through shemittah (sabbatical year) and yovel (jubilee year):"... then shall the land keep a Shabbat to the Lord" (Lev. 25:2). God canceled man's specific rights and forbade him to exploit the soil and to reap its growth. God's rights are rehabilitated in the sabbatical year...Here we grasp one of the most characteristic features of the Jewish anthropological philosophy. The deep feeling of man's basic harmony with organic nature-a harmony emerging from uniformity-is the most salient feature of that philosophical formula. Man may be the most developed form of life on the continuum of plant-animal-man, but the ontic essence remains identical. (46-47)

The Rav is clarifying, in this essay, that not only are plants regarding by God as "full-fledged" living beings which require God's permission to be killed and utilized, but also that man, animal and plant share a common existence and that man needs to be in harmony with the plant world (the earth) in order to fulfill his own nature properly. The Rav explains that the *galut* (exile) is not simply a loss of the Temple and the Torah society but a distancing of the Jewish person from the physical land to which he is bound to from his core being. The Rav states:

The historical curse of galut, of exile, appears to express this tragedy of full freedom, of losing the man-plant trait of communion with the outside. Particularly, man-plant is incapable of meeting his destiny as an uprooted, abstract spiritual being, not having any bonds with primordial Mother earth. God, confined, kivyakhol (as it were) within the cosmos, wants man to be confined. Statehood, or redemption, embodies the return of the primordial man-locus union. This is the rebirth of a man both free and confined, whose task is to redeem nature by living in unison with her dictates and designs. The state cannot be reduced to social interrelationships alone, but must be extended to the mystical communion of man with nature, the renewal of an old friendship, a reconciliation between man and Mother earth. The state commits man to the soil, to nature, chains him to a bounded specific environment, enabling him to take root in an ancient soil out of which the primitive clan emerged, and within whose confines he experienced the unusual encounter with God. (p. 62).

The Rav clarifies that man, regardless of his sophistication and the level of development, is a being that needs to live in harmony and concern for the land to fulfill his role as man. The Rav states:

At this point we may examine the unique relationship that prevails between man and earth. First the earth claims man; he was taken of Mother Earth and to her he must return. "until you return to the ground; for out of it you were taken; for dust you are, and to dust you return" (Gen. 3:19)...God put primordial man in paradise for the specific purpose of tilling and keeping it: "And the Lord God took the man, and put him into the Garden of Eden, to till it and to keep it."(Gen. 2:15). Obviously the prime task of man was to cultivate the ground: "And no plant of the field was yet in the earth, and no herb of the field had yet grown: for the Lord God had not caused it to rain upon the earth, and there was not a man to till the earth (Gen.2:5)." (Page 52-53)

In Chapter 43 of the 3rd Book of the Guide for the Perplexed Maimonides, "the Rambam" provides a detailed analysis of the type and severity of the punishments in the Torah and how they relate to the nature of the sins. This is a lengthy discussion so I will only be able to cite certain sections:

The punishment meted out to anyone who has done wrong to somebody else consists in general in his being given exactly the same treatment that he has given to somebody else. If he has injured the latter's body, he shall be injured in his body, and if he has

injured him in his property, he shall be injured in his property. The owner of the property may be indulgent and forgive. To a murderer alone, however, because of the greatness of his wrongdoing, no indulgence shall be shown at all and no blood money shall be accepted from him: *And the land cannot be cleansed of the blood that is shed therein, but by the blood of him that shed it.* Hence even if the victim remains alive for an hour or for several days, speaks, and is in full possession of his mind and says: Let him who murdered me be dismissed; I have forgiven and pardoned him-this cannot be accepted from him. For necessarily there must be a soul for a soul-the young and the old, the slaves and the free, the men of knowledge and the ignorant, being considered as equal. For among the crimes of man there is none greater than this. The Rambam continues....He who has caused damage to property shall have inflicted upon him damage to his property up to the same amount: "Whom the judges shall condemn, he shall pay double unto his neighbors" (Exodus 22:8)-that is, the thing taken by him and an equal amount taken from the property of the thief. Know that the more frequent a kind of crime is and the easier it is to commit, the greater the penalty for it must be, so that one should refrain from it. On the other hand, the penalty for a thing that happens seldom is lighter. Therefore the fine imposed on him who steals a sheep is double and the fine imposed for the theft of other transportable

objects, I refer to fourfold reparation, the condition being that he has let them go out of his possession by selling them or has slaughtered them. For they have always been stolen in the majority of cases because they were in the fields where they cannot be watched over the way it is possible to watch over things that are in towns....Similarly the law concerning false witnesses is that the thing that they wished to be done unto another shall be done unto them; if they wished the one they bore witness against to be killed, they shall be killed, if they wished him to be flogged, they shall be flogged; and if they wished him to be fined, they shall have a similar fine imposed on them.

The foundation principle that the Rambam is explaining here is that righteousness is based on punishing the violator with the degree and type of damage they inflicted or, in the case of witnesses, intended to inflict, upon the victim of their sin. Variation in this calculation, according to the Rambam, are due to the need to provide stronger incentives in cases of common violations such as stealing sheep, but they are still based on the concept of measure for measure which is the foundation of justice.

TERUMAH

Build Me a Sanctuary

In the parsha of Terumah, the Jewish people are commanded to build the sanctuary (the Mishkan):

And they shall make Me a sanctuary and I will dwell in their midst	**ח.** וְעָשׂוּ לִי מִקְדָּשׁ וְשָׁכַנְתִּי בְּתוֹכָם:
according to all that I show you, the pattern of the Mishkan and the pattern of all its vessels; and so shall you do.	**ט.** כְּכֹל אֲשֶׁר אֲנִי מַרְאֶה אוֹתְךָ אֵת תַּבְנִית הַמִּשְׁכָּן וְאֵת תַּבְנִית כָּל כֵּלָיו וְכֵן תַּעֲשׂוּ:

(Shemot: 25:8-9)

Maimonides ('the Rambam"), in the Mishneh Torah, succinctly states the purpose and definition of the Sanctuary:

It is a positive commandment to construct a House for God, prepared for sacrifices to be offered within. We must celebrate there three times a year, as (Shemot: 25:8) states: "and you shall make Me a sanctuary. (MT, Laws of the Beis HaBechirah: 1:1).

The *mishkan* is essentially a place to offer sacrifices. Why these sacrifices had to be offered in a specific site (the Temple) is explained by the Rambam in the "Guide for the Perplexed" He states:

It is known that these people (idolaters) built temples for the stars and that in that temple an idol whose worship was agreed upon was set up, I mean an idol assigned to a certain star or to a portion of a Sphere. Consequently we were commanded to build a temple for Him, may He be exalted, and place in it the ark within which were the two Tablets (the luchot) containing the word "I am the Lord" and "Thou shalt not have (any other gods)."

The Rambam, in keeping with his approach in the "Guide", is explaining the building of the Temple as a method of rectifying an idolatrous tendency within the people of the time to build temples to idols. The Sanctuary and the Temple take these tendencies and habits and rechannels them from idolatrous worship to the worship of the true God and to the rejection of idolatry. This rejection of idolatry is aided by the placing of the tablets given to Moshe, containing the commandments that make clear the unique nature of God and the prohibition to worship any other being. The Rambam has also explained in the "Guide" that the offering of sacrifices serves a similar end of rechanneling the evil habit of idolatrous offerings of sacrifices, by having all sacrifices, required by the Torah, to be offered to God. The Rambam's perspective in the "Guide" of viewing the Torah laws of sacrifices as a concession to the idolatrous tendencies of the people has been met with strong criticism by Nachmanides "the

Ramban" and by Rabbi Joseph B. Soloveitchik ("the Rav"). The Rav states in his essay "Halakhic Mind":

In the Guide, Maimonides sees in sacrifice just an educational method of elevating the Jew above such forms of worship. Previously, sacrifice had been the common practice of the heathens among whom the Jews had lived. In order to direct the Jew towards worship of God, the Torah made the concession of animal sacrifice. Nachmanides severely criticized Maimonides for his rationalization, and introduced his own interpretation. Sacrifice, for him refers actually to man himself. Worship is nothing but mental sacrifice. And animal sacrifice symbolizes the internal act of self-negation. Whatever the merit of Nachmanides' interpretation, one thing is clear. Philosophically it is far superior to Maimonides' explanation. While Maimonides' causalistic aspect in the Guide is pure instrumentalism, Nachmanides' interpretation penetrates the complex concept of sacrifice itself. He has elaborated an idea which may have some modern philosophical merit. (Guide Book III, Chapters 45-46). See also Nachmanides in his Commentary on Leviticus: 1: 9 (Halakhic Mind (footnote 108-page 131).

The Rav's perspective here is that the Rambam, in viewing the sacrifices as only a means to the removal of a negative quality, does not attribute to sacrifices any inherent positive quality. The Rav views the Rambam's characterizing of the sacrifices as simply medicinal for combatting a divine illness, as inadequate, and agrees with Nachmanides that the sacrifices (and the temple) are more accurately viewed on their own merits as a method of positively bringing man close to God. In the Rav's essay, "The Emergence of Ethical Man" he provides a deep insight into the Sanctuary as expressing aspects of God and man's, dynamic movement, so to speak, between "expansiveness" and "contraction". The Rav states:

We cannot help but notice the intent of the Torah to "arrest" divinity within concrete bounds. The Sinaitic revelation demonstrated the inapproachability of God, His otherness and destructiveness on the one hand, and divine urgency and impetus on the other. Immediately thereafter, God commanded Moses, "And let them make Me a Sanctuary; that I may dwell among them" (Ex.25:8). Apparently, the Torah knew that while the dreadfulness and transcendental repulsion free divinity from all existing ties with this world, the moment of fascination and attractiveness tries to achieve almost the impossible - to introduce God into a concrete confine or abode. There is a definite tendency to imprison the infinite, transcendental deity within the bounds of our concrete universe. The source of this concept is Ezekiel's famous epiphany: "*barukh kevod Hashem mi-midomo*" (3:12) – God has a "*makom*", a place. God imposes voluntary imprisonment on Himself, by His

own free will arrests Himself within the confines of a cosmic order in general, and within the hollowed abode in particular. Solomon asked this impertinent question: "Then spoke Solomon: The Lord said that He would dwell in the thick darkness. I have surely built You a house to dwell in, a settled place for You to abide in forever... For will God indeed dwell on the earth? Behold the heavens, and heaven of heavens cannot contain You: how much less this house which I have built" (I Kings 8:12-13).

According to the Midrash (Numbers, Midrash Rabbah 12:3), the Rav states: **"Moshe could not reconcile God's transcendence with self-limitation. "He who dwells in the sacred place of the most high shall abide under the shadow of the Almighty" with "I shall dwell in their midst" (Shemot 25:8). According to the Midrash, God revealed to him the mystery of *tzimtzum* ("contraction"). Apparently, life is expressed in the polarity of freedom and confinement, continuous movement and arrest within a bounded environment. It applies equally to both God and man.**

The Rav explains in this essay that there is, within our relationship to God, a dimension in which God in his boundless holiness, has no relation to man, and the human being can only stand in total ignorance and awe before the Creator. But, amazingly through the process of "*tzimtzum*" ("contraction"), God can, so to speak, confine His infiniteness to the Universe and even to the small confines of the Sanctuary. It is this "*tzimtzum*" that allows man to relate to God and serve and supplicate to Him through prayer, service and obedience. The Rav explains that the human being, in his own manner, also moves constantly between expansiveness, through his creativity and accomplishments and contraction, through the many limitations and defeats of human life. This dichotomy is a major theme and foundation of the Rav's writings, expressed powerfully in the essay, "The Lonely Man of Faith".

TETZAVEH

Clothes Make the Man

In the parsha of Tetzaveh the Torah describes the appointment of the *Kohanim* (priests) and the requirement for the unique clothing of the *Kohane Gadol* (the high priest).

1. And you bring near to yourself your brother Aaron, and his sons with him, from among the children of Israel to serve Me [as kohanim]: Aaron, Nadab, and Abihu, Eleazar, and Ithamar, Aaron's sons.

א. וְאַתָּה הַקְרֵב אֵלֶיךָ אֶת
אַהֲרֹן אָחִיךָ וְאֶת בָּנָיו אִתּוֹ
מִתּוֹךְ בְּנֵי יִשְׂרָאֵל לְכַהֲנוֹ לִי
אַהֲרֹן נָדָב וַאֲבִיהוּא
אֶלְעָזָר וְאִיתָמָר בְּנֵי אַהֲרֹן:

2. You shall make holy garments for your brother Aaron, for honor and glory.

ב. וְעָשִׂיתָ בִגְדֵי קֹדֶשׁ
לְאַהֲרֹן אָחִיךָ לְכָבוֹד
וּלְתִפְאָרֶת:

Maimonides ("The Rambam") explains in the "Guide for the Perplexed":

In order to exalt the Temple, the rank of its servants was exalted, the Priests and Levites were singled out, and the Priests wore the most splendid, finest, and most beautiful garments: Holy garments…*for splendor and for beauty*" (Exodus: 28:2). And it was commanded that *someone who has a blemish* should

not be employed in divine service; not only one who is afflicted with an infirmity, but also those afflicted with deformities *are disqualified from being Priests* (Vayikra 21:16-21) as is explained in the regulations of legal science dealing with this commandment (Mishnah, Berachot 7). For to the multitude an individual is not rendered great by his true form (the rational soul or intellect) but by the perfection of his limbs and the beauty of his clothes; and what is aimed at is that the Temple and its servants should be regarded as great by all. (Guide, Book 3, Chapter 45)

The Rambam explains here that the distinguishing and separating out of the *Kohanim* and the *Leviim* from the other Jewish people is for the purpose of bringing honor to the Temple. It seems that were this not required, the functions of the *Kohanim* and the *Leviim* could be carried out by all of the Jewish people. The Rambam explains that by the Jewish people observing this distinguished and privileged group (privileged to serve in the Temple and to receive the gifts of the sacrifices) honor is brought to the Temple. The Rambam has stated elsewhere in the "Guide" that the people had been involved in building idolatrous temples. This desire was rechanneled and rectified by having the Jewish people build a single temple that reflected the one true God. So, according to the Rambam, the *Kohanim* and the *Leviim* are a means to bringing honor to the Temple and the Temple is a means to bringing honor to God. In the Rambam's view, the institutions of the *Kohanim* and the

Temple take their forms, in part, as concessions to the flawed nature and history of the Jewish people.

The Rambam also explains here that the requirement that the *Kohane* must have a normal, healthy body, as well as the requirement of the *Kohane's* special clothing, are for the purpose of creating respect and honor in the eyes of the people. He states that the people, in general, err in judging a person by physical attractiveness and fine clothing as opposed to his or her true nature (the possession of wisdom and understanding). This being the case, the *Kohanim* were provided with special clothing and the *Kohane Gadol* was provided with the most beautiful and special clothing. The Rambam seems to hold that the requirements of splendid clothing and that of a healthy body without defect, would not be needed if all the people were wise and discerning. The term used in translation of the "Guide" for the people that require this concession is "the multitude", which is similar to the more contemporary term of "masses". It is in response to the masses misconception of the value of outward appearance that the requirements of the *Kohane's* bodily form and clothing are required, according to the Rambam.

In contrast to the Rambam's depiction of the *Kohane Gadol's* outward form as being a concession to the unenlightened masses, Rabbi Joseph B. Soloveitchik ("The Rav") states in the essay "Before Hashem":

Toward the end of the Avodah Service, when the scarlet turned white, the piyyut describes how the nation exuded happiness, expressing pleasure and delight, a feeling of closeness to Hashem….The description of the Avodah culminates in this majestic piyyut "Maray Kohane" which describes the luminous appearance of the Kohen Gadol after successfully, completing the Avodah. Why the happiness in reciting Maray Kohane ("The Appearing of the Kohane") ? Why was it sung with such a happy tune? The answer is that the Kohen reflected the radiance of the Shechinah. Through witnessing the radiant appearance of the Kohen Gadol, there could be no doubt about Hashem's acceptance of Klal Yisrael's prayer (Before Hashem 148-149).

The Rav, in this explanation, informs us of an addition significance to the *Kohane Gadol's* illustrious appearance. It is not only for the purpose of bringing honor to the Temple, as the Rambam describes in the "Guide for the Perplexed". According to the Rav, the *Kohane Gadol* stands in, so to speak, for the *Shechinah* during the Avodah service and, as such, his appearance must reflect, on a human scale, that which is most perfect and most beautiful. From the Rav's perspective, the beauty of the Kohane Gadol reflects the glory of the *Shechinah* and is therefore necessary and appropriate and not a concession to the masses overvaluing of external beauty.

The Rav, in the text "Noraot HaRav", provides the following explanation regarding the changing of the clothing or "vestments" of the Kohane Gadol during the Avodah service of Yom Kippur. The Rav states:

"He would remove his clothes, immerse himself": **The Kohen Gadol immersed himself five times on Yom Kippur. The first immersion was required in order to purify him, changing his status from 'tamai" (impure) to "tahur" (pure), just as anyone who enters the Temple must first immerse himself, as stated by the Gemara in *Yoma(30a).* The other four immersions, on the other hand, were required in order to sanctify the Kohen Gadol as he was elevated to higher levels of holiness. (Noraot HaRav, Volume 6, pp. 31-34)**

The Rav also explains the effect of the *Kohen Gadol's* putting on of the golden vestments on Yom Kippur.

"And don golden vestments": **The clothing worn by the Kohane Gadol allowed him to fulfill the imperative of dressing *"for the honor and splendor",* the very purpose of the priestly garments, as identified in the Torah (Shemot 28:2). As a result, the Kohen Gadol provided a form of atonement every moment that he wore the eight vestments of gold, since each of the eight pieces of clothing, as explained by the Gemara in *Zevachim* (89b), provided atonement for different sins committed by Jewish people. (Noraot HaRav, Volume 6, p. 64)**

The Gemara in Zevachim states that just as the sacrifices offered by the Kohane Gadol were an atonement for the Jewish people, so too the *Kohane Gadol's* wearing of the golden garments atoned. The Rav often stated the position of Nachmanides, ("The Ramban") that sacrifices are an expression of man's sacrifice of his body and soul to God's will. Perhaps the *Kohane Gadol's* wearing of the gold vestments and the taking upon himself of the demanding and terrifying role of High Priest is another manner by which man sacrifices his personal self to fulfill the will of the Creator. In this way the vestments, like the sacrifices, atone.

KI TISSA

God's Loving Kindness Towards Man

In the parsha of Ki Tissa Moshe ascends Mount Sinai and receives the second set of tablets from God. The first were broken by Moshe when he descended and observed the Golden Calf that had been made in his absence. After Moshe forms the second set of tablets, God communicates with Moshe, revealing to him what is known as "the 13 attributes of mercy". These are the revelation of how the Jewish people are to request mercy from God. The parsha states in Exodus 34:6-7

6. And the Lord passed before him and proclaimed: Lord, Lord, benevolent God, Who is compassionate and gracious, slow to anger and abundant in loving kindness and truth,

ו. וַיַּעֲבֹר יְ־הֹוָ־ה עַל פָּנָיו
וַיִּקְרָא יְ־הֹוָ־ה יְ־הֹוָ־ה
אֵל רַחוּם וְחַנּוּן אֶרֶךְ
אַפַּיִם וְרַב חֶסֶד וֶאֱמֶת:

7. preserving loving kindness for thousands, forgiving iniquity and rebellion and sin; yet He does not completely clear [of sin] He visits the iniquity of parents on children and children's children, to the third and fourth generations."

ז. נֹצֵר חֶסֶד לָאֲלָפִים
נֹשֵׂא עָוֹן וָפֶשַׁע וְחַטָּאָה
וְנַקֵּה לֹא יְנַקֶּה פֹּקֵד עֲוֹן
אָבוֹת עַל בָּנִים וְעַל בְּנֵי
בָנִים עַל שִׁלֵּשִׁים וְעַל
רִבֵּעִים

The Rav in his essay, "And From There You Shall Seek", explains that the concept of loving kindness of the Creator for the creation is a foundational tenet of Judaism and distinguishes it from the Aristotelean conception of a God that is a Prime Mover with no "concern" for the happening of His creation. The Rav also makes a very strong statement that Maimonides ("The Rambam") is often misunderstood as agreeing with the Aristotelian view that love between God and man goes only "one-way" (i.e., that man loves God but that God does not love man). The Rav states:

I would like to call the reader's attention to one thing in order to prevent misunderstanding on the part of those who study our master's (Maimonides') teachings in depth. Love in Aristotelian philosophy is one-way: the world yearns for the Prime Mover, without experiencing reciprocal love. The Prime Mover is aloof from the world and does not long for it. His relationship to the world is that of a teleological and necessary cause, without desire or intention. Since there is no directed providence in Aristotle's view, the love of the Prime Mover for the world is abolished. Moreover, the world's love for the pure form is not an intentional act but an immanent function that sets the cosmic process in motion. The Torah, which bases all of Judaism on the principle of creation and providence, but also on the principle of the chosenness of the Jewish people, introduced into the center of our world

the concept of loving kindness and of love as a reciprocal process. The creation of the world is the embodiment of God's grace. God's providence over His creatures in general, and His choice of the congregation of Israel in particular, is a manifestation of infinite love. Anyone who says that Judaism commands the individual to love God but does not promise him reciprocal love is a heretic.

Up to this point, the Rav has been clarifying that the concept of God's involvement with His creation is an act of love. Divine love is different than human love, but the term "love" as the human mind conceives it, is relevant and true in relation to God's relationship to the world. The Rav holds this is fundamental to Judaism. The Rav makes this crystal clear in stating that, "Anyone who says that Judaism commands the individual to love God but does not promise him reciprocal love is a heretic." In stating this, the Rav is clarifying that the belief in God's loving kindness is not a philosophical position that a Jew can agree with or not, but is a fundamental truth of our *mesorah* ("tradition"). The Rav continues with a clarification of the Rambam's position on this point, dispelling the misconception by some that the Rambam agreed with Aristotle and those who deny God's loving kindness towards His creatures.

How unfortunate it is that many scholars pursued folly and suspected that Maimonides, Heaven forbid, agreed with the teachings of Aristotelian philosophy

that the yearnings of the world for God are one-way, without any reciprocal yearnings. Maimonides does indeed say the following in the "Guide for the Perplexed": ***We have already made it clear to you that that intellect which overflowed from Him, may He be exalted, towards us is the bond between us and Him. You have the choice: if you wish to strengthen and fortify this bond, you can do so; if, however, you wish gradually to make it weaker and feebler until you cut it, you can also do that (Book 3, Chapter 51)".*** **As a result, many scholars claimed that God does not care about maintaining a love relationship between Himself and His creatures. But such an interpretation is wrong, and locating the error does not require deep investigation. The principle of free will makes it necessary for man to have the ability to loosen his ontic link with God. If people can sin, why can't they abolish God's love for them? But there is not even the slightest hint here of a lack of divine love.**

The Rav is clarifying that although Maimonides statement, quoted above from the "Guide", might be read by some as the "passivity" of God regarding man's connection to Him and it is only man that acts in this relationship, this is not so. The Rambam, the Rav explains, is only clarifying that man can break the bond between himself and God, not that God has no "interest", so to speak, in the connection. The Rav then brings multiple references within the Torah and "*Tanach*" (the Bible) regarding God's love for His creation and includes statements from the Rambam in his work, the "Mishnah Torah". The Rav states:

Maimonides himself mentions the attribute of love in many places in his code of Jewish law:"....because God loves us and is keeping his vow to our Father Abraham" (Laws of Idolatry 1:3); "God Himself loves *gerim* (coverts to Judaism) as it is written, 'And He loves the "ger" (Laws of Character Traits 6:4); "Great is repentance, for it brings one near to the *Shekhinah*.... Yesterday he was hated by the Deity, abhorred and distanced from Him, and today he is beloved, desirable, and a close friend....Moreover, they (penitents) are eagerly desired" (Laws of Repentance 7:6-7). Maimonides calls the second book of his code "The Book of Love". It is unimaginable that Maimonides, the pillar of Halakhah, was influenced in a fundamental issue like this by Arabic philosophical inquiry, which was somewhat affected by Aristotle's view.

The Rav continues his essay with an important elucidation of the Rambam's understanding of the relationship of reason to the emotions. He explain that the Rambam does not hold that wisdom results from fully isolating reason from the emotions. The Rav states the Rambam's position to be that there is a mutual enrichment between reason and emotions that results in the true love of God.

What Maimonides wanted to do was to establish an enduring conjunction of the psyche with the intellect. Reason conjoins with emotion and is enriched by it. Reason supports emotion but is also nourished by it; there is reciprocity here. On the one hand, when the affects blend with the intellect, their nature changes, and they become less passive. In place of involuntary impression, free activity blossoms. When cognition absorbs emotion, it converts it and subsumes it under free action and creation. Cognition bestows some of its glory onto emotion-the glory of free action and the desire for accomplishment. On the other hand, cognition too is elevated through its melding with emotionality. The unity of the knower and the known, which is one of the main principles of Maimonides theory (Guide 1:68), occurs only in a cognition imbued with love and desire.... *'There is an identity of love and cognition: "one only loves God with the knowledge with which one knows Him. According to the knowledge will be the love. If the former be little or much, so will the latter be little or much'* - from the Mishneh Torah Laws of Repentance 10:6. (from text "And From There You Shall Seek" by Rav Soloveitchik)

The Rav makes a bold statement here regarding Maimonides perspective on the nexus between emotions and reason. Instead of holding that the Rambam saw the emotions as pure impediment to clarity of reason, the Rav explains that the Rambam saw reason as being "elevated" by a person's melding of his or her reason with a love and desire for God. He also makes the point that the emotions are imbued with the quality of "free action" once they are beautified by reason. A love without reason is a lower form of love and reason without love lacks a dimension in its understanding.

VAYAKEL

Making the Mishkan- The Wisdom of Betzalel

In this week's Torah reading we see the appointment of Betzalel and Oliahav by Moshe to the position of master artisans of the *mishkan* (tabernacle). The Torah states in Vayakhel (36:2):

ב. וַיִּקְרָא מֹשֶׁה אֶל בְּצַלְאֵל וְאֶל אָהֳלִיאָב וְאֶל כָּל אִישׁ חֲכַם
לֵב אֲשֶׁר נָתַן יְ־הֹוָ־ה חָכְמָה בְּלִבּוֹ כֹּל אֲשֶׁר
נְשָׂאוֹ לִבּוֹ לְקָרְבָה אֶל הַמְּלָאכָה לַעֲשֹׂת אֹתָהּ

And Moses called Bezalel and Oholiab and every wise hearted man into whose heart the Lord had given wisdom, everyone whose heart lifted him up to approach the work to do it.

Bezalel and Oholiab's creation of the *mishkan* (sanctuary) was a divinely, sanctioned creation of beauty. The *mishkan* is the vehicle the draws man closer to God and creating a "home" for the Divine presence. But what was the "wisdom of the heart" (*chacham lave*) that God gave to Bezalel and Oholiab and those who participated in the creation of the *mishkan*? Perhaps this was more than simply a technical craft. Just as in the performance of studying Torah, when the scholar pursues the discovery of God's truth, this discovery is filtered through each scholar's unique mind and perspective, so too the redeemed artist seeks a beauty that has its source in God, though each artist will express this truth in a unique way. Had someone other than Bazalel and Oholiab led the effort to construct the *mishkan* it would have been done according to command, but with a different, unique outcome. Objective truth has its source in God as does objective beauty. Both the sanctioned, redeemed scholar and artisan "channel" this truth through the uniqueness of his or her individual, and unique soul and personality to participate in bringing the creation to fruition.

Rabbi Soloveitchik ("the Rav") discusses the "redemption of the aesthetic" in the text, "Worship of the Heart". He cautions that the aesthetic personality initially chooses pleasantness and beauty over truth and the good. But this impulse can be redeemed and serve God, who is the source of beauty as well as wisdom. Once redeemed, beauty and the aesthetic experience not only lose their demonic quality, but become a uniquely powerful and sanctioned manner of exalting God, as man understands that God is not only the source of all knowledge but that "absolute beauty rests in God" (page 60). The Rav states:

Thus beauty has been linked up with transcendental and absolute Being and freed from the contingency of a volatile, passing and conditional world arrangement. God sanction not

only the true and the good but also the beautiful. It is delightful and fair because it reflects eternal glory and majesty. In beautiful things, the transcendental hint (to something beyond) is inherent. Beauty is not hemmed in on all sides by the boundaries of finitude (page 60).

Maimonides in "The Guide for the Perplexed" provides an extensive explanation of the multiple meanings of the word "*chochma*" wisdom which is relevant to our discussion about Bezalel who is described by the Torah as an "*ish chacham lav*" – a wise-hearted man. Maimonides states:

The term wisdom ("chochma") is applied in Hebrew in four senses. It is applied to the apprehension of true realities, which have for their end the apprehension of Him, may He be exalted. It says, "But wisdom, where shall it be found...(Job: 28:12). It says: "If thou seek her as silver...(Proverbs: 2:4). The usage is frequent. The term is applied to acquiring arts, whatever the art might be: "And every wise-hearted among you" (Exodus 35:10). "And all the women that were wise-hearted" (Exodus 35:25). It is applied to acquiring moral virtues: "And teach his elders wisdom" (Psalms 105:22). "Is wisdom with aged men?" (Job: 12:12)-for the thing that is acquired through mere old age is a disposition to achieve moral

virtues. It is applied to the aptitude for stratagems and ruses: "Come, let us deal wisely with them" (Exodus 1:10).

In clarifying that the term "*chochma*" has these four meanings: 1) knowledge of God 2) technological capability (craft) 3) knowledge of the moral virtues and 4)strategies and problem-solving, we must ask what all these four have in common, seeing that a single term is used for such a broad spectrum of qualities. In the beginning of Chapter 37, Book 3 of Maimonides' "Guide for the Perplexed" he describes how the Active Intellect which emanates from God is the source of intelligence in the human being, at times impacting the rational faculty and at times the imaginative faculty or both of these. He states:

It is necessary to consider the nature of the divine influence, which enables us to think , and gives us the various degrees of intelligence. For this influence may reach a person only in a small measure, and in exactly the same proportion would then be his intellectual condition, while it may reach another person in such a measure that, in addition to his own perfection, he can be the means of perfection for others. The same relation may be observed throughout the whole Universe...In some cases the influence of the (Active) Intellect reaches only the logical and not the imaginative faculty;

either on account of the insufficiency of that influence, or on account of a defect in the constitution of the imaginative faculty, and the consequent inability to receive that influence: this is the condition of wise men or philosophers. If, however, the imaginative faculty is naturally in the most perfect condition, this influence may, as has been explained by us and by other philosophers, reach both his logical and his imaginative faculties: this is the case with prophets. But it happens sometimes that the influence only reaches the imaginative faculty on account of the insufficiency of the logical faculty, arising from a natural defect, or from a neglect in training. This is the case with statesmen, lawgivers, diviners, charmers, and men that have true dreams, or do wonderful things by strange means and secret arts, though they are not wise men: all belong to the third class.

This passage requires much reflection but we can see that the divine influence which impacts the reasoning and the imaginative faculties of man can take many forms, some superior to others, but varied nonetheless. Perhaps the multiple meanings of the term "*chochmah*" ("wisdom") refers to varied human mental experiences that results from the influence of the Active Intellect on a person and that the variety of outcomes are determined by the nature of the person's inherent abilities, training, study and free will choices which determines which portion of the Active Intellect he or she receives.

PEKUDAI

The Mishkan and the Redeeming of Beauty

In this week's Torah reading, there is a description of the details of Moshe's setting up of the Mishkan.

33. He set up the courtyard all around the Mishkan and the altar, and he put up the screen at the entrance to the courtyard; and Moses completed the work.

לג. וַיָּקֶם אֶת הֶחָצֵר סָבִיב לַמִּשְׁכָּן וְלַמִּזְבֵּחַ וַיִּתֵּן אֶת מָסַךְ שַׁעַר הֶחָצֵר וַיְכַל מֹשֶׁה אֶת הַמְּלָאכָה:

34. And the cloud covered the Tent of Meeting, and the glory of the Lord filled the Mishkan.

לד. וַיְכַס הֶעָנָן אֶת אֹהֶל מוֹעֵד וּכְבוֹד יְ־הֹוָ־ה מָלֵא אֶת הַמִּשְׁכָּן:

35. Moses could not enter the Tent of Meeting because the cloud rested upon it and the glory of the Lord filled the Mishkan.

לה. וְלֹא יָכֹל מֹשֶׁה לָבוֹא אֶל אֹהֶל מוֹעֵד כִּי שָׁכַן עָלָיו הֶעָנָן וּכְבוֹד יְ־הֹוָ־ה מָלֵא אֶת הַמִּשְׁכָּן:

(Shemot: 39:32)

Maimonides ("the Rambam") clarifies, in his "Guide for the Perplexed", the multiple meanings of the terms "Glory of God" used in the Torah. The Torah utilizes the Tetragrammaton (four letter unspeakable name of God) in this phrase "Glory of God" ("*kavod Hashem*"). I will refer to this name as the Tetragrammaton or "Y.K.V.K." in the quotes from the Rambam. In Chapter 64 of the first book of the "Guide" he discusses the meanings of the Tetragrammaton as well as the phrase "the Glory of God".

Know that the name Y.K.V.K. sometimes is intended to signify the name exclusively, as in His saying: *"Thou shalt not take the name of the Lord thy God in vain"* (Exodus, 20:7)...This occurs innumerable times. The term is sometimes intended to signify the essence and true reality of Him, may He be exalted, as for instance: "*And they shall say to me. What is His name?"* (Exodus, 23:21)...Similarly "*the glory of Y.K. V.K.* " is sometimes intended to signify the created light that God causes to descend in a particular place in order to confer honor upon it in a miraculous way: *"And the glory of Y.K. V.K abode upon Mount Sinai, and (the cloud) covered it, and so on; (Exodus: 24:16), "And the glory of Y.K. V.K. filled the tabernacle".* (Exodus: 40:34). The expression is sometimes intended to signify His Essence and True Reality, may He be exalted, as when he says, *"Show me, I pray Thee, Thy glory",* and was answered: *"For man shall not see Me and live".*

The Rambam clarifies that in the statement in this week's reading "and the glory of Y.K.V.K. filled the tabernacle", the term "glory of Y.K.V.K." signifies the miraculously created light that was "to confer honor upon it miraculously". As the Rambam was dedicated to explaining Torah terms that could be misinterpreted as expressing physical qualities of God, he is dispelling the idea that God actually, in some way, resided within the mishkan. Instead the "glory of Y.K.V.K." is "a light that was created by God, miraculously, to confer honor upon the location". This light is a creation like the earth and stars and the "glory of Y.K.V.K" which does have a location, does not represent

God in any direct manner, but this light He created. Only those existences with a physical quality (i.e., a body) have a location, such as being located in the tabernacle, and this, the Rambam makes clear, does not apply to God.

And Moses called Bezalel and Oholiab and every wise hearted man into whose heart the Lord had given wisdom, everyone whose heart lifted him up to approach the work to do it.

ב. וַיִּקְרָא מֹשֶׁה אֶל בְּצַלְאֵל וְאֶל אָהֳלִיאָב וְאֶל כָּל אִישׁ חֲכַם לֵב אֲשֶׁר נָתַן יְ־הֹוָ־ה חָכְמָה בְּלִבּוֹ כֹּל אֲשֶׁר נְשָׂאוֹ לִבּוֹ לְקָרְבָה אֶל הַמְּלָאכָה לַעֲשֹׂת אֹתָהּ

Rabbi Joseph B. Soloveitchik ("The Rav") in the essay "Exaltation of God and Redeeming the Aesthetic", (found in the text of his essays on prayer "The Worship of the Heart") presents a unique clarification on the relationship of the aesthetic/artistic dimension of human creativity and how it can be either a source of evil or, once redeemed, can be an important way to serve and exalt the Creator. I would strongly recommend this essay to anyone who is interested in understanding the relationship between aesthetics and Torah. In this week's Torah reading we see the appointment of Betzalel and Oliahav by Moshe to the position of master artisans of the mishkan (tabernacle). The Torah states in Vayakhel (36:2):

The Rav explain in the above essay that the unredeemed aesthetic desire is at the heart of sin.

Sin, according to our world formula, is engendered when the aesthete emerges victorious from the conflict

described above, and primacy is accorded to the experience of beauty. Whenever acts of charity and cognitive occupation become aesthetic performance, stripped of the teleological aspiration-self-centered, self-indulgent and self-pleasing, then sin is born." (page 46)

The placing of man's desire for a beautiful and pleasant existence (aesthetic) over an ethical-cognitive one is at "the root of sin". Even acts such as charity and study can become tools of the desire for beauty and form, when outer structure and appearance become the essence of their performance and the desired end. Charity can become a "charity event" whose true purpose is to create a beautiful evening with the charitable benefit as an excuse to hold the affair. Even the pursuit of knowledge can become part of a pleasant structure of life, with academia often being more of a "lifestyle" than a dedicated pursuit of truth and insight. The Rav explains that the aesthetic desire for beauty and pleasantness must be "redeemed" by having as its purpose a transcendent element and having the aesthetic experience serve the pursuit of what is true and what is good. The Rav states:

What is required is the awakening of the skeptic, the rise of a critique of the aesthetic judgment and beauty-appreciation. Though the emergence of doubt-the thought that everything experienced as beautiful is perhaps not beautiful at all-the catharsis of beauty is made possible. When the aesthete begins to wonder whether everything which is apprehended as beauty and as pleasant expresses indeed genuine beauty, when he thinks that the aesthetic act can be critically

examined and its worth objectively ascertained, in a manner similar to our critical attitude toward the cognitive and ethical gestures, then beauty is redeemed. (page 56)

Once redeemed, beauty and the aesthetic experience not only lose their demonic quality, but becomes a uniquely powerful and sanctioned manner of exalting God, as man understands that God is not only the source of all knowledge but that "absolute beauty rests in God" (page 60). The Rav states:

Thus beauty has been linked up with transcendental and absolute Being and freed from the contingency of a volatile, passing and conditional world arrangement. God sanctions not only the true and the good but also the beautiful. It is delightful and fair because it reflects eternal glory and majesty. In beautiful things, the transcendental hint (to something beyond) is inherent. Beauty is not hemmed in on all sides by the boundaries of finitude (page 60).

VAYIKRA

AND HE CALLED TO MOSES, AND THE LORD SPOKE TO HIM FROM THE TENT OF MEETING, SAYING, SPEAK TO THE CHILDREN OF ISRAEL, AND SAY TO THEM: WHEN A MAN FROM [AMONG] YOU BRINGS A SACRIFICE TO THE LORD; FROM ANIMALS, FROM CATTLE OR FROM THE FLOCK YOU SHALL BRING YOUR SACRIFICE. (VAYIKRA: 1:1-2)

VAYIKRA

The Temple Offering –God, Man and Sacrifice

At the beginning of the parsha Vayikra the Torah states:

And He called to Moses, and the Lord spoke to him from the Tent of Meeting, saying,

א. וַיִּקְרָא אֶל מֹשֶׁה וַיְדַבֵּר יְ־הֹוָ־ה אֵלָיו מֵאֹהֶל מוֹעֵד לֵאמֹר:

2. Speak to the children of Israel, and say to them: When a man from [among] you brings a sacrifice to the Lord; from animals, from cattle or from the flock you shall bring your sacrifice.

ב. דַּבֵּר אֶל בְּנֵי יִשְׂרָאֵל וְאָמַרְתָּ אֲלֵהֶם אָדָם כִּי יַקְרִיב מִכֶּם קָרְבָּן לַי־הֹוָ־ה מִן הַבְּהֵמָה מִן הַבָּקָר וּמִן הַצֹּאן תַּקְרִיבוּ אֶת קָרְבַּנְכֶם:

The Torah then describes a number of different sacrifices and the details of how each is to be properly offered. There is much to ponder in the area of sacrifices as its purpose is obscure and the details of the sacrificial rites are even more difficult to fathom. Maimonides ("the Rambam") in "The Guide for the Perplexed" gives a general explanation of why different types of offerings were brought for different types of sins. He states:

The greater the sin which a person had committed, the lower was the species from which the sin-offering was brought. The offering for worshipping idols in ignorance was only (exclusively) a she-goat whereas for other sins an ordinary person brought either a ewe-lamb

or a she-goat (Vayikra 4:27-35), the females being, as a rule, in every species, inferior to the males. There is no greater sin than idolatry, and also no inferior specifies, than a she-goat. The offering of a king for sins committed ignorantly was a he-goat (Vayikra 4:22-26) as a mark of distinction. The high priest and the Sanhedrin, who only gave a wrong decision in ignorance, but had not actually committed a sin, brought a bull for their sin-offering (Vayikra 4:3-21), or a he-goat, when the decision referred to idolatry (Bamidbar, 15:22-26). The sins for which guilt offerings were brought were not as great as transgressions that required a sin offering. The guilt offering was therefore a ram, or a lamb, so that the species as well as the sex were superior in this latter case, for the guilt offering was a male sheep. For this same reason we see the burnt offering which was entirely burnt upon the altar was selected from the superior sex; for only male animals were admitted as burnt offerings. It is in accordance with the same principle that ornament and incense were absent from oblations of a sinner. (Vayikra 5:11)

There are a number of questions that one could ask about this passage. First, the Rambam's explanation that a more severe sin would require a lower level of animal to be sacrificed is somewhat counterintuitive. Usually the greater the sin, the greater the punishment. If one views the sacrifice as a payment of sorts by the sinner, it seems that the greater sin should require the greater animal. Even in terms of price (at least, currently- the bull is about 3 times the cost of a cow and I assume the same is true for other farm animals.) So why would a more severe sin have a lesser animal as sacrifice? There are many scholars, including the Ramban and the Rav that see the offering of a sacrifice as symbolic of the offering of oneself to atone for the sin. From this perspective the Rambam's explanation is logical, as the person with the greater sin views him or herself as more lowly and therefore, represented by the lowlier animal. Curiously, the Rambam explains the purpose for the sacrifices as being a method of weaning the Jewish people away from idolatrous sacrifices and does not state that the sacrifices have an inherent cathartic impact or symbolic quality for the person. However, the Rambam may still hold that the sacrifices don't have this effect.

Rabbi Soloveitchik ("The Rav") wrote a detailed letter to Reverend James S. Walsh who was assigned to the Park Street Catholic Information Center in Boston in 1947. In the letter the Rav responds to Reverend Walsh's inquiry regarding the redemption of the first born ("*pidyon haben*"). The Rav's letter includes an explanation of the concept of sacrifice in Judaism. The letter is included in the text "Community Covenant and Commitment". The Rav states:

The whole Judaic cult ritual and ethos revolve about this theme. To live in accord with God's word is identical with living a sacrificial life. To act morally is

synonymous with sacrificial action. God summoned man into His sacrificial service: "Speak unto the children of Israel, and say unto them, if any man of you brings an offering unto the Lord..." (Lev. 1:2). What did man bring as an offering? What was man called upon to sacrifice? Judaism gave a straightforward answer to this basic theological and ethical question. Man must offer everything he possesses. Nothing is to be spared and nothing is to be saved for man. The logic of this answer is self-evident. A sacrificial action consists in restoring that which man heretofore considered his own to its rightful owner and in returning to the Master whatever belongs to Him which was entrusted to man's care and of which he erroneously and impudently took possession. Since there is nothing within the reach of man which he does not have in trust for and from God, there is nothing whose return to God would not be considered a hallowed sacrificial service. Judaism has insisted upon the total sacrificial gesture on the part of man....Judaism fought relentlessly against the heathen curse of human sacrifice, "Thou shalt not do so unto the Lord thy God: for every abomination to the Lord which He hateth have they done unto their gods; their sons and their daughters they have burned in the fire to their gods (Deut. 12:31). This ruthless cult was condemned and stamped as murder by Judaism only as an ecclesiastical institution at the level of a temple service and a concrete sacerdotal performance. At an

experiential spiritual level, however, this type of sacrifice is the fundamental one for Judaism. The brutal cult of perpetuating murder and of extinguishing the physical existence of man as an object in honor of God is pagan and abominable. Yet the offering of the spiritual personality of the human metaphysical existence to God is a great heroic act, in which Judaism believe man finds his unique charismatic fulfillment. (Pages 298-299).

The Rav, in explaining the fundamental concept of the sacrificial act in Judaism clarifies that the offering of a sacrifice is a method of offering up oneself, at least in a symbolic manner. But the bringing of a sacrifice is more than symbolic, the Rav explains, since the Jew, by accepting the "yoke of Heaven," accepts that all he or she is and possesses belongs to God. Even though actual human sacrifice is abhorrent to Judaism and absolutely forbidden, the concept of sacrifice of one's life's energy, will and possessions to God, is fundamental to our faith. There are even certain circumstances where a person is enjoined to give up his or her actual life for God, although not as a temple sacrifice, but in a martyr's death. We are commanded to love God with all our heart, all our soul and all our possessions. Jewish history is, unfortunately, filled with the blood of martyrs who had to sacrifice their lives for the sake of God. The bringing of the sacrifice and that sacrifice being killed in a holy act, is something of an affirmation by the person that their dedication to God is total and that nothing is held back. We are supposed to be in a state of willingness at all times to return to God all we possess - even our bodies, our children and our possessions. This is, as I understand the Rav, a fundamental and core perspective of the Jew. Bringing a sacrifice confirms a person's willingness to sacrifice all for God at any time.

TZAV

The Holiness of Life and the Rejection of Death

In the 7th chapter of parsha Tzav the Torah states:

21. And a person who touches anything unclean, whether uncleanness from a human or an unclean animal [carcass] or any unclean [carcass of an] abominable creature, and then eats of the flesh of a peace offering to the Lord, that soul shall be cut off from its people.

כא. וְנֶפֶשׁ כִּי תִגַּע בְּכָל טָמֵא בְּטֻמְאַת אָדָם אוֹ בִּבְהֵמָה טְמֵאָה אוֹ בְּכָל שֶׁקֶץ טָמֵא וְאָכַל מִבְּשַׂר זֶבַח הַשְּׁלָמִים אֲשֶׁר לַי־הוָ־ה וְנִכְרְתָה הַנֶּפֶשׁ הַהִוא מֵעַמֶּיהָ:

One becomes "*tamei*" (imperfectly translated as "unclean") through contact with certain objects. Becoming "*tamei*" restricts a person's ability to enter holy areas such as the mishkan and requires immersion in a "*mikveh*" (ritual bath) and a waiting period to become "tahor", (often translated as "clean" or "ritually clean"). Maimonides ("The Rambam") in his great work the Mishneh Torah explains:

A human corpse imparts ritual impurity that persists for a minimum of seven days when it is touched or carried or when one is under the same structure (*ohel*). The impurity imparted by touching a corpse or being under the same structure is explicitly mentioned in

the Torah, as Numbers 19:11 states: "One who touches a corpse of any human being will be impure for seven days" and *ibid.*:14 states: "Anyone who enters the tent and anything in the tent will be impure for seven days. (MT: Tumat Meit 1:1)

The halacha of "*tamai*" and "*tahor*" (ritually clean and unclean) may at first seem to be the result of some substance or physical transfer that takes place between the corpse and the person who touches it. But the Rambam clarifies that this is not the case by explaining that contact between the corpse, or a part of the corpse, and the internal organs of a living person does not communicate "*tuma*" ("ritual restriction") He states:

The impurity incurred by touching mentioned in all situations, whether involving a human corpse or another source of impurity, is brought about by a person touching the source of impurity itself.... If, however, a person took a source of impurity, skewered it with a weaving needle, and inserted it into the throat of a person who is ritually pure without it touching his tongue or inserted it within the womb of a woman from below without touching her flesh, the person who swallowed the source of impurity does not become impure because his inner organs came in contact with the source of impurity. The rationale is that contact between a source of impurity and one's inner organs is not considered as touch. (MT: Tumat Meit 1:3)

The Rambam clarifies here that the phenomenon of "*tamei*" is not some form of physical transfer. If this was the case the contact between the corpse and the internal part of the living person would certainly result in a transfer and a state of "*tamei*" is the living person. But this is not the case. Certainly if a person's internal organs came in contact with a source of physical infection there would be a transfer, even more so than from an exterior touch. It is clear that "*tamei*" is a status imparted by the structure of halakhic law and that it does not describe the physical transference of a contaminating substance.

Rabbi Soloveitchik ("The Rav") in his essay "Halakhic Man" makes clear that Judaism and the Torah are highly "life-focused" and center on the holiness of earthly life. Unlike other religions that base the goodness of this life on the world to come, Torah sees a unique goodness in man's life on Earth where he is capable of utilizing his free will, creativity and struggle against his desires to serve God. From this perspective the Rav explains that "*tumat meit*" "(ritual restriction due to contact with a dead body") is a halakhic expression of the Torah's negative view of death. The Rav states:

Judaism has a negative attitude towards death; a corpse defiles; a grave defiles; a person who has been defiled by a corpse is defiled for seven days and is forbidden to eat any sacred offering or enter the Temple.....Many religions view the phenomenon of

death as a positive spectacle, in as much as it highlights and sensitizes the religious consciousness and "sensibility". They therefore sanctify death and the grave because it is here that we find ourselves at the threshold of transcendence, at the portal of the world to come. Death is seen as a window filled with light, open to an exalted supernal realm. Judaism, however proclaims that coming in contact with the dead precipitates defilement. Judaism abhors death, organic decay and dissolution. Authentic Judaism as reflected in halakhic thought sees death in a terrifying contradiction to the whole of religious life. (HM: Page 31)

The Rav is not at all negating the greatness of the next world. But on the other hand, there is a unique goodness to this world that is lacking in the world to come. It is from this perspective that death is seen as negative. He explains:

The world to come is a tranquil, quiet world wherein a man will receive the reward for the commandments which he performed in this world. However, the receiving of a reward is not a religious act; therefore, halakhic man prefers the real world to the transcendent existence because here, in this world, man is given the opportunity to create, act, accomplish, while there, in the world to come, he is powerless to change anything at all.....The task of the religious individual is bound up with the performance of commandments, and this

performance is confined to this world, to physical, concrete reality, to clamorous, tumultuous life, pulsating with exuberance and strength. (HM 33).

Judaism and the system of the Torah confirm life as being a good in itself and not simply a preparation for the good of the world to come. The Rav clarifies that only a religion that values earthly life an inherently valuable can be truly merciful and just. If this life is purely preparatory for the next world then the only justice and mercy would be that which assists in attaining the next world. This has been the "reasoning" of many cruel and unjust initiatives such as the Inquisition and forced conversions. The Rav states:

The teachings of the Torah do not oppose the laws of life and reality, for were they to clash with this world and were they to negate the value of concrete, physiological-biological existence, then they would contain not mercy, loving kindness, and peace but vengeance and wrath.

The Rav's insight brings out the deeper meaning of the Jewish people's focus on the very preciousness of life ("chai") in a manner that is unique among the religions of the world.

SHEMINI

A Foreign Fire Before the Lord

In the parsha of Shemini, the Mishkan service is transferred to Aaron and his sons. In the inaugural week of the Mishkan, Moshe had functioned as the Kohane Gadol, the high priest. As the parsha states:

1. And it was on the eighth day, that Moses summoned Aaron and his sons and the elders of Israel.

א. וַיְהִי בַּיּוֹם הַשְּׁמִינִי קָרָא מֹשֶׁה לְאַהֲרֹן וּלְבָנָיו וּלְזִקְנֵי יִשְׂרָאֵל:

2. And he said to Aaron, "Take for yourself a bull calf as a sin offering, and a ram as a burnt offering, [both] unblemished, and bring [them] near before the Lord.

ב. וַיֹּאמֶר אֶל אַהֲרֹן קַח לְךָ עֵגֶל בֶּן בָּקָר לְחַטָּאת וְאַיִל לְעֹלָה תְּמִימִם וְהַקְרֵב לִפְנֵי יְ־הֹוָ־ה:

It is during this first offering of the sacrifices in the Mishkan that Aaron's sons transgress in the manner of their offering in some way and are punished by a fire descending and killing them. The parsha states:

Chapter 10

1. And Aaron's sons, Nadab and Abihu, each took his pan, put fire in them, and placed incense upon it, and they brought before the

א. וַיִּקְחוּ בְנֵי אַהֲרֹן נָדָב וַאֲבִיהוּא אִישׁ מַחְתָּתוֹ וַיִּתְּנוּ בָהֵן אֵשׁ וַיָּשִׂימוּ עָלֶיהָ קְטֹרֶת וַיַּקְרִבוּ

Lord foreign fire, which He had not commanded them. לִפְנֵי יְ־הֹוָ־ה אֵשׁ זָרָה אֲשֶׁר לֹא צִוָּה אֹתָם:

2. And fire went forth from before the Lord and consumed them, and they died before the Lord. ב. וַתֵּצֵא אֵשׁ מִלִּפְנֵי יְ־הֹוָ־ה וַתֹּאכַל אוֹתָם וַיָּמֻתוּ לִפְנֵי יְ־הֹוָ־ה:

There is much speculation by the commentators regarding what unauthorized act Nadav and Avihu did to cause their death. It is difficult to understand how people of their level could be worthy of such punishment. Maimonides (the Rambam) in the "Guide for the Perplexed" states that Nadav and Avihu were among the highest level of the prophets. The Rambam states:

"At to the revelation on Mount Sinai, all saw the great fire, and heard the fearful thunderings, that caused such an extraordinary terror: but only those of them who were duly qualified were prophetically inspired, each one according to his capacities. Therefore it is said, "Come up unto the Lord, thou and Aaron, Nadav and Abihu". Moshe rose to the highest degree of prophecy, according to the words, "And Moshe alone shall come near the Lord." Aaron was below him and Nadav and Avihu below Aaron, and the seventy elders below Nadav and Avihu, and the rest below the later, each one according to his perfection."

Rabbi Soloveitchik ("The Rav") in his great essay "Catharsis" describes the heroic aspect of Aaron in his restraint from mourning for his son here and, it seems, even emotionally allowing himself to focus on the tragedy. This severe requirement was due to the status of the Kohane Gadol. The Rav states:

The Torah demanded cathartic action, not only in the hedonic (desires), but in the emotional world of man, as well. In the carnal hedonic realm, catharsis expresses itself in the movement of recoil from something extraneous; e.g. the retreat of the bridegroom from the bride, or the renunciation of food by the hungry man. In the emotional sphere, however the cathartic act consists in retreating or disengaging from oneself, from one's own inner world, in renouncing something that is part of oneself, such as a sentiment, a mood or a state of mind. Can we indeed withdraw from ourselves, rejecting the feeling which grips us with enormous force, dismissing an experience which at times is overpowering? Halacha says yes. The Torah formulated laws, governing the deeds of man; such as "thou shalt not murder,", though shalt not hate thy brother," are as integral a part of the Halachic normative system as are those related to human external action. In a word, the Halacha thinks there is an ethic, not only of action, but of feeling, as well. Man is the master over his own emotional world, capable of disowning feelings or

emotions, however compulsive or powerful, if they seem to be disruptive; and conversely, of assimilating redemptive emotion into his personality. Catharsis in the emotional sphere, according to Halacha, consists in active human interference with the emotive experience.

The Rav exemplifies this heroic mastery of one's emotional life in the case of Aaron's response to the death of Nadav and Avihu. In the same essay, "Catharsis" the Rav states:

Let me illustrate the Halachic idea of inner withdrawal or emotional catharsis. Aaron the high priest met with disaster. On the most joyous day of his life, when the Tabernacle was dedicated and he was inaugurated into his office, two of his sons died. Death is always the great evil which man cannot accept. It is certainly unacceptable to a father whose grief over the loss of a son is limitless. How much more so the unreasonable death of two sons, who had entered the sanctuary to worship and to serve the Lord and were devoured by a fire from the Lord. Moses addressed the following words to Aaron immediately after the disaster struck: "Let not the hair on your head go loose, neither rend your garments; lest ye die, lest wrath come upon all the people. But let your brethren, the whole house of Israel, bewail the burning which the Lord hath kindled. Ye shall not go out from the door of the Tabernacle, list ye die; for the anointing oil of the Lord

is upon you." Moses enjoined Aaron and his children from mourning for Nadav and Avihu. Aaron and his two surviving sons were enjoined from shedding a tear for them. Why? Because the priests constituted a community of the anointed who were consecrated exclusively to the service of the Lord. The inalienable right, to which every parent is entitled, of mourning the death of a child was denied to Aaron and his sons. The commitment or consecration of a priest of God is ultimate, all demanding and all inclusive. God lays unrestricted claim not to a part but to the whole of the human personality. Existence *in toto,* in its external, and inward manifestations, is consecrated to God. Aaron belonged to no one, not even to himself, but to God. Therefore he was not even free to give himself over to the grief precipitated by the loss of his two sons; he had no private world of his own. Even the heart of Aaron was divine property.

The Rav clarifies that the halacha requires not only man's acts to be consecrated to him, but his internal, emotional life as well. All belong to God and His possession of us is all encompassing. At certain times in a person's life he or she may be required to be heroic and exhibit a special strength ("*gevurah*") and disown even the most cherished aspects of his deepest feelings and personality.

TAZRIA

Maternity and the Separation from God

The parsha of Tazria begins with a description of the separation of the women from her husband after childbirth and from the sanctuary and from holy objects. The Torah states (Vayikra: 12:1-7):

1. And the Lord spoke to Moses, saying:

א. וַיְדַבֵּר יְהֹוָה אֶל מֹשֶׁה לֵּאמֹר:

2. Speak to the children of Israel, saying: If a woman conceives and gives birth to a male, she shall be unclean for seven days; as [in] the days of her menstrual flow, she shall be unclean.

ב. דַּבֵּר אֶל בְּנֵי יִשְׂרָאֵל לֵאמֹר אִשָּׁה כִּי תַזְרִיעַ וְיָלְדָה זָכָר וְטָמְאָה שִׁבְעַת יָמִים כִּימֵי נִדַּת דְּוֹתָהּ תִּטְמָא:

3. And on the eighth day, the flesh of his foreskin shall be circumcised.

ג. וּבַיּוֹם הַשְּׁמִינִי יִמּוֹל בְּשַׂר עָרְלָתוֹ:

4. And for thirty three days, she shall remain in the blood of purity; she shall not touch anything holy, nor may she enter the Sanctuary, until the days of her purification have been completed.

ד. וּשְׁלשִׁים יוֹם וּשְׁלֹשֶׁת יָמִים תֵּשֵׁב בִּדְמֵי טָהֳרָה בְּכָל קֹדֶשׁ לֹא תִגָּע וְאֶל הַמִּקְדָּשׁ לֹא תָבֹא עַד מְלֹאת יְמֵי טָהֳרָהּ:

5. And if she gives birth to a

ה. וְאִם נְקֵבָה תֵלֵד

female, she shall be unclean for two weeks, like her menstruation [period]. And for sixty six days, she shall remain in the blood of purity.

וְטָמְאָה שְׁבֻעַיִם כְּנִדָּתָהּ וְשִׁשִּׁים יוֹם וְשֵׁשֶׁת יָמִים תֵּשֵׁב עַל דְּמֵי טָהֳרָה:

6. And when the days of her purification have been completed whether for a son or for a daughter, she shall bring a sheep in its first year as a burnt offering and a young dove or a turtle dove as a sin offering, to the entrance of the Tent of Meeting, to the kohen.

ו. וּבִמְלֹאת | יְמֵי טָהֳרָהּ לְבֵן אוֹ לְבַת תָּבִיא כֶּבֶשׂ בֶּן שְׁנָתוֹ לְעֹלָה וּבֶן יוֹנָה אוֹ תֹר לְחַטָּאת אֶל פֶּתַח אֹהֶל מוֹעֵד אֶל הַכֹּהֵן:

Rabbi Soloveitchik ("the Rav") in the text "Family Redeemed-Essays on Family Relationships" discusses the nature of a woman's desire for a child and its tragic and noble dimensions. He describes two levels of motherhood, the first as part of the "natural community" and the second as part of the "covenantal community". In the natural community, in which the desire for a child is a powerful, emotional drive, the woman finds herself in a difficult, conflictual situation which is significantly more intense than the man's interest in having a child. The Rav states:

In the natural community, the woman is more concerned with motherhood than the man with

fatherhood. Motherhood, in contrast to fatherhood, bespeaks a long-enduring peculiar state of mind. The nine months of pregnancy, with all its attendant biological and psychological changes, the birth of the child with pain and suffering, the nursing of the baby and, later; the caretaking of and attending to the youngster- all form part of the motherhood experience. In a word, the woman is bound up with the child and she experiences her motherhood role in all her thought and feeling. The father, if he wants, can deny his fatherhood and forego responsibility. The mother is bound up with the child; the father can roam around forgetting everything. Motherhood is an experience – unredeemed and hence brutish, yet an experience. Physically, fatherhood implies nothing tangible and memorable. The male, bodily and mentally, does not experience his fatherhood....Motherhood is a fact that is foisted upon a woman. That is why the name of woman was derived from her role as a mother, while Adam's name has nothing in common with his fatherhood. 'Can a woman forget her baby or disown the child of her womb? (Isaiah 49:5). (The Family Redeemed, p. 107)

At the natural stage, the woman is compelled to sacrifice her own self-centered existence and to become child-centered. Her needs are subsumed in those of the child. The man, according to Rav is not impacted in this way by fatherhood and remains significantly self-centered, even with the birth of the child. The Rav then explains that the role and essence of motherhood and fatherhood changes with the Covenant that was communicated by God to Avraham and Sara to create a holy nation. From this point the mothering and fathering of a child became an ethical act, sanctified and redeemed by God as bringing the child into the world and raising it becomes an act of fulfilling this covenant and contributing to the mission of "*tikkun haolam*" (repairing the world). Eve, who represents the natural mother is replaced by Sarah, the covenantal mother. The Rav states:

The freely committed universal mother supplanted the instinctually involved natural mother. Eve was "the mother of all living"; Sarah, the mother of nations and kings. Eve's motherhood consisted in giving life (in a natural) sense to her child. It lacked, however, the element of leadership. Her motherhood was a result of a biological pressure, the culmination of a natural process. Sarah's was due to a great vision, to a new mission she took on. She and "all the persons they had acquired in Haran" (Gen. 12:5) – her children/pupils- formed a covenantal community, one founded on education, a living tradition and commitment. Sarah redeemed the motherhood experience by taking a factum, a natural reality, and changing it into a commitment; natural entanglement was elevated to a normative choice. The woman herself rose from a receptive to an active role. And the most important

dimension which was added is that of universality, the capacity to assume motherhood vis-à-vis all children. (The Family Redeemed, p. 108)

The Rav also clarifies that covenantal parenthood completely transforms the role of the father as well. He is now brought into the child-raising in a manner that has equal importance and dedication to that of the mother. The Rav states:

With the emergence of Abraham and the founding of a new kind of community, the covenantal one, the vague role of fatherhood and the all-absorbing experience of motherhood were redeemed. New commitments were accepted; man began to live not only for himself, but for others as well. He became concerned with the destiny of others, and discovered in himself responsiveness not only to biological pressure but to the call of conscience, through which God addresses Himself to him. The fatherhood idea was redeemed, purged of its orgiastic-hedonic element, infused with life, and turned into a central reality on par with that of motherhood.

The woman's separation during this time is one that can, at first blush, seem baffling or even offensive. Why should the woman be separated from the sanctuary and all holy objects due to birth for 41 days in the case of a male infant and 80 days in the case of a female infant? The birth of a child is the fulfillment of the mitzvah of "be fruitful and multiply" and is certainly viewed as a sanctioned act, aligned with God's will. Also, why is the length of separation longer for the girl infant than the boy?

Reflecting on the Rav's explanation of the natural and the redeemed mother, we can speculate as follows. Upon birth, the ontic bound between the mother and child is an all-encompassing one. There is nothing of importance in the world except the nurturing, protecting and caring for this infant. The intensity of the impulse to do so makes all other aspects of life simply insignificant. The separation from the holy objects and the sanctuary acknowledges this natural and sanctioned shift that occurs when a mother finds herself with her newborn child. To participate in that which is holy, requires an acknowledgment of the centrality of God and the objective truth of things. A mother in the intense initial days of caring for the infant is not able to focus on the awe and love of God to the extent that is necessary for the entry into the sanctuary and contact with the objects of holiness. Her focus in the physical, material world in the form of the infant child. With regard to the longer length of separation for the girl infant, we can speculate that perhaps the bris requirement of the boy after 8 days accelerates the process of the mother's being able to see the child in the context of the covenant and not simply as the biological offspring to be nurtured and protected. It is this transition from the natural mother to the covenantal mother that needs to be completed before the woman can return to fully partaking of the holiness of the sanctuary and its objects.

In Chapter 33 of Book 3 of the Guide for the Perplexed, Maimonides explains that the laws of "sanctity and purity" are focused on restriction from the sensual aspects of life such as unrestricted sexuality and gluttony and the removal of dirt from the body and garments as these "outer purifications" lead one to a refine their thoughts and perspective, which the Rambam call "the purification of the inner". He states:

Consequently, He states clearly that sanctity consists in renouncing sexual intercourse, just as He states explicitly that the giving-up of the drinking of wine constitutes sanctity, in what He says about the Nazarite: "He shall be saintly". (BaMidbar 6:5)...Cleaning garments, washing the body, and removal of dirt also constitute one of the purposes of this Law. But this comes after the purification of the actions and the purification of the heart from polluting opinions and polluting moral qualities. For to confine oneself to cleaning the outward appearance through washing and cleaning the garment, while having at the same time a lust for various pleasures and unbridled license in eating and sexual intercourse, merits the utmost blame. (Guide, Book 3, Chapter 33).

What may be offensive to some is the idea that a mother and her newborn child may in some way be categorized along with those who come in contact with the dead or who are "*tamei*" due to sexual activity. What is the commonality among these disparate phenomena? All of them focus the mind intensely on the physical aspects of life and turn one's from attention to focus on the Creator. This does not mean that these actions are not sanctioned. The act that makes someone "*tamei*" can be a mitzvah in itself, such as sexual intercourse to have children or the giving birth to a child. Also, the burying of the dead is considered "chesed shel emes" (true kindness) and pushes off all other Torah obligations. However whether we are reflecting on the reality of our own mortality, experiencing or reflecting on marital relations or even tenderly caring for a helpless infant, all of these focus the mind on the intensely physical aspects of the human experience and place the reflection on eternal, abstract truths to the periphery of the mind. For this reason, perhaps, these varied experiences restrict one from contact with the sanctuary and the holy objects until the time that a separation can be made from these thoughts and activities at which time one can regain the status of "*tahor*" and return to focus on God and the eternal truths as the center of one's being.

METZORA

Death and Defilement

In chapter 15 of parsha Metzora it states:

16. A man from whom there is a discharge of semen, shall immerse all his flesh in water, and he shall remain unclean until evening.	**טז.** וְאִישׁ כִּי תֵצֵא מִמֶּנּוּ שִׁכְבַת זָרַע וְרָחַץ בַּמַּיִם אֶת כָּל בְּשָׂרוֹ וְטָמֵא עַד הָעָרֶב:
19. If a woman has a discharge, her flesh discharging blood, she shall remain in her state of menstrual separation for seven days, and whoever touches her shall become unclean until evening.	**יט.** וְאִשָּׁה כִּי תִהְיֶה זָבָה דָּם יִהְיֶה זֹבָהּ בִּבְשָׂרָהּ שִׁבְעַת יָמִים תִּהְיֶה בְנִדָּתָהּ וְכָל הַנֹּגֵעַ בָּהּ יִטְמָא עַד הָעָרֶב:

Maimonides (the "Rambam") in his work "The Guide for the Perplexed" describes the restrictions of those who are "*tamei*" (translated as "unclean" above) regarding entering into the Sanctuary. The Rambam explains this restriction as a method of instilling a sense of reverence for the Sanctuary. He states:

We have already explained that the whole intention with regard to the Sanctuary was to affect those that came to it with a feeling of awe and of fear; as it says: ' *Ye shall fear My Sanctuary (Lev. 19:30).* Now if one is

continually in contact with a venerable object, the impression received from it in the soul diminishes and the feeling it provokes becomes slight....This being the intention, He, may He be exalted, forbade the unclean to enter the Sanctuary in spite of there being many species of uncleanness, so that one could - but for a few exceptions - scarcely find a clean individual. For even if one were preserved from touching a carcass of a beast, one might not be preserved from touching one of the eight creeping animals, which often fall into dwellings and into food and drink and upon which a man often stumbles in walking. And if one were preserved from that, one might not be preserved from contact with a menstruating woman or a woman or a man having a running issue or a leper or their bed. And if one were preserved from that, one might not be preserved from sexual intercourse with one's wife or from nocturnal pollution. And even if one were cleansed from these kinds of uncleanness, one would not be allowed to enter the Sanctuary till after sunset. (Book 3, Chapter 47)

Here the Rambam is stating his position that the many forms of being "*tamei*" ("ritually restricted") that the Torah contains, are for the purpose of creating a sense of reverence for the Sanctuary and making it a rare occurrence that one finds him or herself in a state of ritually purity which is required to enter into it. As the well-known saying goes, "familiarity breeds contempt". To me this implies that the Rambam did not see the state of "*tamei*" as something inherently evil or diminishing, but that, by making it so difficult to be able to enter the Sanctuary, it increased the honor and respect the person imparted to this experience. Worthy of note is that a Jew is permitted to remain "*tamei*" for his or her entire life and it is not a violation of Jewish law. Regarding the choice of those things which impart the state of "*tamei*" the Rambam explains in the same chapter:

Also, all these things are disgusting - I mean menstruating women, a man or a woman having a running issue, a leper, and a corpse, a carcass of a beast, a creeping animal, and issue of semen. Accordingly, many purposes are achieved by means of these laws. One of them is to keep men away from disgusting things. The second is to safeguard the Sanctuary.

I think the "Also" the Rambam states here means that, in addition to bringing people to a greater reverence for the Sanctuary, the laws of "*tamei*" provided guidance to people that they should minimize their contact with situations that would bring the mind's focus to the purely physical aspects of life, these being certain bodily fluids and contact with the dead of human or animals. Deterring this contact, the Rambam saw as edifying. I do not think he is implying anything unnatural or wrong with these things, only that contact with them brings a person's thoughts to the physical and mortal aspects of existence, which he sees as something a person should strive to minimize.

Rabbi Joseph B. Soloveitchik ("the Rav"), in his major essay "Halakhic Man", clarifies a fundamental aspect of Judaism as it relates to "*tumah*" (ritual restriction) and provides a united principle for the underlying structure of the law in this area. He explains that the source of "*tumah*" is contact with the dead and that this halakhic structure reflects the "this-worldly" focus of Judaism and that life, in all its physical, mortal aspects, is precious and holy. The Rav states:

Judaism has a negative attitude toward death; a corpse defiles; a grave defiles; a person who has been defiled by a corpse is defiled for seven days and is forbidden to eat any sacred offering or enter the Temple; a Nazarite who has been defiled by a corpse cancels his previous count and must carry out the shavings of his head for defilement and bring an offering; the priests of God are forbidden to defile themselves with the dead. He whose holiness is of a higher order than the holiness of his fellow is subject to a more severe prohibition against defilement…Death is the symbol of the most intense defilement; therefore he who is holy unto the Lord must keep far away from such defilement. (pgs. 31-32)

We can speculate about how this "defilement of death" relates to the punishment of "*tzaras*". The person with "*tzaras*" has sinned either with slander or in some other way and, as a result, receives a lesion that defiles and renders the person unable to enter the sanctuary or even to live among his or her fellow Jews. Death and sin are closely related according to the Torah. As King David states in Psalm 101:5: **"Whoever slanders his neighbor secretly I will destroy. Whoever has a haughty look and an arrogant heart I will not endure."** Meaningful, truly human life has at its core the person's experiencing of the presence of God. Sin as the primary cause of a person's separation from God, is a diminishment of life for the person. This is stated beautifully in a Midrash on the verse in parsha Vayishlach (31:4) **"Hashem said to Moshe: behold, your days are drawing near to die."** The Midrash derives from the structure of the sentence that, just as days do not die, neither to the righteous. The Midrash state: **"The righteous are considered alive, even in death, while the wicked are viewed as lifeless and dead even when they are alive."**

"*Tzaras*" renders the person into a type of living corpse. The sins the person has committed have reached the point where he or she is so distant from the presence of God that the person is "dead even when they are alive". They are defiled as well as a powerfully defiling influence on other who come in contact with them, similar to the defilement resulting from the contact with a dead body. By punishing the person with "*tzaras*" many positive outcomes are accomplished. The person who is involved in slander (according to Maimonides) is separated from the community, which minimizes the person's ability to continue to damage other with slander. The person is given a powerful, disturbing and clear sign of his sin and his need to repent. The person with "*tzaras*" is given the opportunity to see how their actions are removing them from life in the presence of God and making them more dead than alive, as their existence lacks the true essence of the human being's purpose and desire.

ACHAREY MOS

Unequal Opportunity, Repentance and Pardon

In chapter 16 of parsha Acharei Mos, the Torah describes the method by which Aaron, the High Priest ("the Kohane Gadol"), takes the two male goats on Yom Kippur for sin offerings:

7. And he shall take the two he goats, and place them before the Lord at the entrance to the Tent of Meeting.

ז. וְלָקַח אֶת שְׁנֵי הַשְּׂעִירִם וְהֶעֱמִיד אֹתָם לִפְנֵי יְ־הֹוָ־ה פֶּתַח אֹהֶל מוֹעֵד:

8. And Aaron shall place lots upon the two he goats: one lot "For the Lord," and the other lot, "For Azazel."

ח. וְנָתַן אַהֲרֹן עַל שְׁנֵי הַשְּׂעִירִם גּוֹרָלוֹת גּוֹרָל אֶחָד לַי־הֹוָ־ה וְגוֹרָל אֶחָד לַעֲזָאזֵל:

9. And Aaron shall bring the he goat upon which the lot, "For the Lord," came up, and designate it as a sin offering.

ט. וְהִקְרִיב אַהֲרֹן אֶת הַשָּׂעִיר אֲשֶׁר עָלָה עָלָיו הַגּוֹרָל לַי־הֹוָ־ה וְעָשָׂהוּ חַטָּאת:

10. And the he goat upon which the lot "For Azazel" came up, shall be placed while still alive, before the Lord, to [initiate] atonement upon it, and to send it away to Azazel, into the desert.

י. וְהַשָּׂעִיר אֲשֶׁר עָלָה עָלָיו הַגּוֹרָל לַעֲזָאזֵל יָעֳמַד חַי לִפְנֵי יְ־הֹוָ־ה לְכַפֵּר עָלָיו לְשַׁלַּח אֹתוֹ לַעֲזָאזֵל הַמִּדְבָּרָה:

It is through the goat that is "for Azazel" that the sins of the people are atoned. As the Torah states:

21. And Aaron shall lean both of his hands [forcefully] upon the live he goat's head and confess upon it all the willful transgressions of the children of Israel, all their rebellions, and all their unintentional sins, and he shall place them on the he goat's head, and send it off to the desert with a timely man.

כא. וְסָמַךְ אַהֲרֹן אֶת שְׁתֵּי [ידו] יָדָיו עַל רֹאשׁ הַשָּׂעִיר הַחַי וְהִתְוַדָּה עָלָיו אֶת כָּל עֲוֹנֹת בְּנֵי יִשְׂרָאֵל וְאֶת כָּל פִּשְׁעֵיהֶם לְכָל חַטֹּאתָם וְנָתַן אֹתָם עַל רֹאשׁ הַשָּׂעִיר וְשִׁלַּח בְּיַד אִישׁ עִתִּי הַמִּדְבָּרָה:

22. The he goat shall thus carry upon itself all their sins to a precipitous land, and he shall send off the he goat into the desert.

כב. וְנָשָׂא הַשָּׂעִיר עָלָיו אֶת כָּל עֲוֹנֹתָם אֶל אֶרֶץ גְּזֵרָה וְשִׁלַּח אֶת הַשָּׂעִיר בַּמִּדְבָּר:

Maimonides ("The Rambam") is his great work, the Mishneh Torah, explains that the goat that is sent to "Azazel" and dies while tumbling down the cliff, atones for the sins of the Jewish people, even without repentance, with the exception of certain major transgressions. He states:

Since the goat sent [to Azazel] atones for all of Israel, the High Priest confesses upon it as a spokesman for all of Israel as [Leviticus 16:21] states: "He shall confess upon it all the sins of the

children of Israel." The goat sent to Azazel atones for all the transgressions in the Torah, the severe and the lighter [sins]; those violated intentionally and those transgressed inadvertently; those which [the transgressor] became conscious of and those which he was not conscious of. All are atoned for by the goat sent [to Azazel]. This applies only if one repents. If one does not repent, the goat only atones for the light [sins]. Which are light sins and which are severe ones? The severe sins are those for which one is liable for execution by the court or *karet.* False and unnecessary oaths are also considered severe sins even though they are not [punished by] *karet.* [The violation of] the other prohibitions and [the failure to perform] positive commandments that are not punishable by *karet* are considered light [sins].

What is most interesting about the Rambam's explanation is his holding that the goat sent to Azazel achieves pardon for all the Jewish people's "light" sins, even those done intentionally, although the person does not repent. Pardon without repentance seems basically unjust. There are approaches to address this difficult position. Perhaps the person who does not repent receives a pardon from punishment in this world, but regarding the state of the person's soul, which will determine his or her place in the world to come, the goat to Azazel has no impact without repentance. This explanation may reduce the injustice, but it doesn't answer the basic question. The Meiri addresses this issue by positing that participation by an individual in the Temple service of Yom Kippur was so impactful that it effectuates a penitent change in the soul without the person having to go through the regular process of repentance (except in the case of "heavy sins"). Both the above explanations retain the concept that the full "return" of a person requires inner transformation and that the Temple ceremony on Yom Kippur cannot, in itself, bring the sinner truly back to God. This would certainly seem reasonable. But perhaps one could make a case for a miraculous pardon effectuated by the Temple rite on Yom Kippur. Perhaps there are metaphysical miracles, just as there are physical ones, that defy the natural structure of the world and that the goat to Azazel brought about what could be termed "a miraculous pardon" that was created by God to allow the Jewish people to achieve their purpose. This requires more thought as to whether God performs miracles in the area of pardon.

Rabbi Soloveitchik ("The Rav") understands the Rambam's explanation of the goat sent to Azazel ("the scapegoat") as meaning that the goat will achieve pardon for the Jewish nation as a whole, even without repentance, but that this will most definitely <u>not</u> achieve a pardon for each individual Jew. He states:

...the acquittal afforded by the scapegoat when the Temple existed was not meant for the individual. The individual derived no benefit from this sacrifice.

Atonement was for the owner of the offering only, in this case the community as a whole. Indeed, if we read carefully, we shall see that regarding sacrifices it is written: 'and it expiated for him… and for the entire community of Israel', meaning for Knesset Israel as a single entity…This is what Maimonides wished to point out in his opening passage on the scapegoat as quoted 'Since the *se'ir hamishtaleach* (the scape goat) is destined to serve as an atonement for the whole of Israel, it is confessed over by the High Priest in the name of the whole of Israel.' He (Maimonides-RB) wanted to stress here that it was not the confession of the individual, or of many individuals that was made, but that of the entire community of Israel…..The High Priest was not the delegate of any individual, not even of millions of individuals. He acted in the name of all of Israel. So the atonement afforded by the se'ir hamishtaleach is not for individuals as such; they can only derive benefit from it via the pipelines of the community. (On Repentance, pages 119-120)

The Rav is clarifying that there is a judgment of the Jewish people as a nation. It is this judgment that is impacted by the pardon of the scapegoat. We see many times in the Torah that the Jewish people are judged as a single entity. For example, at the time of the golden calf, when God spoke to Moshe about destroying the Jewish people and, of course, in Egypt where God saved the nation. The Rav explains that the Jewish people are more than just the sum of the individuals that make it up. It is an entity that has its own separate status and it is judged, punished, rewarded, condemned or pardoned as such. This entity of Bnei Yisrael is afforded pardon through the process of the scapegoat's death. But for the individual, according to the Rav himself as well as his reading of the Rambam, repentance is always necessary, in order for pardon to be given. This was the case, he explains, even in the time of the Temple when the scapegoat was sent to Azazel.

KEDOSHIM

Love of the "Other"

God commands the Jewish people in parsha Kedoshim to love the "stranger" *("gair")* as he does himself. From Rashi it is clear that the "*gair*" is a convert to Judaism. The parsha states:

Chapter 19

33. When a stranger sojourns with you in your land, you shall not taunt him.	**לג.** וְכִי יָגוּר אִתְּךָ גֵּר בְּאַרְצְכֶם לֹא תוֹנוּ אֹתוֹ:
Rashi: you shall not taunt him: Heb. לֹא תוֹנוּ. [This refers to] tormenting with words [as opposed to torment through other means, e.g., financially (see Rashi Lev. 25:14)]. [For instance,] do not say to him, "Only yesterday you were an idol worshipper, and now you come to learn Torah, which was given over by the Almighty God Himself! ". — [Torath Kohanim 19:82]	**לא תונו:** אונאת דברים. לא תאמר לו אמש היית עובד עבודה זרה ועכשיו אתה בא ללמוד תורה שנתנה מפי הגבורה:

34. The stranger who sojourns with you shall be as a native from among you, and you shall love him as yourself; for you were strangers in the land of Egypt. I am the Lord, your God.

לד. כְּאֶזְרָח מִכֶּם יִהְיֶה לָכֶם הַגֵּר | הַגָּר אִתְּכֶם וְאָהַבְתָּ לוֹ כָּמוֹךָ כִּי גֵרִים הֱיִיתֶם בְּאֶרֶץ מִצְרָיִם אֲנִי יְהוָֹה אֱלֹהֵיכֶם:

Rashi: for you were strangers: Do not accuse your fellow man with your own defect. - [B.M. 59b]

כי גרים הייתם: מום שבך אל תאמר לחברך:

I am the Lord, your God: [Here, the word for "your," אֱלֹהֵיכֶם, is in the plural; thus, regarding the stranger, Scripture reminds you:] I am Your God and his God!

אני ה' אלהיכם: אלהיך ואלהיו אני:

This requirement to "love the stranger" a convert to Judaism, not born of a Jewish mother, is at the heart of the Torah system. According to the Talmud (Baba Metzia 59b) it is stated that the command not to oppress a stranger appears, according to Talmud Baba Matzia 59b, at least 36 times in the Tannach (Jewish Bible). In these statements the command is tied to the fact that the Jews were strangers in the land of Egypt. One can ask why our previous status as strangers or outsiders is so closely wedded to this prohibition. What if we were not slaves in the land of Egypt? Would it then be permissible to oppress the convert? Rabbi Soloveitchik ("The Rav") discusses the centrality of the Egyptian servitude in shaping the eternal character of the Jewish psyche and compares it with the salvation of the people in Persia which we celebrate on the Purim holiday. The Rav states:

Egypt is a central experience that underlies the very morality of the Jew. The unique morality of the Jew is rooted in a very sensitive, exceptionally tender, and warm approach to man. The Torah is concerned with *kevod haberiyot*, human dignity. The latter must not be abused. It must not be denied to the weak and the helpless. Sensitivity and compassion are the central axis of our moral experience. To hurt the feelings of a person by uttering some innocuous remark is a severe transgression. We have two terms for kindness-mercy and compassion, *rahamim* and *rahmanut.* The term *rahamim* is derived from the verb *rahem,* which basically means to love. A *merahem* is one who sympathizes. *Rahamanut* is derived from *rahaman.* The latter is an adjectival noun meaning one who is compassionate. The difference between *merahem* and *rahaman* is the following. *Merahem* describes an act, not a disposition. Whoever engages in loving or commiseration is called merahem, not matter how kind or merciful he is by nature. *Rahaman* describes

not an action, but a trait, a temper, a bent in one's character, a disposition. The *rahaman* cannot help himself but to love. Even when he wants to be strict and rigid, he cannot do it, since his very personality is overflowing with love. *Rahamanut* means that love, and only love, ought one to give to people. The fact that in Egypt we were exposed to all kinds of chicanery, that we were treated there like objects and not people, the fact that later in Persia we were sold by the king to the prime minister for slaughter and annihilation, engendered in us a sensitivity and emotional tenderness not to be found in anyone else. The Jew is saturated with compassion and mercy. We all know what a Jew feels when he says this boy is an orphan, this woman is a widow. The laws pertaining to the treatment of those lonely people bear witness to our sympathetic understanding and involvement in the travail of others. Without the experience of Egypt and Persia, we would have remained emotionally coarse and tough. That is the reason for the frequent mention of the Exodus whenever the Torah speaks of our duty to respect the feelings of others, particularly the feelings of the defenseless, helpless, and lonely people. The Torah always reminds us that we were aliens in Egypt. (Days of Deliverance, pgs. 22-23)

The experience of Egypt, and the "re-experiencing" of Egypt which we are commanded to carry out at Pesach, is, according to the Rav, essential to Jew being a *rahaman*. This sense of love and compassion for others – especially those who are in a vulnerable and downtrodden state, has its root in the experience and collective memory of the Jewish people of being in that state during the Egyptian servitude. Knowledge of the Torah and its directive to act with compassion may make one a *merahem* (one who acts with compassion) but will not, in itself make one a *rahaman* (one who possessive the quality of tenderness and compassion) as a core personality trait. For this the experience of Egypt must impact the personality. The Rav has stated that it is incumbent upon the Jews to not only tell to story of Egypt but to re-experience or relive it. In addition to this reliving of the event making the redemption personal for us, it also can be seen as important for imprinting the quality of rahamanut permanently onto the Jewish soul. The Rav describes in the text "Festival of Freedom", this process of re-experiencing the servitude and redemption from Egypt:

We celebrate the festival of Yeziat Mizrayim not only because we remember it, nor just because we re-experience it, but rather because it is a permanent drama. Every generation lives through the actual experience of Yezi'at Mizrayim. Hence, before we start reciting, commenting on, and explaining the parshah of Arammi oved avi, we inform the listener that our method is one of total interpretation, of translating the past into the present, of identifying memory with reality. The parshah tells us that we are lonely people, that we are all a band of wandering

Arameans facing hostility, that our very existence is a miracle. The story of the Exodus is the story of our destiny! ("Festival of Freedom")

Maimonides states in the Mishneh Torah the following regarding the requirement to love the covert. He states there in Chapter 6 of Hilchot Deot ("The Laws of Character Traits"):

Halacha 4

Loving a convert who has come to nestle under the wings of the *Shechinah* [fulfills] two positive commandments: one for he is [also] included among the "neighbors" [whom we are commanded to love] and one because he is a convert and the Torah (Deuteronomy 10:19) states: "and you shall love the converts." [Thus, God] has commanded us concerning the love of a convert just as He has commanded us concerning loving Himself as [Deuteronomy 11:1] states: "and you shall love God, your Lord." The Holy One, blessed be He, Himself, loves converts as [Deuteronomy 10:18] states: "and He loves converts."

In his *Sefer HaMitzvot* (*positive Mitzvah 207.*) Maimonides states regarding this commandment:

The 207th *mitzvah* is that we are commanded to love converts. The source of this commandment is G-d's statement (exalted be He), "You must love the

convert." Since the convert spoken of here is a *ger tzedek*, he is included in the commandment for the entire Jewish people, "You must love your neighbor." Nevertheless, since he has now entered the Jewish religion, G-d shows him additional love and added an extra commandment [to love him]. This is similar to the prohibition of mistreating him, where in addition to the prohibition [regarding all Jews], "You shall not mistreat one another," G-d also said, "Do not mistreat a convert." The Gemara explains that one who mistreats a convert transgresses both, "You shall not mistreat one another," and, "Do not mistreat a convert." We are similarly commanded to love him, [both] by the commandment, "You must love your neighbor as [you love] yourself," and the commandment, "You must love the convert." This is obvious and not hidden, and I am not aware of anyone among those who have compiled the list of commandments who has failed to realize this. In many Midrashim is it explained that G-d has commanded us regarding the convert, as He has commanded us regarding Himself (exalted be He). This [is evident] from the verse, "Love G-d your Lord," and the verse, "You must love the convert."

In both the Mishneh Torah and the Sefer HaMitzvot, Maimonides makes the intriguing comparison between loving the convert and loving God. At first reflection there does not seem to anything congruent between God and the convert. Loving God is quite a different phenomenon than one treating a person with compassion and understanding. The love of God is grounded in a faulty but moving recognition of God as the True Existence and the source of all being and wisdom. The love of the convert is based on a recognition of his status as a fellow Jew and a person who has sacrificed much to join the Jewish people. Where is the similarity that would lead to Maimonides equating the two? Perhaps the fact that both God and the convert are both "other". God is different from us in an absolute sense. God is the ultimate "other" and our fathoming this "otherness" to greater and greater degrees is the essence of Maimonides "negative theology" in which we gain a clearer and clearer sense of how God does not resemble us or any created thing in any manner. The covert also partakes of a quality of "otherness". In the case of the convert we are faced with a person from a different culture, religion and background who enters into Judaism. Here too we must love and connect with that which is different from ourselves-not in the ultimate sense as in the case of God, but in a psychological/emotional sense the love of the convert must move beyond identification and compassion for that which is most like ourselves to value and treat him or her from a sense of his or her true worth and not a psychological feeling of connection from culture, background or family. Here too me are commanded to love the "other"- a person who is different from us but still a cherished member of the community.

EMOR

Sanctifying God's Name by Saving Ourselves

In Chapter 22 of parsha Emor the Torah states:

32. You shall not desecrate My Holy Name. I shall be sanctified amidst the children of Israel. I am the Lord Who sanctifies you,	**לב.** וְלֹא תְחַלְּלוּ אֶת שֵׁם קָדְשִׁי וְנִקְדַּשְׁתִּי בְּתוֹךְ בְּנֵי יִשְׂרָאֵל אֲנִי יְ־הֹוָ־ה מְקַדִּשְׁכֶם:
33. Who took you out of the land of Egypt, to be a God to you. I am the Lord.	**לג.** הַמּוֹצִיא אֶתְכֶם מֵאֶרֶץ מִצְרַיִם לִהְיוֹת לָכֶם לֵאלֹהִים אֲנִי יְ־הֹוָ־ה:

Maimonides ("The Rambam") is his great work, the Mishneh Torah brings this verse as the source of the mitzvah of sanctifying God's name. As he states at the beginning of chapter 5 of the "Laws of the Foundations of the Torah" ("*Hilchot Yesodai HaTorah*"):

The entire house of Israel are commanded regarding the sanctification of [God's] great name, as [Leviticus 22:32] states: "And I shall be sanctified amidst the children of Israel." Also, they are warned against desecrating [His holy name], as [the above verse] states: "And they shall not desecrate My holy name."

What is most interesting is that the Rambam in the next halacha, when explaining how sanctification is carried out describes the cases when a person does not allow him or herself to be killed rather than violate the law. The person compelled upon death to break the law, does so and lives. This is clearly described as a path of sanctifying God's great name. As the Rambam explains:

What is implied? Should a gentile arise and force a Jew to violate one of the Torah's commandments at the pain of death, he should violate the commandment rather than be killed, because [Leviticus 18:5] states concerning the mitzvot: "which a man will perform and live by them." [They were given so that] one may live by them and not die because of them. If a person dies rather than transgress, he is held accountable for his life.

How is saving one's self an expression of sanctification of God's name? Sanctification of God's name, it seems, is not limited to the sacrifice of one's life or property. It seems from the Rambam that the sanctification of God's name is an act that expresses ones obedience to God's will and effectively communicates a fundamental concept of God's will. In this case, the allowing of oneself to live shows the love of God for mankind and that the Torah was not given to people to oppress or abuse them for the sake of God. According to the Rambam, one is absolutely not permitted to martyr oneself in the above case and would be held accountable for suicide if he did so (other authorities disagree with this position). The Rambam, I believe, is explaining that to allow oneself to die in this case would communicate a falsehood about the Torah and what God wants of man and would be a desecration.

Rabbi Joseph B. Soloveitchik ("the Rav") in a shiur brought down in Rabbi Sirkin's text "Harerey Kedem" addresses this same verse in parsha Emor to explain an aspect of the laws of Chanukah. In general, with regard to positive mitzvot there are limitations to what a person is required to sell or do in order to carry out a mitzvah. The rule brought down in the *Shulchan Orach* is that a person is required to spend up to a fifth of his wealth to carry out the positive mitzvah. But the Rav explains that there is an exception with regards to a positive mitzvah which fulfills the obligation to publicize God's miracle ("*persumay neesah*"). These positive mitzvot include the 4 cups of wine for the Pesach seder and the purchase of oil for the Hanukah lighting. In these cases there is agreement that one must even forfeit ones whole wealth and go begging in order to carry out the mitzvah.

The Rav explains that the pasuk we quoted earlier (Vayikra 22:32) is the source of this unique requirement of positive mitzvot that include publicizing God's miracles. This type of positive mitzvah is given a quality of equivalence with the requirement of not to desecrate God's name. This is why the pasuk includes both refraining from desecration and sanctification as, in a sense, describing two aspects of the same thing. As the verse states: **You shall not desecrate My Holy Name. I shall be sanctified amidst the children of Israel. I am the Lord Who sanctifies you."** Not sanctifying God's name when one has the opportunity to do so is equivalent, in some sense, to desecrating his name. So since there are cases, such as idolatry, murder and incest, where a person does have to sacrifice even their life to sanctify God's name and, I believe, it is required for one to forfeit all of their goods in order to not desecrate God's name, so too in order to have the opportunity to sanctify God's name through publicizing a miracle, the Torah requires one to give up all of one's wealth and even go begging door to door to obtain the funds for the mitzvah.

The Rav brings down an explanation of the Sifra on the pasuk we have been discussing. The Sifra states:
"And you will not desecrate - this is called sanctification" ***('Vlo t'chilayl ehmore kiddush*)**.**

This is an important concept that is often found in Jewish law and practice. When a person has the opportunity to sanctify God's name and refrains from doing so, it is not considered to be a neutral act. It is judged by the Torah as an act of desecration of God's name. For example, the rabbis tell us that a person who does not speak Torah at a meal is like one who worships idols. At first reflection this seems to be extremely far-fetched. If a person sits downs and has a meal and simply does not speak any words of Torah, it doesn't seem to be an act of desecration. Nothing has been said either for good or for bad. Where is the desecration? But the point is that the sin of "omission" can be just as powerful and communicative as a positive act of disdain. To not say something or do something when it is called for is an expression of denial or a devaluing of that which should have been recognized. For example, if a person would receive some award or accomplish something significant in his or her life, and not mention in the acceptance speech anything about the people who assisted in making the award possible, it would be a "desecration" and gross act of injustice and disdain for those people. In a more profound sense, when a person gathers with other Jews at a meal and partakes of the enjoyments of the world God has provided and makes no mention of God, either in saying a blessing or reflecting on and thanking God for the opportunities of partaking of life's enjoyments, it is a profound omission and one that reflects a fundamental flaw in the person's worldview.

BEHAR

The Holiness of Life in All Its Forms

In the text "The Emergence of Ethical Man" Rabbi Joseph B. Soloveitchik ("The Rav") writes remarkably about the similarity of God's relationship to all life on Earth- plant, animal and human. He states:

Sacrifices are drawn from the animal realm because the very idea of offering suggest the surrender of life to its rightful master, to God. But offerings are also drawn from the vegetable realm: wine, oil and flour take a most prominent place in the sacrificial lists. That all organic existence is on one continuum is a postulate of Judaism. But the Torah does not apply uniform standards to all organic life. Human life is evaluated as the apex of the bio-pyramid - what was termed tzelem-and plant as its base. But the difference consists only in degree, not in kind. Therefore all organic life was included in the sacral act of offering life to God. (page 44-45)

The Rav's statement here and the motif of this unique essay, is that there is a profound distinction between life (organic) and non-life (inorganic) in the creation. Although man is on a unique level, animal and even plant life shares the exalted position of living things and, as such, are the sole possession of God. Man may possess, it seems, inorganic matter completely, put not anything that possesses life. The Rav continues to clarify this shared status of all life in his explanation about *bikkurim* (the Temple offering of the first fruits of trees) :

It is critical that the idea that the *bekhor* belongs to God, expressing the unique intimacy between God and any living creature, includes vegetative life as well- *bikkurim*, first fruits. Thus, Numbers mentions *bikkurim* together with the firstborn of man and animal (18:12-17). *Terumah* (priestly due) and *hallah* (dough given to the priest) express the same idea; vegetative life, to be consumed by man, but first to be consecrated to God, who is the source of all life. The logic is identical to that in regard to the slaughtering of animals in the desert: life-even of the plant-can only be claimed by God, and man has no right to destroy it. Of course, the Torah has granted man the privilege of using the plant, of destroying its life, only for his own sustenance. (pages. 45-46)

This concept that man has no ownership, but only "tenancy rights" of life on earth, regardless of its form, is expressed perhaps most clearly in the laws of *shemittah*. The Rav continues his statement:

Yet it is only tenancy-rights that man holds in regard to vegetative life. It may never be acquired absolutely by him, an idea expressed regularly through shemittah (sabbatical year) and yovel (jubilee year): "then shall the land keep a Shabbat to the Lord" (Leviticus: 25:2)

God canceled man's specific rights and forbade him to exploit the soil and to reap its growth; God's rights are rehabilitated in the sabbatical year. To sum up, in Judaism we cross the threshold of life upon entering the vegetative realm. Plant is a living creature and enjoys to a certain extent many prerogatives Judaism grants a being endowed with life, for sacrifice means the return of life to its rightful owner. God does not lay any claim to inorganic, dead matter. (page 46)

Maimonides, ("The Rambam"), states in his great work, the Mishneh Torah, with regard to the laws of Shemittah:

It is a positive commandment to divest oneself from everything that the land produces in the Sabbatical year, as [Exodus 23:11] states: "In the seventh [year], you shall leave it untended and unharvested." Anyone who locks his vineyard or fences off his field in the Sabbatical year has nullified a positive commandment. This also holds true if he gathered all his produce into his home. Instead, he should leave everything ownerless. Thus everyone has equal rights in every place, as [*ibid.*] states: "And the poor of your people shall partake of it." One may bring a small amount into one's home, just as one brings from ownerless property, five jugs of oil, fifteen jugs of wine. If he takes more than that, it is permitted. (Mishnah Torah, Laws of Shemittah: 4:24)

It is interesting to note the Rambam's language in the beginning of this halachah, " It is a positive commandment to divest oneself from everything that the land produces in the Sabbatical year". From this statement it does not seem that it is the land, so much as the produce of the land that one is making ownerless. This statement is consonant with what we stated earlier from Rabbi Soloveitchik that the shemittah laws are related to the concept of the sole possession by God of all life –in this case- plant life. It is not so much the land, but the produce of the land that is returned to God. As Rabbi Soloveitchik made clear, it is fundamentally important that man understand that all life belongs to God in a manner more intimately than his possession of the world as a whole. Perhaps we can say that man can own the land, but never the produce of the land. The produce is God's and man only makes use of through an allowance of the Creator. In the Rambam's philosophical work, "The Guide for Perplexed" he explains the impact that the Shemittah laws have on developing a person's compassion for the needs of the poor and for all creatures . He States:

With regard to all the commandments that we have enumerated in *Hilchot Shemita ve'Yovel* (Laws concerning the Sabbatical Year and the Jubilee), some are meant to lead to pity and help for all men - as the Torah states: "That the poor of the people may eat; and what they leave, the beasts of the field shall eat ..." (Shemot 23:11) - and are meant to make the earth more

fertile and stronger through letting it fallow." (Book 3: Chapter 39)

The Torah laws, in their perfection, simultaneously convey profound truths to its adherents while at the time structuring a society that is just and merciful. The laws of shemittah teach people of the unique nature of God's "rights" , so to speak, to all life, while at the same time refining and shaping the personality of the Jewish people and assisting those who are in need. It is important to read the "Guide for the Perplexed" not as an explanation of the reasons behind the mitzvot, but as a clarification of the benefits that the rational mind can discern regarding them. I do not believe that the Rambam held that man, with his limited intelligence can understand the complete purpose or benefits of the Torah laws. But I do believe the Rambam held that it is important and necessary to search for reasons and benefits for those mitzvot that we can understand in our limited manner. Clarifying and expressing these benefits sanctifies God in the eyes of the Jewish people and the people of the world. Through this process people can discern the wisdom of the Creator and holiness of the Torah.

BEHAKOSAI

Hester Panim and Divine Punishment

In the parsha of Behosai warns the Jewish people of the dire punishments that will result from the Jewish people not following the commandments of God once they enter the land of Israel.

22. I will incite the wild beasts of the field against you, and they will bereave you, utterly destroy your livestock and diminish you, and your roads will become desolate.	**כב.** וְהִשְׁלַחְתִּי בָכֶם אֶת חַיַּת הַשָּׂדֶה וְשִׁכְּלָה אֶתְכֶם וְהִכְרִיתָה אֶת בְּהֶמְתְּכֶם וְהִמְעִיטָה אֶתְכֶם וְנָשַׁמּוּ דַּרְכֵיכֶם:

God also warns that if, when they are punished the Jewish people don't view these events as being punishments, but instead as events that occurred due to random situations or those that were due to circumstances unrelated to God's punishment, (*"v'halachtem eemee kehree"*), then the punishments will increase tremendously. The Torah states in BaMidbar 26:22-25:

23. And if, through these, you will still not be chastised [to return] to Me, and if you [continue to] treat Me happenstance,	**כג.** וְאִם בְּאֵלֶּה לֹא תִוָּסְרוּ לִי וַהֲלַכְתֶּם עִמִּי קֶרִי:

24. Then I too, will treat you as happenstance. I will again add seven punishments for your sins:

כד. וְהָלַכְתִּי אַף אֲנִי עִמָּכֶם בְּקֶרִי וְהִכֵּיתִי אֶתְכֶם גַּם אָנִי שֶׁבַע עַל חַטֹּאתֵיכֶם:

25. I will bring upon you an army that avenges the avenging of a covenant, and you will gather into your cities. I will incite the plague in your midst, and you will be delivered into the enemy's hands,

כה. וְהֵבֵאתִי עֲלֵיכֶם חֶרֶב נֹקֶמֶת נְקַם בְּרִית וְנֶאֱסַפְתֶּם אֶל עָרֵיכֶם וְשִׁלַּחְתִּי דֶבֶר בְּתוֹכְכֶם וְנִתַּתֶּם בְּיַד אוֹיֵב:

The intensification of God's punishment, from one that is severe, but bearable, to one that is an unimaginable level of torment, is analyzed by Rabbi Soloveitchik ('the Rav"). There is a level of punishment by God which is not due to his direct structuring of the punishment, but instead due to his withdrawal, so to speak, from the scene, allowing the enemies of God and Israel to operate freely in their sadistic attack and destruction of the Jewish people. This is the situation of "Hester Panim" (hiding of the Face) and is described by Rabbi Avraham Besdin is his series of essays on the Rav's *shiurim*. Rabbi Besdin writes in the text "Reflections on the Rav":

Rabbi Joseph B Soloveitchik ("the Rav") explains the unique severity of the punishment that results from "*hester panim*" (God's hiding of his face) as opposed to *middat hadin*

(Divine judgment) and how this was the punishment that resulted in the Holocaust. He explains:

There are two levels of Divine punishment, *Middat Hadin* and *Hester Panim.* The former involves measure for measure punishment, commensurate with one's sins. It does not signify God's withdrawal; on the contrary, it reflects His involvement and concern, intended to stimulate *teshuvah* (repentance). *Middat Hadin,* therefore, never inflicts annihilation or total extermination, *kelayah. Hester Panim,* however, is a temporary suspension of God's active surveillance. He turns His back, so to speak, on events and leaves matters to chance. Under such circumstances, the usual vulnerability of the Jew invites the threat of total extermination. This is strikingly conveyed by the words *vehyahale-ekhol,* "they shall be devoured." What ensues is not circumscribed by consideration of measure for measure, and the magnitude and severity can be devastating. Without God's governing control, events may simply go berserk....The *Asarah Haruge Malkhut* (martyrs-RB*)* were victims of *Middat Hadin,* not *Hester Panim.* It was a measured *onesh* (punishment-RB)*,* but it indicated God's involvement, *gezarah hi milefanai.* It is related in the *Eleh Ezharah* piyyut of the Yom Kippur Musaph service that, when the angels protested against the torturing to death of the Sages, a heavenly voice replied: 'If I hear further protest, I will force the world to revert to water. I will

reduce the world to *tohu vavohu' (*RB-chaos and disorder*)* God threatened the *tohu vavohu* of *Hester Panim* if the *Middat Hadin* of controlled retribution were not accepted. The Holocaust was *Hester Panim.* We cannot explain the Holocaust but we can, at least, classify it theologically, characterize it, even if we have no answer to the question "why?" The unbounded horrors represented the *tohu vavohu* anarchy of the pre-*yitzirah* state. This is how the world appears when God's moderating surveillance is suspended. The State of Israel, however, reflects God's return to active providence, the termination of *Hester Panim.*" (Reflections on the Rav-Abraham Besdin- pages 36-37)

There is a clear sense of absolute din or justice here where the Jewish people are treated with the same neglect that God has been treated by them. Man's complete withdrawal from the presence of God and the interaction with God through the mitzvot, results in God's withdrawal from man and in carrying out His providential role. There are limitations to God's withdrawal. Even in these times of *Hester Panim* we are promised that ultimately the promise to Avraham will be fulfilled and the Jewish people will return in repentance.

44. But despite all this, while they are in the land of their enemies, I will not despise them nor will I reject them to annihilate them,

מד. וְאַף גַּם זֹאת
בִּהְיוֹתָם בְּאֶרֶץ
אֹיְבֵיהֶם לֹא מְאַסְתִּים
וְלֹא גְעַלְתִּים לְכַלֹּתָם

thereby breaking My covenant that is with them, for I am the Lord their God. לְהָפֵר בְּרִיתִי אִתָּם כִּי אֲנִי יְהֹוָה אֱלֹהֵיהֶם:

45. I will remember for them the covenant [made with] the ancestors, whom I took out from the land of Egypt before the eyes of the nations, to be a God to them. I am the Lord. מה. וְזָכַרְתִּי לָהֶם בְּרִית רִאשֹׁנִים אֲשֶׁר הוֹצֵאתִי אֹתָם מֵאֶרֶץ מִצְרַיִם לְעֵינֵי הַגּוֹיִם לִהְיוֹת לָהֶם לֵאלֹהִים אֲנִי יְהֹוָה:

In the famous essay "Kol Dodi Dofek" the Rav focuses on what he sees as the miracle of the establishment of the State of Israel after the Holocaust as the removal of the state of "Hester Panim" that existed in time of the Nazi Holocaust. He states:

Eight years ago in the midst of a night of terror filled with the horrors of Maidanek, Treblinka, and Buchenwald, in a night of gas chambers and crematoria, in a night of absolute divine self-concealment (*hester panim muhlat*) in a night ruled by the satan of doubt and apostasy which sought to sweep the maiden from her house into the Christian Church in a night of continuous searching, of questing for the Beloved (God) in that very night the Beloved appeared. God who conceals himself in dazzling hiddenness "suddenly manifested Himself and began to knock at the tent of His despondent and disconsolate love,

twisting and convulsively on her bed, suffering the pains of hell. As a result of the knocks on the door of the maiden, wrapped in mourning the State of Israel was born. " (Kol Dodi Dofek, p. 68)

Maimonides ('the Rambam"), in his great philosophical work the "Moreh Nevukim" ("Guide for the Perplexed"), analyzed the area of God's providence in a number of places in the text. In the third book of the Guide where the Rambam divides the mitzvot of the Torah into 14 classes or categories. These 14 classes correspond with the 14 books of the Rambam's "Mishneh Torah" which was divided into these 14 areas, or 14 books. He states in the 1st class termed "Yesodai HaTorah":

...the commandment to cry to God in time of trouble, "to blow an alarm with the trumpets" (Num. x.9), belongs to this class. We are told to offer up prayers to God, in order to establish firmly the true principle that God takes notice of our ways, that He can make them successful if we worship Him, or disastrous if we disobey Him , that (success and failure) are not the result of chance of accident. In this sense we must understand the passage, "If you walk with me by chance or accident. (Lev. 26:21). i.e., if I bring troubles upon you for punishment, and you consider them as accidents, I will again send you some of these accidents as you call them, but of a more serious and troublesome character. This is expressed in the words:

"If you walk with me by chance: then I will walk with you also in the fury of chance". (ibid. verses 27, 28). For the belief of the people that their troubles are mere accidents causes them to continue in their evil principles and prevents them from abandoning their evil ways. (Book 3: Chapter 36).

Maimonides states here that the purpose for obligatory prayer is as a means to inculcating the idea that God's affects the lives of individuals and nations and that occurrences are not the result of random or chance events. This misperception would include the widely held secular perspective that events occur due to the fixed laws of nature governing the physical world and that they have no connection to divine reward or punishment. Maimonides is quite contemporary in his assessment of this secular view which holds even the most dire occurrences are due to these fixed laws with, perhaps, the impact of free choice on the part of individuals. However many do not even hold that human free choice exists. The contemporary assessment that the events that occur to a person or group are without any "input" from the Creator has made people today exceptionally bold and stubborn in their continuance of evil behaviors even in the face of terrible adversity. The belief in a God that intervenes, rewards and punishes is essential to a person's ability to repent and reform their actions.

BAMIDBAR

THE LORD SPOKE TO MOSES IN THE SINAI DESERT, IN THE TENT OF MEETING ON THE FIRST DAY OF THE SECOND MONTH, IN THE SECOND YEAR AFTER THE EXODUS FROM THE LAND OF EGYPT, SAYING: TAKE THE SUM OF ALL THE CONGREGATION OF THE CHILDREN OF ISRAEL, BY FAMILIES FOLLOWING THEIR FATHERS' HOUSES; A HEAD COUNT OF EVERY MALE ACCORDING TO THE NUMBER OF THEIR NAMES (BAMIDBAR 1:1-2)

BAMIDBAR

The 3 Desert Camps: A Blueprint for the Temple

Ezra HaSofer established the practice of reading the parsha of Bamidbar on the Shabbos before Shavuos. Rabbi Yoseph B. Soloveitchik ("The Rav") analyzed the purpose of this enactment. He explains that central to the parsha of Bamidbar is its explanation of the setting up of the camps of the Jewish tribes, surrounding the Sanctuary ("Mishkan"), with concentric circles and different degrees of holiness ("kedusha") in each of the three camps. The first chapter of the parsha states (Bamidbar 1:52-54):

52. The children of Israel shall encamp, each man by his own camp and each man by his division.	**נב.** וְחָנוּ בְּנֵי יִשְׂרָאֵל אִישׁ עַל מַחֲנֵהוּ וְאִישׁ עַל דִּגְלוֹ לְצִבְאֹתָם׃
53. The Levites shall encamp around the Mishkan of the Testimony, so that there be no wrath upon the congregation of the children of Israel and the Levites shall keep the charge of the Mishkan of the Testimony.	**נג.** וְהַלְוִיִּם יַחֲנוּ סָבִיב לְמִשְׁכַּן הָעֵדֻת וְלֹא יִהְיֶה קֶצֶף עַל עֲדַת בְּנֵי יִשְׂרָאֵל וְשָׁמְרוּ הַלְוִיִּם אֶת מִשְׁמֶרֶת מִשְׁכַּן הָעֵדוּת׃
54. And the children of Israel did according to all that the Lord had commanded Moses thus did they do.	**נד.** וַיַּעֲשׂוּ בְּנֵי יִשְׂרָאֵל כְּכֹל אֲשֶׁר צִוָּה יְ־הֹוָ־ה אֶת מֹשֶׁה כֵּן עָשׂוּ׃

The Rav explains that the 3 different camps in the desert were: 1) the camp of the *Shechinah* ("Place of God's Presence") at the center with the Sanctuary containing the

Holy Ark (the "Holy of Holies"); 2) the camp of the *Leviim* surrounding the *Miskan*, and 3) the camp of the other tribes of Israel surrounding the camp of the *Leviim*. The Rav notes that Maimonides ("The Rambam") describes these 3 camps (The Camp of the *Shechinah*, the Camp of the *Leviim* and the Camp of the *Yisraelim* (the other tribes), as the future "blueprint" for the Holy Temple, which includes the Temple Mount and the neighborhoods surrounding it where the tribes would live in the City of Jerusalem.

The Rambam describes the desert encampments in the Mishneh Torah:

The [encampment of the Jewish people] in the desert [was divided into] three areas: the camp of Israel, which was itself subdivided into four camps; the camp of the Levites about which [Numbers 1:50] states: "They shall camp around the Sanctuary;" and the camp of the *Shechinah* [which included the area] beginning at the entrance to the courtyard of the Tent of Meeting inwards. Correspondingly, for [future] generations *("ookuhgoan l'doros")*. [The area] from the entrance to Jerusalem to the Temple Mount is comparable to the camp of Israel.[The area] from the entrance to the Temple Mount until the entrance to the Temple Courtyard, the gate of Nicanor, is comparable to the camp of the Levites. [The area] from the entrance to the Temple Courtyard inward, is comparable to the camp of the *Shechinah*. (Laws of Beis Habechira: 7:11)

According to the Rav, the Rambam is clarifying the point that Jerusalem does not have the status of simply a city in Israel. Jerusalem had, and still has, the status of being the"*Machane Yisrael*"- the camp of Israel - just as it was in the desert. *Har habayit* (The Temple Mount) has the status of "*Machane Leviya*" – the camp of the Leviim and the *Beit HaMikdash*-("the Holy Temple") is a continuation of the "*Machane Shechinah*"- the Place of the God's Presence" , as it was in the desert. The Rav interprets the Rambam as stating that the holiness of the Temple is not due to its own inherent holiness but instead attributed to its being a continuation of the holiness of the "*Machane Shechinah*"- the Place of God's Presence" in the desert. This idea is brought out by the Rambam's statement in the Mishneh Torah stated above where, after describing the structure of the three levels of camps in the desert, he states: "**correspondingly, for [future] generations ("*ookahgoan l'doros*")**". The Rav explains this statement of the Rambam to mean that the "*Machane Shechina*" that existed in the desert was the source of all *kedushah* in the camps surrounding it in the desert, as well as in the Holy Temple and Jerusalem. From this, the Rav goes on to explain the reading the parsha of Bamidbar on the holiday Shavuos.

The focus of the parsha Bamidbar is the description of the 3 *machanot* in the desert and their levels of holiness. Shavuos is the holiday celebrating the giving of the Torah at Mount Sinai. The Rav explains that at the time of the giving of the Torah, Mount Sinai had the status of the Holy Temple. There were three levels of holiness related to Mount Sinai at the time of the giving of the Torah: 1) the top of the mountain-the place of God and Moshe-this was the *Machane Shechina* (the first camp); 2) the second machine that included Aharon and the 70 elders. This was "*Machane Leviya*" –"the camp of the Leviim (the second camp); 3) the third *machane* consisting of the rest of the Jewish people – "the *Bnei Yisrael*" who surrounded the mountain-this was "*Machane Yisrael*". For this reason, the Rav explains, Moshe had to clearly demarcate these three areas and assure that no one went beyond their camp, which corresponded to their level of holiness. Parsha Bamidbar explains the different levels of the *machanot* in the desert and is read on Shavous because the levels of kedusha of these *machanot* reflect the *kedushah* of the 3 *machanot* that existed on Mount Sinai at the giving of the Torah on Shavuos.

Why, I would ask, doesn't the Holy Temple have its own inherent *kedushah*? Why, according the Rav's understanding of the Rambam, does the *kedushah* of the Temple and its surrounding area derive from the *machanot* of the desert which, in itself, is a reflection of the *machanot* at Mount Sinai at the time of the giving of the Torah? Perhaps there is an important diminishment of the Temple's status expressed in this formulation of the law. The Holy Temple is not holy due to its structure, its materials nor from its beauty or exalted location. The Temple is holy because it is a place of meeting. It is a place where God "camps", so to speak with

His people. Its function is one of communication and meeting between the infinite, perfect God and his finite and imperfect people. This is, perhaps, the source of its holiness. And of all the meetings that were ever convened between God and his people, the ultimate and paradigmatic one was, of course, *matan Torah* at Mount Sinai. It was at this time and at this time only, that God met directly with each and every Jew and directly communed with him or her. It was this meeting which created the holiness of the place. At that place where God entered the camp of the Jewish people and conveyed His will to them, holiness of place was created. One might conclude that holiness in this world, is not the result of qualities within a person, place or thing, but derives from the ability of something or someone to facilitate the communication between God and His creation. In this way the Holy Temple derives its kedusha from its facilitating the meeting of man with his God, and God with His people. Mount Sinai at the time of Shavuos was the true Holy of Holies as it bridged the infinite chasm between God and man to a degree that had never occurred before and the likes of will never occur again.

NASO

The Nazir: Restriction from Distraction

The parsha of Naso describes the vow of the Nazir and the restrictions of *Naziris*:

Chapter 6

2. Speak to the children of Israel, and you shall say to them: A man or woman who sets himself apart by making a nazirite vow to abstain for the sake of the Lord.

ב. דַּבֵּר אֶל בְּנֵי יִשְׂרָאֵל וְאָמַרְתָּ אֲלֵהֶם אִישׁ אוֹ אִשָּׁה כִּי יַפְלִא לִנְדֹּר נֶדֶר נָזִיר לְהַזִּיר לַי־הוָ־ה:

3. He shall abstain from new wine and aged wine; he shall not drink [even] vinegar made from new wine or aged wine, nor shall he drink anything in which grapes have been steeped, and he shall eat neither fresh grapes nor dried ones.

ג. מִיַּיִן וְשֵׁכָר יַזִּיר חֹמֶץ יַיִן וְחֹמֶץ שֵׁכָר לֹא יִשְׁתֶּה וְכָל מִשְׁרַת עֲנָבִים לֹא יִשְׁתֶּה וַעֲנָבִים לַחִים וִיבֵשִׁים לֹא יֹאכֵל:

4. For the entire duration of his abstinence, he shall not eat any product of the grape vine, from seeds to skins.

ד. כֹּל יְמֵי נִזְרוֹ מִכֹּל אֲשֶׁר יֵעָשֶׂה מִגֶּפֶן הַיַּיִן מֵחַרְצַנִּים וְעַד זָג לֹא יֹאכֵל:

5. All the days of his vow of abstinence, no razor shall pass over his head; until the completion of the term that he abstains for the sake of the

ה. כָּל יְמֵי נֶדֶר נִזְרוֹ תַּעַר לֹא יַעֲבֹר עַל רֹאשׁוֹ עַד מְלֹאת הַיָּמִם אֲשֶׁר יַזִּיר לַי־הוָ־ה קָדֹשׁ יִהְיֶה גַּדֵּל פֶּרַע שְׂעַר רֹאשׁוֹ:

Lord, it shall be sacred, and he shall allow the growth of the hair of his head to grow wild.

6. All the days that he abstains for The Lord, he shall not come into contact with the dead.

ו. כָּל יְמֵי הַזִּירוֹ לַי־הֹוָ־ה עַל נֶפֶשׁ מֵת לֹא יָבֹא:

Maimonides (The Rambam) in his work "The Guide for the Perplexed" states regarding the Nazir:

The object of naziris is obvious. It keeps away from wine which has ruined people in ancient and modern times. Man must take of wine only as much as is absolutely necessary. For he who abstains from drinking is called holy; his sanctity is made equal to that of the High priest, in not being allowed to defile himself even for his father and his mother. This honor is given him because he abstains from wine. (Guide for the Perplexed 3:48)

The Rambam's statement is noteworthy in that it focuses on the *nazir's* restriction on drinking wine and attributes the restriction of contact with the dead as being a result of this abstention. The question is why does the Rambam state that "it is obvious" that the object of naziris is to keep people away from wine? The presence of the *nazir's* other restrictions seems to detract from the obviousness of this as the sole purpose of naziris. Also, the *nazir* is permitted alcoholic products derived from non-grape sources (such as beer, scotch, etc.), while restricted from grapes. It is hard to see naziris as simply a halakchic structure to assist a person in restraining from alcohol use. Perhaps we can delve a bit into the Rambam's concept of holiness ("kedushah") which he associates with the *nazir's* abstention and how this holiness relates to a person's restriction from physical pleasures. The Rambam states in the 3rd book of the "Guide for the Perplexed":

The Law is also intended to give its followers purity and holiness; by teaching them to suppress sensuality, to guard against it and to reduce it to a minimum, as will be explained by us. For when God commanded [Moses] to sanctify the people for the receiving of the Law, and said, "Sanctify them to-day and to-morrow" (Exod. xix. 10), Moses [in obedience to this command] said to the people, "Come not at your wives" (*ibid.* ver. 15). Here it is clearly stated that sanctification consists in absence of sensuality. But abstinence from drinking wine is also called holiness; in reference to the Nazarite it is therefore said, "He shall be holy" (Num. vi. 5). According to Siphra the words, "sanctify yourselves and be ye holy" (Lev. xx. 7), refer to the sanctification effected by performing the divine commands. As the obedience to such precepts as have been mentioned above is called by the Law sanctification and purification, so is defilement applied to the transgression of these precepts and the performance of disgraceful acts, as will be shown. (The Guide for the Perplexed: Book 3: Chapter 33).

The Rambam held that the refinement of the rational faculty was the path to attaining closeness to God. The Rambam's position was that the Torah's laws were, in part, a preparatory system by which a person could wean himself or herself away from sensuality and emotionality and achieve the psychological balance and mental skills needed to embark on contemplation of God, to the extent possible with our limited human intellect. Seen in this context, the Nazir is not simply refraining from wine for the purpose of limiting "bad behavior" or the physical, emotional or social destruction that often results from drunkenness. The *nazir's* interest is to refine his or her emotions and desires in a manner which will allow the mind a greater degree of development and the Nazir to experience a closer relationship with God. This perspective could also explain the logic of the *nazir's* restriction from contact with the dead and hair cutting. Perhaps the Rambam sees them as subcategories of the wine restriction. Both contact with the dead and hair grooming can be significant sources of distraction. Contact with the dead brings one to contemplate death which is a source of despair and depression. Concern with appearance can also be profoundly distracting to one's thought and study. These distractions are removed for the *nazir*. Freed from these distractions and desires, the Nazir has a greater opportunity to experience an intensified period of refinement and contemplation of God.

Rabbi Joseph B. Soloveitchik ("The Rav"), in his work "Halakhic Man", describes in detail the negative perspective the Torah has towards death and explains this as the reason that contact with the dead is the fundamental source of defilement ("*tumah*") in Jewish law and distracts man from his work in the "world of the living". Regarding the *nazir*, the Rav states:

The task of the religious individual is bound up with the performance of commandments, and this performance is confined to this world, to physical, concrete reality, to clamorous, tumultuous life, pulsating with exuberance and strength. Therefore, holiness need keep itself far away from death. The priest, the Nazarite, the Temple court, the holy offering are all removed, as if by an iron wall, from the realm of death. (Halakhic Man, p. 33).

There are distractions of the sensual and the psychological kind. Wine distracts us from God by accentuating sensuality, while contact with the dead distracts through feelings of sadness and despair.

BEHAALOTECHA

The Beef About Manna

The parsha of Behaalotecha relates the Jewish people's rejection of the manna that God provided for them in the desert, and describes their craving for meat. The parsha states (BaMidbar 10:4-8):

4. But the multitude among them began to have strong cravings. Then even the children of Israel once again began to cry, and they said, "Who will feed us meat?	**ד.** וְהָאסַפְסֻף אֲשֶׁר בְּקִרְבּוֹ הִתְאַוּוּ תַּאֲוָה וַיָּשֻׁבוּ וַיִּבְכּוּ גַּם בְּנֵי יִשְׂרָאֵל וַיֹּאמְרוּ מִי יַאֲכִלֵנוּ בָּשָׂר:
5. We remember the fish that we ate in Egypt free of charge, the cucumbers, the watermelons, the leeks, the onions, and the garlic.	**ה.** זָכַרְנוּ אֶת הַדָּגָה אֲשֶׁר נֹאכַל בְּמִצְרַיִם חִנָּם אֵת הַקִּשֻּׁאִים וְאֵת הָאֲבַטִּחִים וְאֶת הֶחָצִיר וְאֶת הַבְּצָלִים וְאֶת הַשּׁוּמִים:
6. But now, our bodies are dried out, for there is nothing at all; we have nothing but manna to look at."	**ו.** וְעַתָּה נַפְשֵׁנוּ יְבֵשָׁה אֵין כֹּל בִּלְתִּי אֶל הַמָּן עֵינֵינוּ:
7. Now the manna was like coriander seed, and its appearance was like the appearance of crystal.	**ז.** וְהַמָּן כִּזְרַע גַּד הוּא וְעֵינוֹ כְּעֵין הַבְּדֹלַח:
8. The people walked about and gathered it. Then they ground it in a mill or crushed it	**ח.** שָׁטוּ הָעָם וְלָקְטוּ וְטָחֲנוּ בָרֵחַיִם אוֹ דָכוּ בַּמְּדֹכָה וּבִשְּׁלוּ בַּפָּרוּר וְעָשׂוּ אֹתוֹ

in a mortar, cooked it in a pot and made it into cakes. It had a taste like the taste of oil cake.

עֻגוֹת וְהָיָה טַעְמוֹ כְּטַעַם לְשַׁד הַשָּׁמֶן:

God responds to this request: (Vayikra 10:19-20):

19. You shall eat it not one day, not two days, not five days, not ten days, and not twenty days.

יט. לֹא יוֹם אֶחָד תֹּאכְלוּן וְלֹא יוֹמָיִם וְלֹא חֲמִשָּׁה יָמִים וְלֹא עֲשָׂרָה יָמִים וְלֹא עֶשְׂרִים יוֹם:

20. But even for a full month until it comes out your nose and nauseates you. Because you have despised the Lord Who is among you, and you cried before Him, saying, "Why did we ever leave Egypt?

כ. עַד חֹדֶשׁ יָמִים עַד אֲשֶׁר יֵצֵא מֵאַפְּכֶם וְהָיָה לָכֶם לְזָרָא יַעַן כִּי מְאַסְתֶּם אֶת יְ־הֹוָ־ה אֲשֶׁר בְּקִרְבְּכֶם וַתִּבְכּוּ לְפָנָיו לֵאמֹר לָמָּה זֶּה יָצָאנוּ מִמִּצְרָיִם:

Rabbi Joseph B. Soloveitchik ("The Rav") explains in his essay "The Emergence of Ethical Man" that the language used by God in response to this "meat-craving" reflects a fundamental truth regarding the preciousness of all life and the negative Torah perspective on the taking of animal life for pleasure. The Rav states: **"So much disdain and contempt we find in no other story. The insistence upon flesh, this lusty carnal desire, arouses divine wrath".** The eating of flesh, the Rav explains, is termed "*ta-avah*"-"lust, an illicit demand".

The Rav goes on to explain that there is an equivalence that exists among all life and, in this regard, the slaying of any life is an act of violation. However, Judaism allows, and even requires the slaying of animals and the eating of meat within its halakchic structure. The Rav clarifies:

Animal hunters and flesh-eaters are people that lust. Of course it is legalized, approved. Yet it is classified as *taavah*, lust, repulsive and brutish. The real motif that prompts such an unquestionable antagonism toward slaying of animals is the aboriginal Jewish thought that conceives man on a natural-vegetant-animal plane. Particularly man and animal are almost identical in their organic dynamics that is equated with life, and there is no justifiable reason why one life should fall prey to another. Why should a cunning intelligence that granted man dominion over his fellow animals also give him license to kill? (The Emergence of Ethical Man: page 37)

In this essay the Rav goes on to explain that the original dispensation of the Jew's restriction on eating meat was limited to only sacrificial meat. The Jews, in the desert, were required to maintain a level of holiness that would abhor the simple killing and eating of animal flesh. Only when this slaughter and eating was connected to the sacrificial act of the Mishkan was it sanctified. The Rav states:

Non-ceremonial taking of animal life was forbidden. Only sacral killing of an animal was sanctioned: "To the end that the children of Israel may bring their sacrifices, which they offer in the open field, that they may bring them to the Lord, to the door of the Tent of Meeting, to the priest and offer them for peace offerings to the Lord" (Vayikra:17:6). The animal is

designated by divine law as an offering to God." (page 38).

The Rav goes on to explain that this restriction was modified when the Temple worship was centralized in Israel. This central location created too great a hardship for those Jews living far from its location. But even in stating this removal of the restriction of eating only sacrificial meat, the Rav points out, the term "*teavah*" (lust desire) is used. **"When the Lord your God shall enlarge your borders, as He promised you, and... you long to eat meat; you may eat meat to your heart's desire (te'avah nafshekha)" (Devarim:12:20-21).** The implication being that a Jew's eating meat, though now permissible, has its source in a contemptible part of his nature.

Maimonides ("The Rambam") makes mention of the holiday requirement to eat meat along with drinking wine in the Mishneh Torah in the Laws of Yom Tovim (6:17-18). He states:

On these days, a person is obligated to be happy and in good spirits...Men should eat meat and drink wine, for there is no happiness without partaking of meat, nor happiness without partaking of wine.

The Rambam, in stating the requirement of meat and wine for a person to truly rejoice, explains that the eating of meat, for men at least, is at the core of the state of rejoicing. The Rambam's statement can be seen as in consonance with the position of the Rav in the following way: For man to be "*mesamayach*" (in a state of true rejoicing) all elements of his being must be satiated. This includes those which elements of the human personality that have their source in the appetitive, aggressive, lustful area, as well as his desire for *emes* (truth) and *mishpat* (justice). The eating of meat (and drinking of wine) are the optimal means of satiating these lustful parts of man's nature and so are not only permitted, but required for proper whole-hearted rejoicing on the Yom Tov.

SHELACH

Destiny Derailed by A Few Poorly Chosen Words

The parsha of Shelach describes the report of the twelve princes of Israel (one from each tribe) who went to scout out the land of Canaan. Ten of the twelve who went, returned with words that brought fear and despondency to the Jewish people. Only Yehoshua and Calev did not participate in this "evil report" and tried to dispel the negative impact of the others. The Torah states in Bamidbar 13:31-33:

31. But the men who went up with him said, "We are unable to go up against the people, for they are stronger than we.

לא. וְהָאֲנָשִׁים אֲשֶׁר עָלוּ עִמּוֹ אָמְרוּ לֹא נוּכַל לַעֲלוֹת אֶל הָעָם כִּי חָזָק הוּא מִמֶּנּוּ:

32. They spread an [evil] report about the land which they had scouted, telling the children of Israel, "The land we passed through to explore is a land that consumes its inhabitants, and all the people we saw in it are men of stature.

לב. וַיּוֹצִיאוּ דִּבַּת הָאָרֶץ אֲשֶׁר תָּרוּ אֹתָהּ אֶל בְּנֵי יִשְׂרָאֵל לֵאמֹר הָאָרֶץ אֲשֶׁר עָבַרְנוּ בָהּ לָתוּר אֹתָהּ אֶרֶץ אֹכֶלֶת יוֹשְׁבֶיהָ הִוא וְכָל הָעָם אֲשֶׁר רָאִינוּ בְתוֹכָהּ אַנְשֵׁי מִדּוֹת:

33. There we saw the giants, the sons of Anak, descended from the giants. In our eyes, we

לג. וְשָׁם רָאִינוּ אֶת הַנְּפִילִים בְּנֵי עֲנָק מִן הַנְּפִלִים וַנְּהִי בְעֵינֵינוּ

seemed like grasshoppers, and so we were in their eyes.	כַּחֲגָבִים וְכֵן הָיִינוּ בְּעֵינֵיהֶם:

The evil report of these 10 princes, and the Jewish people's fearful response to it, was the cause of the Jewish people's remaining in the desert for 40 years, although the journey to Canaan should have only required a few weeks to complete. The Torah states in Bamidbar 14:22-23:

22. that all the people who perceived My glory, and the signs that I performed in Egypt and in the desert, yet they have tested me these ten times and not listened to My voice,	**כב.** כִּי כָל הָאֲנָשִׁים הָרֹאִים אֶת כְּבֹדִי וְאֶת אֹתֹתַי אֲשֶׁר עָשִׂיתִי בְמִצְרַיִם וּבַמִּדְבָּר וַיְנַסּוּ אֹתִי זֶה עֶשֶׂר פְּעָמִים וְלֹא שָׁמְעוּ בְּקוֹלִי:
23. if they will see the Land that I swore to their fathers, and all who provoked Me will not see it.	**כג.** אִם יִרְאוּ אֶת הָאָרֶץ אֲשֶׁר נִשְׁבַּעְתִּי לַאֲבֹתָם וְכָל מְנַאֲצַי לֹא יִרְאוּהָ:

Rabbi Soloveitchik ("The Rav"), describes the flaw of these 10 princes in the text "the Rav Speaks" by Abraham R. Besdin. He explains that they did not understand the nature of the unique relationship between the Jewish people and the land of Israel. It was this failure that made these princes, and those that followed them, unfit to inhabit the holy land and it was for this that they were condemned to die in the desert. The Rav states:

Jewish destiny is linked with this land; we have no other. Only in this land, our Sages say, does the Shekhinah dwell and only therein does prophecy flourish. This *segulah* (a unique positive quality-RB) attribute of the land is no more rationally explicable than the *segulah* of the people. These are qualities certified by our faith, and history has corroborated the singularity of both people and the land. (page 120).

The 12 princes who scouted the land made the error of assessing the land in a standard manner; in a sense, comparing it to other lands for its inhabitability and military characteristics. The Rav explains that since the land of Israel is the unique, singular land for the Jewish people, the scouting party's proper role was not to assess or compare the land with other lands, but to only acquaint oneself with the land and experience its qualities. The Rav relates this to the Jewish law that a Jewish man is required to meet and to know one's bride before making the marriage commitment. The Rav explains:

...the reason Moses was told to send scouts into the land (was) not to gather intelligence, but to have the distinguished heads of each tribe explore the land bring back reports of its singular character. The instructions Moses gave them defined their mission, viz. to make the acquaintance of the land. By entering the land, the people were being wedded to it and,

despite Divine assurances of its quality, they had to experience it through their princes before the commitment could be deeply rooted and irrevocably assumed. (page 122)

The Rav explains that the sin of the spies was that:

Their report was that of spies, not that of scouts; they balanced debits against credits and declared the entire enterprise hopeless. With grandeur looking down on them, all they could see was the mundane. (page `123)

Maimonides ("The Rambam") has a very different understanding of the "evil report" of the 10 spies. He views the incident as a necessary event by which God justified to the Jewish people their 40 year journey through the desert. This period of time, according to the Rambam, was required for the inevitably slow development to take place and transform a slave nation into one that was capable of fulfilling its noble role in the land of Israel. The Rambam states in the "Guide for the Perplexed":

It was the result of God's wisdom that the Israelites were led about in the wilderness till they acquired courage. For it is a well-known fact that traveling in the wilderness, and privation of bodily enjoyments, such as bathing, produce courage, whilst the reverse is the source of faint-heartedness; besides, another generation rose during the wanderings that had not

been accustomed to degradation and slavery. ("Guide for the Perplexed": Friedlander translation: Book 3: Chapter 32)

The Rambam explains in this chapter that this process of gradual change is found throughout God's interaction with the Jewish people and explains the structures of many Jewish laws by which a people who began as idolatrous slaves were transformed into a courageous, holy nation. The Rambam also brings examples from nature by which organisms develops and grow through gradual steps in development. From the Rambam's explanation we can see the spies' evil report of the land and the mass rebellion it caused as an expected event that revealed that the people were not ready to enter the land so shortly after the redemption from slavery. Had the Jewish nation been denied entrance into the land for 40 years without the incident of the spies, it would have been perceived by them as unnecessary and unjust. However though the incident of the spies, it was made clear that the gradual development of the desert was necessary to prepare the next generation to conquer the land. However, taking Maimonides perspective of the necessity for the gradual transformation in the desert, one could ask the question of why the report of spies and the Jewish people's response was portrayed as such a great sin and one that resulted in the death of the spies and punishment of the Jewish people. Perhaps although the gradual development of the people from slaves to conquerors is the normal way things occur. However, with the unique experience the Jewish people had in the redemption from Egypt and the receiving of the Torah, there was an opportunity for them to accelerate this development and take a bold step of total transformation. Our history has many examples of individuals who change it seems, in an instant to a different person. Elisha left all things of his life in a moment of great decision to follow Eliyahu. Rabbi Soloveitchik at the conclusion of his great essay, "The Lonely Man of Faith" describes Elisha's transformation. He states:

While he was engaged in the most ordinary, everyday activity, in tilling the soil, he encountered God and felt the transforming touch of God's hand. The strangest metamorphosis occurred. Within seconds, the old Elisha disappeared and a new Elisha emerged. (p. 112)

The unprecedented revelation of God's might and providence that had brought the people to this point of decision was negated and defeated by the *lashon hara* of the spies. The plagues, the splitting of the sea, the manna, the awe and the enlightenment of Sinai were all swept away by a few words of discouragement. It is a cautionary tale of the power of speech to destroy and change the destiny of a person or a people. It is certainly true, what the Rambam states in the Guide regarding "gradualism" being the natural course of change. But the Jews had been given a unique opportunity to "jump levels" and transform without the normal course of time and development. This flash of transformation did not occur for the Jewish people and they were relegated to the "normal way of things" by which they would gradually develop over years and generations into the nation that was capable of conquering the land.

KORAH

What Was Korah's Sin?

The parsha of Korach describes the rebellion of Korah and his 250 followers (Bamidbar 16:1-3):

1. Korah the son of Izhar, the son of Kohath, the son of Levi took [himself to one side] along with Dathan and Abiram, the sons of Eliab, and On the son of Peleth, descendants of Reuben.	**א.** וַיִּקַּח קֹרַח בֶּן יִצְהָר בֶּן קְהָת בֶּן לֵוִי וְדָתָן וַאֲבִירָם בְּנֵי אֱלִיאָב וְאוֹן בֶּן פֶּלֶת בְּנֵי רְאוּבֵן:
2. They confronted Moses together with two hundred and fifty men from the children of Israel, chieftains of the congregation, representatives of the assembly, men of repute.	**ב.** וַיָּקֻמוּ לִפְנֵי מֹשֶׁה וַאֲנָשִׁים מִבְּנֵי יִשְׂרָאֵל חֲמִשִּׁים וּמָאתָיִם נְשִׂיאֵי עֵדָה קְרִאֵי מוֹעֵד אַנְשֵׁי שֵׁם:
3. They assembled against Moses and Aaron, and said to them, "You take too much upon yourselves, for the entire congregation are all holy, and the Lord is in their midst. So why do raise yourselves above the Lord's assembly?"	**ג.** וַיִּקָּהֲלוּ עַל מֹשֶׁה וְעַל אַהֲרֹן וַיֹּאמְרוּ אֲלֵהֶם רַב לָכֶם כִּי כָל הָעֵדָה כֻּלָּם קְדֹשִׁים וּבְתוֹכָם יְ־הֹוָ־ה וּמַדּוּעַ תִּתְנַשְּׂאוּ עַל קְהַל יְ־הֹוָ־ה:

Rabbi Joseph B. Soloveitchik ("The Rav") explains the approach taken by Korah and his followers and how it is essentially similar in form to current day reproaches of the Torah system of laws. This attack is on both the structure of Jewish law and the need for experts to determine the application of the law in a particular case. Korah assumed that Jewish law did not require the intuitive and refined thinking of an expert to derive the law, but only a "common sense" understanding of the facts of the case. The Rav states in the essay "The Common Sense Rebellion Against Torah Authority" in the sefer "Reflections on the Rav" by Rabbi Avraham Besdin:

Korah's rationale can be understood more readily if we clarify three terms denoting the various levels of reason and intelligence. "*Hokhmah*" refers to specialized knowledge and scholarship which are acquired by extensive and detailed study. "*Bina*" is the capacity to analyze, to make distinctions, to draw inferences and apply them to various situations. When "*binah*" is combined with *"hokhmah"*, we have the especially gifted and creative thinker. *"Daat"* deals with common sense, basic intelligence, and sound practical judgment. Korah's appeal to common sense in Judaism was basically a claim that only *daat* and not *hokhmah*, is involved in the application of Halakhah….

A second dimension of Korah's attack on Moshe's leadership was his claim that Moshe misunderstood the structure of

Jewish law. Specifically, Korah denigrated Moshe's understanding the structure of the legal obligation to be separate from the desired outcome or "reason" for the law. Korah derided Moshe for holding that a room full of Torah required a mezuzah and a garment of blue color required the blue thread of the *tzitzit*. The Rav explains how Korah tried to formulate the law to make the Torah's system of laws as explained by Moshe seem absurd. He states:

On the basis of Korah's theory, the mitzvah would have to correspond to the mood that prompts it. The value of the mitzvah is to be found not in its performance, but in its subjective impact upon the person, its ability to arouse a devotional state of mind… If these mitzvoth ceased having this impact upon people, their observance would be open to question and new rituals, more responsive to changing sensitivities, should be enacted. What follows from his reasoning is that the mitzvah may be modified according to changing times or even according to individual temperaments of different people. There is to him, no inherent redemptive power in the mitzvah beyond its therapeutic effects, its capacity to evoke a subjective experience.

The Rav explains that the Torah law's obligations are not altered in a particular case to achieve an outcome that is perceived as more aligned with the supposed reason or purpose for the mitzvah. The law must remain consistent in all cases, regardless of the particular outcome. Rabbi

Soloveitchik was quite consistent in his view that halakchic observance has its own validity as a means to the human being "walking with: God and achieving holiness within one's earthly life. Halacha is not to be understood or to receive its validity from its efficaciousness according to some other system of truth. Kashrut is not validated because it may have health benefits; prayer is not validated because it has psychological benefits. Halacha is valid within its own objectives of drawing man close to God and providing human beings with a way to serve the Creator. Halachic authorities would not deny that halakchic observance may have extra-halakchic benefits, but these are neither the purpose of the system or its source of value or validity. If a doctor prescribed exercise to a person to improve the person's health and it happened to help them work better at business and be more productive, this ancillary benefit would not impact the medical benefit of the exercise, for which it was prescribed. Rabbi Jonathan Sacks comments on the Rav's work "Halachic Mind" in his essay, "Rabbi Joseph B. Soloveitchik's Early Epistemology". Rabbi Sacks states:

The central argument of The Halakhic Mind is that religion constitutes an *autonomous cognitive domain.* R. Soloveitchik has no taste for apologetics, for the justification of religion in terms drawn from outside itself. He (the Rav) notes "the passionate desire of every philosopher of religion to legitimate the cognitive validity and truthfulness of religious propositions. Yet the problem of evidence in religion will never be solved. The

believer does not miss philosophic legitimation; the skeptic will never be satisfied with any cognitive demonstration" ("Exploring the Thoughts of Rabbi Joseph B. Soloveitchik", edited by Rabbi Marc D. Angel).

Korah, according to the Tanchuma brought down by Rashi, did more than rebel against the leadership of Moshe. He also attacked Moshe by attacking the Torah itself, portraying certain laws as absurd. The Tanchuma states:

He clad them (Korach dressed his 250 followers) in garments made entirely of blue wool, they came and stood before Moses, and said to him; A garment made entirely of blue wool, does it require fringes or is it exempt? Moses said o them: It does require. They began to laugh at him: Is it possible that with a garment made of another material, one thread of blue wool exempts it (makes it ritually correct) yet this which is made entirely of blue wool shall not exempt itself?

In the case that was brought down in this Tanchuma we should note that the question itself is not the sin. One is permitted and encouraged to question one's teacher, even if the teacher is Moshe Rebbenu, regarding a Jewish law. This is seen endlessly in the Talmud where debate and discussion are intense and a law is clarified by questions about unusual cases that are brought into the discussion. In the case of Korah and his followers this was certainly not the case. The situation of dressing the group in the blue garment and the laughter the Tanchuma mentions when Moshe explains that the blue wool garment requires the *techielis* (blue fringe) show clearly that this question was one brought to Moshe, not for clarification, but as a means for disparagement of him and the Torah itself.

The Torah and rabbinic laws of how the student conducts himself before his teacher are described by Maimonides in the 5th chapter of the Mishneh Torah, "Hilchos Talmud Torah" (Laws of Torah Study). When asking questions of his teacher there are many parameters of how to do it in a respectful and efficient manner. Questioning is, nonetheless encouraged and praised. Maimonides states:

...A student should take care of his students and love them, because they are like sons who bring him pleasure in this world and in the world to come. Students increase their teacher's wisdom and broaden his horizons. Our Sages declared: "I learned much wisdom from my teachers and even more from my colleagues. However, from my student (I learned) most of all. Just as a small branch is used to light a large bough, so a small students sharpens his teacher's (thinking process), until, though his questions, he brings forth brilliant wisdom. (Hilchos Talmud Torah 6:12-13)

The honor afforded one's teacher is greater even than that given to a parent and include specific prohibitions regarding the issuing of an halakchic ruling in the presence of one's teacher. The violation of the honor of the teacher, although Maimonides does not bring down a court-based punishment, does result in the person's being deserving of death and the loss of one's portion in the world to come. Maimonides states:

There is no greater honor than that due a teacher, and no greater awe than that due a teacher. Our Sages declared: "Your fear of your teacher should be equivalent to your fear of Heaven." Therefore, they said, "Whoever disputes the authority of his teacher is considered as if he revolts against the Divine Presence, as implied (BaMidbar 26:9) ...who led a revolt against God." (Hilchos Talmud Torah 5:1)

The pasuk quoted (26:9) describes the rebellion of Korah. Maimonides continues in this Halacha:

Whoever engages in controversy with his teacher is considered as if he engaged in controversy with the Divine Presence, as implied (BaMidbar 20:13): "...where the Jews contested with God and where he was sanctified." Whoever thinks disparagingly of his teacher is considered as if he thought disparagingly of the Divine Presence, as implied by (BaMidbar 21:5): "And the people spoke out against God and Moses" (Hilchos Talmud Torah 5:1)

Maimonides continues, in the next halacha to describe what is meant by disputing the authority of one's teacher. He states:

A person who establishes a house of study where he (the teacher) sits, explains and teachers without his teacher's

permission in his teacher's lifetime. This applies even when one's teacher is in another country. It is forbidden to ever render a halachic judgment in one's teacher's presence. Whoever renders a halachic judgment in his teacher's presence is worthy of death. (Hilchos Talmud Torah 5:2)

Maimonides adds in the 4th Halacha of this chapter,

Any student who is not worthy of rendering a halachic judgment and does so is foolish, wicked and arrogant. (Mishlei 7:36) "She has cast down many corpses" applies to him. (Hilchos Talmud Torah 5:4)

There are also strict laws of respect for any Torah sage, even if he is not one's own teacher. Maimonides states in the 6th chapter of the Mishneh Torah: Hilchos Talmud Torah):

It is a mitzvah to respect every Torah sage, even if he is not one's teacher as (Vayikra 19:32) states: "Stand up before a white-haired (man) and respect an elder." (The word) *"zakane"* (translated as "elders", alludes to the Hebrew words meaning) "one who has acquired wisdom"....(Hilchos Talmud Torah 5:4).

Maimonides continues later in this chapter regarding the sin of disgracing or hating a Torah scholar.

It is a great sin to disgrace Torah sages or to hate them. Jerusalem was not destroyed until (its inhabitants) disgraced its sages, as implied by (II:Chronicles 36:16)

"And they would mock the messengers of God, despise His words, and scoff at His prophets" – i.e., they would scorn those who taught His words. Similarly the Torah's prophecy (Vayikra 26:16): "If you despise My statutes" (should be interpreted): "If you despise the teachers of My statues." Whoever disgraces the sages has no portion in the world to come and is included in the category: "Those who scorn the word of God" (Bamidbar 15:31). Even though a person who disgraces a Torah sage will not receive a portion in the world to come, if witnesses come (and testify that) he disgraced him, even if only verbally, he is placed under a ban of ostracism. (Hilchos Talmud Torah 5:4)

It seems to me that Korah certainly violated the laws of disrespecting his teacher, as Moshe was Moshe Rebbenu and the teacher of all of Israel at that time. He also violated the law of disgracing and hating the Torah scholar through his disparaging of Moshe and laughing at his answer regarding the *techeiles* required on a garment of blue wool. But he violated another law for which the punishment is much more severe. Korah denied the validity of the Oral law. Moshe is his lifetime was the absolute authority of the oral law and the original source of its communication to the Jewish people. To deny the validity of Moshe's halakchic ruling was a clear denial of the validity of the Oral Law. In the beginning of the 3rd chapter of "Hilchos Mamrim" ("Laws of the Rebellious Ones") in the Mishneh Torah, Maimonides states:

A person who does not acknowledge (the validity) of the Oral Law is not the rebellious elder mentioned in the Torah. Instead he is one of the heretics and should be put to death by any person. Since it has become known that such a person denies the Oral Law, he may be pushed into a pit and may not be helped out. He is like all the rest of the heretics who say that the Torah is not Divine in origin, those who inform on their fellow Jews, and the apostates. All of these are not considered as members of the Jewish people....To whom does the above apply? To a person who denied the Oral Law consciously, according to his perception of things. He follows after his frivolous thoughts and capricious heart and denies the Oral Law first, as did Tzadok and Beitus, and those who erred in following them. (Hilchos Mamrim: 3:1-3)

This violation would certainly apply to Korah and his followers who disputed and rejected Moshe explanation of the law of *tzitzit* and the situation which required the *techeilis* thread. By rejecting and disparaging Moshe Rebbenu's position, they were more than rejecting Moshe as a teacher or sage - they were rejecting the very validity of the Oral Law which rested on the validity of Moshe Rebbenu as the primary source of the Oral Law communication to the Jewish people.

CHUKAS

The Enigma of the Red Heifer

The parsha of Chukas describes the details of the "*para adumah*" (the red heifer), whose ashes are required to remove "*tumah*" (ritual restriction) from a person who has come in contact with a dead body. The Torah states: (Bamidbar, Chapter 19):

9. A ritually clean person shall gather the cow's ashes and place them outside the camp in a clean place, and It shall be as a keepsake for the congregation of the children of Israel for sprinkling water, [used] for cleansing.....	**ט.** וְאָסַף אִישׁ טָהוֹר אֵת אֵפֶר הַפָּרָה וְהִנִּיחַ מִחוּץ לַמַּחֲנֶה בְּמָקוֹם טָהוֹר וְהָיְתָה לַעֲדַת בְּנֵי יִשְׂרָאֵל לְמִשְׁמֶרֶת לְמֵי נִדָּה חַטָּאת הִוא:
18. A ritually clean person shall take the hyssop and dip it into the water and sprinkle it on the tent, on all the vessels, and on the people who were in it, and on anyone who touched the bone, the slain person, the corpse, or the grave.	**יח.** וְלָקַח אֵזוֹב וְטָבַל בַּמַּיִם אִישׁ טָהוֹר וְהִזָּה עַל הָאֹהֶל וְעַל כָּל הַכֵּלִים וְעַל הַנְּפָשׁוֹת אֲשֶׁר הָיוּ שָׁם וְעַל הַנֹּגֵעַ בַּעֶצֶם אוֹ בֶחָלָל אוֹ בַמֵּת אוֹ בַקָּבֶר:

The red heifer is described in the Talmud as the most enigmatic of the Torah's laws and the only one that Shlomo

HaMelech did not fathom. Rabbi Joseph B. Soloveitchik ("The Rav"), in the 11th chapter of the text "Man of Faith in the Modern World" (Compiled by Rabbi Besdin) describes the laws of the red heifer and utilizes it to explore the idea of understanding the mitzvot. He states: **Our Sages singled out the *Parah Adumah* (Red Heifer, Num. 19) ritual as the most mystifying of all *hukim*.** (Earlier in the essay, the Rav defines *hukim* as "statutes, which are usually defined as incomprehensible and about which our Sages warned that we may be tempted 'to dismiss as meaningless') However, the Rav explains that the warning by the Torah Sages' that the *hukim* may be impervious to understanding and the Sages statement that one must accept that "It is My (God's) decree and you have no right to question it" does not mean that the meaningfulness of the mitzvah should not be explored, only that this exploration is limited in certain ways. The Rav explains:

There are three types of questions we may ask about any phenomenon. "Why" probes motivations to establish why things are the way they are; "how" seeks explanations as to how they function effectively; and "what" looks for interpretations to establish meaningfulness.

The Rav clarifies that we are unable to legitimately ask the questions of "why" and "how" for *hukim*, such as the *parah adumah*. The "why"question is absurd to ask of God's law. He states:

Asking "why" God issued certain commandments is seeking to comprehend the unfathomable. It is more than simply a matter of being unable to comprehend God's mind and motivation. It is more profound than that. When we ask "why" in the human context, we are truly asking "what motivated Him?" A correct reply would be that in order to achieve objective B, agent A had to be employed, because otherwise B would remain inaccessible. Obviously, one cannot reason in this manner about God, as though He had to overcome some inability or deficiency by using an intermediary agent. All is readily accessible and realized to Him. The best and only answer to any question about God's motivation is "He willed it" *gezerah hi milfanei* (Maimonides "Guide for the Perplexed: 3:13). (Man of Faith in the Modern World, Chapter 9: pages 92-93)

The Rav quotes the section of the "Guide" where Maimonides ("the Rambam") clarifies the different positions on viewing God's creation the world. He explains that God, being without deficiency, gains no benefit from the creation so to view God as doing something for an intended benefit to Him (as is the motivation when man or another living thing does something) is incorrect. There is no benefit to God, who is perfect within Himself. For this reason the "why" question for God's creation of the world or the mitzvot is untenable. The Rambam states:

Even if the universe exists for the sake of man, and the final end of man is, as has been said, to worship God, a question remains to be asked regarding the final end of his worship. For He, may He be exalted, would not acquire greater perfection if He were worshipped by all that He has created and were truly apprehended by them, nor would He be attained by a deficiency if nothing whatever existed except Him. If the answer is given that this is not with a view to His perfection, but to our perfection, for that is the most excellent thing for us- namely, our perfection - the same question follows necessarily: namely, what is the final end of our existence with that perfection? Necessarily and obligatorily the argument must end with the answer being given that the final end is: God has wished it so, or: His wisdom has required this to be so. And this is the correct answer. Accordingly, you will find that the Sages of Israel have inserted into the text of their prayers (Neilah service on Yom Kippur): '*Thou hast set man apart from the beginning and acknowledged* him *that he should stand before Thee. Yet who shall say unto Thee, What dost Thou? And if he be righteous, what boon is this to Thee?*' Thus they have explicitly stated that there does not exist a final end, but only the Will alone. (Guide, Book 3: Chapter 13)

The Rav continues in the same essay, explaining that the "how" question is also unanswerable for *hukim* as their manner of impacting people, although assured, is not understandable by the human mind:

Asking "how" for *hukim* is also nonsensical. How does the sprinkling of watery ashes of the *Parah Adumah* cleanse the ritually unclean (Num. 19)? How does the goat sent to Azazel bring forgiveness on Yom Kippur (Lev. 16)? ...We willingly and reverently accept the incomprehensible "how" even as we dutifully embraced the unfathomable "why"

In contrast to the illegitimacy of the "why" and "how" question, the "what" question is not only reasonable but necessary to properly perform any mitzvah. The Rav explains:
Remaining is the 3rd question, "what" which inquires about the meaningfulness of particular mitzvot to the individual and to society. This is a legitimate pursuit. Nay, it may even be meritorious to inquire, "How can I integrate and assimilate this mitzvah into my religious consciousness and outlook?" "What thoughts and emotions should I feel when the Parah Adumah chapter is read in the synagogue?" How can it help me achieve *devekut*, a greater closeness to God?" Such questions reflect the need to be intellectually and emotionally engaged in the performance of a mitzvah, even of *hukim*. One does not ask, "Why did God legislate *Parah Adumah?*" or "How does it purify the ritually defiled?" but "What is its spiritual message to me?" or "How can I,

as a thinking and feeling person, assimilate it into my world outlook?".

The Rav holds that each individual, although not able to fathom the absolute truth of a mitzvah's purpose, should still be cognizant and reflect on the inner experience that the mitzvah motivates in him or her. Although each person has a unique reaction to a mitzvah, reflection on this response is laudable and has halakhic legitimacy in performing the mitzvah in an optimal manner.

BALAK

The Loneliness of a Nation that Dwells Apart

Maimonides (the "Rambam") wrote in his philosophical work, "The Guide for the Perplexed" that Bilam's miraculous encounter with his donkey was a prophetic experience that occurred within his mind. As the Rambam states:

That which happened to Balaam on the way, and the speaking of the ass, took place in a prophetic vision, since further on, in the same account, an angel of God is introduced as speaking to Balaam." (Guide for the Perplexed- Book 2, Chapter 42). The Rambam, at the beginning of the same chapter, states a general principal about encounters with angels which we read about in the Tannach. He states: "We have already shown that the appearance or speech of an angel mentioned in Scripture took place in a vision or dream. In some cases the account begins by stating that the prophet saw an angel; in others the account apparently introduces a human being, who ultimately is shown to be an angel; but it makes no difference, for if the fact that an angel has been heard is only mentioned in the end, you may rest satisfied that the whole account from the beginning describes a prophetic vision." In the case of Bilam, after threatening to kill his donkey, he sees an angel: "Then Hashem opened the eyes of Bilam and he saw the angel of Hasem standing in the

way, with his sword drawn in his hand and he bowed his head and fell on his face". (Bamidbar 22, 31)-

Nachmanidies the ("Ramban"), in his commentary on the Torah strongly disagrees with this idea. (see Bereishet 18,1)

In the "Guide for the Perplexed" the Rambam describes the different levels of prophecy that human beings experience. Bilam is described as belonging to the second of 12 levels of prophecy, with only Moshe achieving the highest level. Regarding Bilam, the Rambam states:

The second degree is this: A person feels as if something came upon him, and as if he had received a new power that encourages him to speak. He treats of science, or composes hymns, exhorts his fellow-men, discusses political and theological problems; all this he does while awake, and in the full possession of his senses. Such a person is said to speak by the holy spirit.....You must know that Bilam likewise belonged to this class, when he was good; this is indicated by the words, "And God put a word in the mouth of Bilam," (Bamidbar, 23, 5), i.e., Bilam spoke by divine inspiration; he therefore says of himself, "Who hears the words of God (Bamidbar. 24,4).

From the Rambam's explanation it is clear that Bilam was not some puppet or mouthpiece, but instead was imbued with the prophetic insight and wisdom. One is compelled to ask how such a man could desire so much to destroy the

Jewish people that he would go through all of the machinations we see in the parsha to continue his futile attempt to curse Bnei Yisrael. Also, we know that Bilam was the "mastermind" behind the incident where the princes of Israel was brought to depravity by the Midianite women in another attempt to destroy the people. But is it so unusual to turn away from knowledge and embrace baser agendas that come from our need for personal greatness and pleasure? Within our own people many of the greatest minds and creative geniuses have been Israel's greatest detractors. As science uncovers more and more wonders of God's infinite design of the creation, many of the leading scientists, Jewish and otherwise, embrace a strident atheism. Among the Jewish people's leading "intellectuals" we find many of Torah's and Israel's greatest detractors. Greatness of mind is often accompanied with a great sense of personal importance. This need for personal importance is often in conflict with the acceptance and service to God, in whose presence we must realize our relative nothingness. Perhaps this was the struggle that Bilam experienced. A struggle with which he failed.

Rabbi Joseph B. Soloveitchik ("The Rav") noted in a 1954 article in the *Tog Morgen Journal* (in Yiddish) that Bilam expressed in his blessings a fundamental truth about the loneliness and separateness of the Jewish people among the nations. The Rav stated:

The enigma of our existence is primarily revealed through our loneliness and our affliction in all times, the current era included. "Lo, it is a people that shall live alone, and among the nations shall not reckon itself" (Bamidbar, 23:9). The State of Israel did not ignore this unique fate, but quite the contrary, it has given expression to it in a more concrete fashion. No Jew can renounce his part of the unity, which is based upon a fate of loneliness of the Jewish people as a nation. All Jews, Mapai, Mizrahi or Agudah, all are included in one nation, which stands lonesome and in misery in a large and often antagonistic world. The political-historical unity as a nation is based upon the conclusion of the covenant in Egypt, which occurred even prior to the giving of the Torah at Sinai": 'And I shall take you unto me as a nation, and I shall be unto you a G...(Shemos 6:7). And this covenant forced upon us all one uniform fate. The Hebrew word *am,* "nation", is identical to the Hebrew word, *im*, "with". Our fate of unity mainfests itself through a historical indispensable union.

Even today, 60 years later, although the State of Israel has grown in population, prosperity and military might, the loneliness that the Rav attributes to the it is still true – perhaps even more true in some sense, than when he wrote this essay. In what seems to Israelis and observant Jews as an inconceivable assessment, much of the Western world sees Israel as the problem and the cause of the problems of the Middle East conflicts. The Islamic nations and the terrorist groups could not be clearer in their position as aggressor. One thing you can say about Iran and Hamas is that they don't lie about their intent for Israel. But still, even as broader world feels threatened by Islamic terrorism at an unprecedented level, they see Israel as the problem.

Loneliness for an individual or for a nation has its root in being misunderstood. The State of Israel feels itself to be the most misunderstood nation on the planet. We will never be embraced as one of the family of nations until that time of redemption when the Torah too is embraced as the gift of all mankind and the Jewish people as the people chosen not to conquer the world but instead to teach it about the truth of God and that justice, mercy and wisdom are the path to a fully human life in communion with God and ones fellow.

PINCHAS

Different Perspectives on Animal Sacrifices

The parsha of Pinchas describes the animal sacrifices that are to be brought to the mishkan on each weekday, Shabbat and holiday along with the oil, wine and grain offering that accompany them (Bamidbar,28;1-30). These sacrifices and offerings are an eternal part of the Torah and Jewish law and have only ceased in our time due to the destruction of the Temple. Upon the rebuilding of the Temple in Jerusalem, the animal sacrifices will return and be fulfilled in every detail as they were in the past. The Rambam, in his great work the "Guide for the Perplexed" expressed a highly controversial perspective on the purpose and structure of the animal sacrifices and why they are part of Torah law and observance. He states:

But the custom which was in those days general among all men, and the general mode of worship in which the Israelites were brought up, consisted in sacrificing animals in those temples which contained certain images, to bow down to those images, and to burn incense before them; religious and ascetic persons were, in those days, the people were devoted to service in the temples erected to the stars, as has been explained by us. It was in accordance with the wisdom and plan of God, as displayed in the whole Creation, that He did not command us to give up and to discontinue all these manners of service; for to obey

such a commandment it would have been contrary to the nature of man, who generally cleaves to that to which he is used...For this reason God allowed these kinds of service of continue; He transferred to His service that which had formerly served as a worship of created beings, and of thing imaginary and unreal, and commanded us to serve Him in the same manner; e.g. To build unto Him a temple, to have the altar erected to His name, to bow down to Him and to burn incense before Him...(Guide for the Perplexed, Book 3, Chapter 32).

The Rambam understands the provocative nature of his position on this matter as he states in the same chapter: "I know that you will, at first thought, reject this idea and find it strange; How can we suppose that Divine commandments, prohibitions, and important acts, which are fully explained, and for which certain seasons are fixed, should not have been commanded for their own sake, but only for the sake of some other thing;" The Rambam then explains that God led the Jews, upon leaving Egypt, through an indirect route so they would not encounter the Plishtim. He could have instead, miraculously strengthened their nature so that they would be able to endure the Plishtim without fear. So too, God could have miraculously changed the nature of the Jews, so that they would not need to have sacrifices, even though they had them before the Torah. However, this type of miraculous change to man's nature is not part of God's plan. As the Rambam states:

What prevented Him from giving us, as part of our nature, the will to do that which He desires to do and abandon the kind of worship which He rejects?... Although in every one of the signs (related in the Torah) the natural property of some individual being is changed, the nature of man is never changed by God by way of miracle." The Rambam explains that free will is paramount and fundamental to the human being and is not changed by miracles. For this reason the Jews were led by an indirect route around the Plishtim and, for the same reason, the Jewish people were given commandments to continue the sacrificial rituals they were accustomed to, with those sacrifices now directed to God.

Rabbi Soloveitchik ("the Rav"), strongly disagreed with the Rambam regarding this explanation of the sacrifices. He states in his essay "Halakhic Mind":

In the *Guide*, Maimonides sees in sacrifice just an educational method of elevating the Jew above such forms of worship. Previously, sacrifice had been the common practice of the heathens among whom the Jews had lived. In order to direct the Jew toward worship of God, the Torah made the concession of animal sacrifice. Nachmanides severely criticizes Maimonides for his rationalization, and introduced his own interpretation. Sacrifice for him, refers actually to man himself. Worship is nothing but mental sacrifice.

And animal sacrifice symbolizes the internal act of self-negation. Whatever the merit of Nachmanides' interpretation, one thing is clear. Philosophically it is far superior to Maimonides' explanation. While Maimonides' causalistic aspect in the *Guide* is pure instrumentalism, Nachmanides' interpretation penetrates the complex concept of sacrifice itself. He has elaborated an idea which may have some modern philosophical merit. ("Halakhic Mind", page 131 – Notes to Part Four, footnote #108).

Rav Soloveitchik was fundamentally opposed to the approach of viewing mitzvot as deriving their meaning and purpose from an objective outside the system of mitzvot itself. Kashrut is not to be understood in a health context as improving our nutrition and the laws related to sexual prohibitions from the point of view of preserving the family unit. Mitzvot may have these benefits, but they do not explain the purpose of the mitzvah or its primary function. The mitzvot for Rabbi Soloveitchik were a means of serving God and turning all aspects of one's life to that purpose. No mundane benefit could be put forth correctly as the "reason" for the mitzvah. Nachmanidies explanation is more aligned with this view seeing sacrifices as a way to help one subjugate his or her personal will to the will of God.

From what the Rav states above it seems that he holds that Maimonides is attributing the mitzvot of the sacrifices to a purpose of creating a bridge between the idolatrous sacrificial system and the true service of God. Would it not be for the need of human beings to change their pattern of behavior in a gradual manner, there would, it seems, be no animal sacrifices in the Torah system! The Torah had to be given at this juncture in history-perhaps because it was the time when Moshe was alive, or perhaps because the Jews could no longer remain in Egypt. Since at this time of history everyone worshipped through the method of sacrifice, the Torah had to include it and wean the idolatrous element away from the Jewish people's sacrificial actions. But, according the Rambam, if sacrifices had been removed all together, then the Torah system would not have been successful in bringing the people to an appropriate understanding of God. So why, now that humanity does not have any pattern of animal sacrifice, will the mitzvot of animal sacrifice be reinstated at the rebuilding of the Temple? Perhaps the answer is that only Moshe had the level of prophecy by which law could be established. All other prophets, even the messiah are not at this level. There is only one Moshe Rebbenu and therefore only one Torah, eternal and unchanging, regardless of the fact, at least according to the Rambam, that the mitzvot of animal sacrifice were included due to a contemporary issue specific to the time of the giving of the Torah.

MATOS

Acher and the Release from Vows

The parsha of Matos states:

2. Moses spoke to the heads of the tribes of the children of Israel, saying: This is the thing the Lord has commanded.	**ב.** וַיְדַבֵּר מֹשֶׁה אֶל רָאשֵׁי הַמַּטּוֹת לִבְנֵי יִשְׂרָאֵל לֵאמֹר זֶה הַדָּבָר אֲשֶׁר צִוָּה יְהֹוָה:
3. If a man makes a vow to the Lord or makes an oath to prohibit himself, he shall not violate his word; according to whatever came out of his mouth, he shall do.	**ג.** אִישׁ כִּי יִדֹּר נֶדֶר לַיהֹוָה אוֹ הִשָּׁבַע שְׁבֻעָה לֶאְסֹר אִסָּר עַל נַפְשׁוֹ לֹא יַחֵל דְּבָרוֹ כְּכָל הַיֹּצֵא מִפִּיו יַעֲשֶׂה:

Maimonides ("the Rambam") writes in the Mishneh Torah, regarding the taking of an oath:

The following rules apply when a person took an oath *("sh'vuat bitui")* and then regretted having taken the oath. If he sees that he will suffer if he upholds this oath and his intent changes or a factor occurred that was not in his intent originally when he took the oath and he changed his mind because of this, he may appeal (to be released from his oath) from one sage or from 3 ordinary people in a place where there are no sages. His oath is repealed and he is permitted to perform the matter that he took the oath not to do or

not to do the matter that he took an oath to do. This is called the release from the oath." (Mishneh Torah, Shvuot: Chapter 6).

From Maimonides' statement we see that one is allowed to "change one's mind" about an oath for a number of reasons including if unanticipated personal suffering due to the oath changes the oath taker's intention to fulfill the oath, or a new factor occurred that was not part of the oath taker's original intent when taking the oath. For example, if a person took an oath to study 9 hours a day and he finds that because of it he is unable to feed his family, he can rightfully claim that this unintended and unanticipated hardship would have altered his decision to take the oath in the first place. This becomes a means by which he can be released from the oath.

Rabbi Soloveitchik ("the Rav") questions the logic of how the Torah allows for the release of an individual from a vow. In the text "Dreshot HaRav-Selected Lectures of Rabbi Joseph B. Soloveitchik" (summarized and annotated by Arnold Lustiger) it states:

How can one effect a release from vows at all, when the Torah specifically warns "he shall not desecrate (*yahel)* his word; according to whatever comes out of his mouth he shall do." (Numbers 30:3) ? The answer is that when a person shows remorse, there is a halakhic mechanism whereby the vow can be nullified by means of a legal device known as *petah.* Through

***petah*, the person who vows declares that had he known then what he knows now he would never have made the vow. (p. 95)**

The Rav clarifies here that the regret that is required in the nullification of a vow has a particular quality of shame which creates a change in the person who initially made the vow. The person now realizes that the person who took the vow did not represent his or her true self. The error the person made when making the vow is more than simply a mistake or a miscalculation as to the difficulty of carrying out the vow. The vow was not taken, so to speak, by the "real person", so to speak, which is the core persona of the individual. Through this halakchic mechanism which holds that the whole or true person did not make the vow in the first place, the court is able to release the "real person" from the vow as he or she never took it in the first place. The fragment of the verse "*HaAdam b'shavuah*" (Vayikra, 5:4), implies that before one makes a *shvuah* obligation, the complete person (the Adam or the real Adam) in his or her entirety must take on the obligation. Man sometimes assumes commitments that under normal circumstances he would never accept, obligations that will affect the rest of his life. The "real" individual did not make these agreements; "someone else" made them." This allows for the mechanism of *petah* to function. The shame felt by the person is the indication that the true person didn't take the vow in the first place.

In the text, "The Rav Speaks-Five Addresses" which transcribes the 5 presentations given by the Rav to conventions of the Mizrachi Religious Zionist Movement during the period of 1962-1967 he relates this idea of the "real person" versus the "imposter" to the process of teshuvah and the tragic history of Elisha ben Abuya (Aher). The logic of teshuvah must also be justified as it too seems to be illogical. A person does a sin and now through regret and shame is to be pardoned for it! Where is the logic! One should be punished and then, perhaps, be pardoned through teshuvah. But for teshuvah to annul a punishment and provide pardon requires an explanation as does the halakchic mechanism of *petah* did for annulling a vow. The Rav states here:

The Sages relate that R. Meir asked of Aher (Elisha b. Abuya) when he was riding his horse on the Sabbath, "You also, repent"; and according to the Talmud Bavli, Aher answered: "I have heard from behind the curtain, "Return O backsliding children, except for Aher."" According to the Talmud Yerushalmi he said: "I was once riding the horse on Yom Kippur which happened to fall on the Sabbath, behind the Holy of Holies, and I heard a heavenly voice say: 'return O backsliding children, except for Elisha b. Abuya...' The Rav continues: "Do you really think that Aher actually heard what he heard and understood the heavenly voice correctly? Can then a heavenly voice decide against one of the fundamentals of Jewish faith,

against the halachah which declares that "even if he denied the Divine Presence throughout his life but repented at the end he is accepted, as it is written: Thou brings man to contrition (Ps. 90,3)-to the crushing of his soul.' The Rav continues, "It seems to me that the real intent of the heavenly voice can be found in the different readings of the Talmud Bavli and Talmud Yerushalmi. How did the heavenly voice call to him? By Elisha b. Abuya, his proper name, or by Aher, his pseudonym? The answer is plain. The heavenly voice called him, pleaded with him, drew him to itself; the Divine Presence pampered him like a mother who in all circumstances has only good to say of her child. The sharp "except" for was to Aher, but not to Elisha B. Abuya. The Talmud Bavli gives the exact words of the heavenly voice. The Divine Presence drew Elisha b. Abuya to it, but pushed away Aher. Because the true Tanna, the Sage of the Sages of Israel whose Torah Rabbi quotes in Pirkey Avot, never sinned... Someone else was the traitor; another personality-Aher." (The Rav Speaks –Five Addresses p. 194-195)

So, similar to the manner in which *petah* operates by the principle that the person who took the vow was not the real person and therefore can be released, so too a person who is able to do teshuvah properly shows through his or her shame and regret that the person who committed the sin was some "aher", some other person - not the true self of the person. This allows for teshuvah to effectuate pardon and to eliminate punishment for a committed sin.

MASEI

Torah Law and the Death Penalty for Murder

It states in the parsha (Bamidbar 35:30-31):

30. Whoever [namely the blood avenger] kills a person, based on the testimony of witnesses, he shall slay the murderer. A single witness may not testify against a person so that he should die.	ל. כָּל מַכֵּה נֶפֶשׁ לְפִי עֵדִים יִרְצַח אֶת הָרֹצֵחַ וְעֵד אֶחָד לֹא יַעֲנֶה בְ לָמוּת:

Whoever kills a person...: The one who comes to kill him because he murdered someone.	**כל מכה נפש וגו':** הבא להרגו על שהכה את הנפש:
Rashi: based on the testimony of witnesses: who testify that he murdered him intentionally, after he had been forewarned. [I.e., the blood avenger may not slay the murderer unless there are witnesses that he committed the murder.]- [Sifrei Massei 26]	**לפי עדים ירצח:** שיעידו שבמזיד ובהתראה הרגו:

The Rambam writes in the Mishneh Torah:

Halacha 1: Whenever a person kills a human being, he transgresses a negative commandment, as Exodus 20:13 states: "Do not murder." If a person kills a Jew

intentionally in the presence of witnesses, he should be executed by decapitation. This is implied by Exodus 21:20, which states that when a person kills a servant, "vengeance will certainly be executed." The Oral Tradition explains that this refers to decapitation. Whether he kills the victim with an iron weapon or burns him with fire, the murderer should be executed by decapitation.
Halacha 2: It is a mitzvah for the blood redeemer to kill the murderer, as Numbers 35:19 states: "The blood redeemer shall put the murderer to death." Whoever is fit to inherit the victim's estate becomes the redeemer of his blood. If the blood redeemer did not desire - or was unable - to kill the murderer, or if the victim did not have a relative to redeem his blood, the court executes the murderer by decapitation. (Mishneh Torah: Rotzeach ooShemiras Hanefesh: 1:1-2)

The Rambam makes clear that murderer, when properly convicted by the court, is put to death by the "blood redeemer"- the closest male relative, and that it is a mitzvah for the relative to do so. Only if the relative does not or cannot carry out the execution, is it performed by the court. This structure of the relative being the one to carry out the execution requires some analysis. Wouldn't the court be the best candidate to carry out the execution, being expert and objective, as opposed to the grieving relative? What advantage is afforded by the relative being the executioner? One can only speculate regarding this detail of the law. The

Rambam stated above that "whoever is fit to inherit the victim's estate becomes the redeemer of his blood." Is being the inheritor of the victim's estate what obligates the relative in carrying out the execution? When one commits murder, who is the "injured party"? Does the person who is no longer alive, have a claim anymore? Is the closest relative the most injured party? Who is "owed" compensation? The term 'blood redeemer" (goale ha-dam) seems to imply that the life or the "blood of the person murdered "("the life is in the blood") remains as an entity requiring justice to be done to it. Perhaps the Torah stipulates that the dead person remains a wronged party, even though they no longer exist in this world.

The redemption of the blood of the victim (the murder) is done by the relative, as he serves as the *sheliach*, standing-in and taking the place of the murder victim. Just as he stands in and takes possession of the murdered person's property, he stands in for the victim in punishing the one who committed the murder.

In the Rambam's philosophical work, "The Guide for the Perplexed", he states regarding the punishment of the murderer:

The punishment of him who sins against his neighbor consists in the general rule that there shall be done unto him exactly as he has done: if he injured any one personally, he must suffer personally; if he damaged

the property of his neighbor, he shall be punished by the loss of property. But the person whose property has been damaged should be ready to resign his claim totally or partially. Only to the murderer we must not be lenient because of the greatness of his crime; and no ransom must be accepted of him 'And the land cannot be cleansed of blood that is shed therein but by blood of him that shed it.' (Bamidbar 31:33). Hence even if the murdered person continued to live after the attack for an hour or for days, was able to speak and possessed complete consciousness, and if he himself said, 'Pardon my murderer, I have pardoned and forgiven him," he must not be obeyed. We must take life for life, and estimate equally the life of a child and that of a grown person, of a slave and of a freeman, of a wise man and of a fool. For there is no greater sin than this. (Guide, Book 3, Chapter 41)

Why does the Torah not accept monetary compensation for intentional murder and instead require the execution of the convicted murderer? Again, we can only speculate. However Torah has as its foundation the preciousness of human life. The Sabbath is violated for even the smallest chance of mortal danger by an individual. And, with the exception of idolatry, murder and prohibited sexual intercourse, one, according to the Rambam is commanded to transgress the laws of the Torah to save one's life. This is how one sanctifies the name of God. Maimonides states in the Mishneh Torah, Yesodai HaTorah, Chapter 5:

Halacha 1: The entire house of Israel are commanded regarding the sanctification of [God's] great name, as [Leviticus 22:32] states: "And I shall be sanctified amidst the children of Israel." Also, they are warned against desecrating [His holy name], as [the above verse] states: "And they shall not desecrate My holy name. "What is implied? Should a gentile arise and force a Jew to violate one of the Torah's commandments at the pain of death, he should violate the commandment rather than be killed, because [Leviticus 18:5] states concerning the mitzvot: "which a man will perform and live by them." [They were given so that] one may live by them and not die because of them. If a person dies rather than transgress, he is held accountable for his life.

The preciousness of human life is of paramount value to the Creator and we must "walk in his path" and likewise view it as such. To take monetary compensation as punishment for intentional murder may seem merciful for the murderer and, perhaps is viewed as confirming the preciousness of life in that another life is not taken. However, the taking of money for murder also lowers the value of life in that a price is put on the person's existence and one can somehow equate money with life. This equates something of infinite value (a human life) with something of clearly finite value (a specific amount of money) contrary to the basic system of Torah values. As the Rambam stated in the quote from the "Guide for the Perplexed" quoted above:

We must take life for life, and estimate equally the life of a child and that of a grown person, of a slave and of a freeman, of a wise man and of a fool. For there is no greater sin than this.

Rabbi Soloveitchik ('the Rav") explains in the text "The Emergence of Ethical Man" that murder not only impacts the person killed and those in his or her family and society, but that the murder actually impacts the status of the Earth itself. Murder creates a form of spiritual pollution to the Earth itself, which can result in exile and destruction of the land unless the murdered person's blood is neutralized, so to speak, by the blood of the murderer.

So you shall not pollute the land in which you are, for blood pollutes the land, and the land cannot be cleansed of the blood that is shed therein, but by the blood of him that shed it. And you shall not defile the land which you shall inhabit, in which I dwell: for I the Lord dwell among the children of Israel (Bamidbar 35:33).

The Rav comments on these verses explaining that the reason that a murdered person's blood defiles the land because man is an extension of the Earth, having developed from the Earth into a fully conscious, aware and culpable form. Man is Earth in a sense, or at least the part of the Earth that sins, is punished and atones. The Rav states:

Sin defiles not only human beings, but the earth as well. The earth becomes desecrated, polluted by crime, and needs absolution or atonement. In the case of murder, the atonement can be made to the land only by the blood of the murderer...It is indeed unique to speak of *tumah* (ritual restriction) as attached to Mother Earth. A metaphysical quality is ascribed to her. Sin and atonement apply to both man and earth. Why? Because man is a part of her, man is nature expressed in a meaningful existence. He can never, however, free himself from that union. Earth, nature an man flow into each other. There is a complete identity of man and earth. Let us not forget that by the word "earth", we understand not just the land but nature as a whole, the entire complex of physical conditions that make man's existence possible. As an organism, he depends upon his surroundings, and this dependence spells ontic unity and uniformity. Obedience to God means "Then I will give your rain in due season, and the land shall yield her increase and the trees of the field shall yield their fruit"; disobedience-"and I will make your skies like iron, and your earth like brass, and your strength shall be spent in vain, for your land shall not yield her increase, neither shall the trees of the land yield their fruit (Lev. 26:4, 19-20). When a community refuses to live in

accordance with the divine law, Mother Nature becomes non-cooperative, refusing to subordinate herself to man's rule. With sin, the gap widens. Nature begins to resent the presence of man; in response, man attempts to subjugate an insurgent and malicious nature. The struggle, once begun, ends in man's defeat. Mother earth spits out her unruly son. Man is cast out of his environment. (pgs. 55-56).

The Rav seems to me to be saying that the Earth is not simply a means by which sinning man is punished with hardship and eventually exile. A more accurate analogy which be perhaps that that man and the Earth are harmonious parts of a single whole that converge and attract one another like the positive and negative poles of a magnet –let's say the Earth is positive and man is negative(which attract). When man sins he obtains something of a repellant quality, almost as if his "pole" changes to positive, which is naturally repelled by the positive charge of the Earth. The more he sins the more his "charge" is altered until he is absolutely repelled by the Earth, resulting in exile. The blood of the murderer (the death penalty) atones for the murder and the society remains properly "charged" and can remain in the land.

DEVARIM

THESE ARE THE WORDS WHICH MOSES SPOKE TO ALL ISRAEL ON THAT SIDE OF THE JORDAN IN THE DESERT, IN THE PLAIN OPPOSITE THE RED SEA, BETWEEN PARAN AND TOFEL AND LAVAN AND HAZEROTH AND DI ZAHAV. (DEVARIM 1:1)

DEVARIM

A Heart Hardened Against Teshuvah

In the parsha of Devarim Moshe recounts many of the pivotal events of the Jewish people's forty year odyssey through the desert. Moshe states: "

30. But Sihon, king of Heshbon, did not wish to let us pass by him, for the Lord your God caused his spirit to be hardened and his heart to be obstinate, in order that He would give him into your hand, as this day.	ל. וְלֹא אָבָה סִיחֹן מֶלֶךְ חֶשְׁבּוֹן הַעֲבִרֵנוּ בּוֹ כִּי הִקְשָׁה יְהוָה אֱלֹהֶיךָ אֶת רוּחוֹ וְאִמֵּץ אֶת לְבָבוֹ לְמַעַן תִּתּוֹ בְיָדְךָ כַּיּוֹם הַזֶּה:

The Rambam in the Mishnah Torah explains unique type of punishment in which God blocks the path of repentance for an individual, and brings as examples Pharaoh and Sichon:

It is possible that a person may commit a grave transgression, or several transgressions, such that the True Judge rules that the punishment for this sinner, for the transgressions that he has performed willingly and knowingly, is that teshuva will be withheld from him and he will not be allowed the right to turn from his evil, so that he may die and be lost in the sin that he performs... Therefore it is written in the Torah, "I shall harden Pharaoh's heart": because he first sinned

on his own initiative, and did evil to the Israelites living in his land, as it is written, "Let us deal wisely with them..." - therefore it was ruled that teshuva would be withheld from him so that he may be punished; therefore God hardened his heart. But why does He then send a message to him via Moshe, saying, "Let [My people go] and repent [your evil ways]," if He has already told him, "You will not send them out" - as it is written, "You and your servants I know..." but for this I have placed you?" In order to teach everyone that when God withholds teshuva from a sinner, he is not able to repent; he dies in his wickedness which he performed at first of his own free will. Likewise Sichon: because of his sins he was punished by having teshuva withheld from him, as it is written, "For the Lord your God hardened his spirit and toughened his heart." And likewise the Canaanites: because of their abominations, teshuva was withheld from them and they waged war against Israel, as it is written, "For it was from God that their heart was hardened for battle against Am Yisrael, in order that they may be annihilated...." God did not decree upon Pharaoh to cause evil to Israel, nor did He cause Sichon to sin in his land, nor the Canaanites to perform abominations, nor the Israelites to engage in idolatry. All of these sinned of their own accord, and all were punished by having teshuva withheld from them." (Mishneh Torah, Laws of Teshuva, 6:3)

There are different interpretations of what is meant by the "hardening of the heart" and whether it means that *teshuva* is completely prevented by God or only impeded and made more difficult. The Rambam also brings in Chapter 4 of the Laws of Repentance the "5 things ("*deveraim*") that cause the path of repentance to be locked ("*HaNoahleem*") before those that commit them". These 5 are:

1-One who separates themselves from the community;
2-One who contradicts the words of the sages.
3-One who scoffs at mitzvot.
4-One who demeans his teachers.
5- One who hates admonishment.

God's impeding or preventing of repentance for an individual is a difficult concept to understand, as the repentance from sin is a fundamental tenant of Judaism. Even the terrible sinner on his or her death bed can repent, receive pardon and merit a portion in the world to come. So why are the 5 acts listed above, as well as Pharaoh's and Sichon's sins, so unique? These 5 sins all share a common flaw of self-exaltation. The person is so overwhelmed with their sense of self-importance that they have no patience or tolerance for working with the community. They cannot endure the humbling aspect of community participation. The "reality check" we experience when other disagree with us or inform us that perhaps we are not as clever or wonderful as we would like to believe. This profound hubris is also behind the contradicting of a Torah sage, the scoffing at a mitzvah and the demeaning of one's teacher.

All of these bespeak a high-heartedness ("*govah lave*") on the part of the person. But the clearest example of this inability to endure humility is being a person who hates admonishment. These individuals like Sichon and Pharaoh were so full of themselves that it would have required specific intervention by God to provide them with an opportunity to see things differently and, perhaps, do teshuvah. Their punishment was that this was not afforded them and their own closed-off haughtiness "locked them" from teshuvah. By not intervening and providing the precise situation that would have leveraged their path to teshuvah, God impeded their teshuvah, but did not absolutely prevent it.

The Rav (Rabbi Yoseph B. Soloveitchik) explains the concepts of man's sinning and repenting as being the difference between man functioning as an object or functioning as an subject. The Rav explains:

Sin transforms a person into someone who is acted upon or influenced. In response to the very first sin, when HaShem confronted Adam after eating from the tree of knowledge, Adam's response was, "The woman who You gave to be with me, she gave it to me…"(Beresheit,3:12). When HaShem confronted Eve in turn, the response was similar, "The snake tricked me and I ate" (Beresheit 3:13). Both emphasized their helplessness in overcoming an external influence that "forced" their fall….Regarding sin, an analogy is made

to sleep. Sleep is an absolute passive state, in which man is pure object. The insistent demand of the shofar, according to the Rambam, is the imperative to awaken oneself....Through sin one is an object, while teshuvah allows one to again become a subject. ("Before HaShem You Shall Be Purified" Annotated by A. Lustiger, page 32-33).

V'ETCHANAN

Conquered by God and Redeemed

At the opening of this week's parsha Moshe implores God to allow him to enter the holy land and rescind the punishment for striking the rock. Moshe states:

23. I entreated the Lord at that time, saying,	**כג.** וָאֶתְחַנַּן אֶל יְהֹוָה בָּעֵת הַהִוא לֵאמֹר:
24. "O Lord God, You have begun to show Your servant Your greatness and Your strong hand, for who is [like] God in heaven or on earth who can do as Your deeds and Your might?	**כד.** אֲדֹנָי יֱהֹוִה אַתָּה הַחִלּוֹתָ לְהַרְאוֹת אֶת עַבְדְּךָ אֶת גָּדְלְךָ וְאֶת יָדְךָ הַחֲזָקָה אֲשֶׁר מִי אֵל בַּשָּׁמַיִם וּבָאָרֶץ אֲשֶׁר יַעֲשֶׂה כְמַעֲשֶׂיךָ וְכִגְבוּרֹתֶךָ:
25. Pray let me cross over and see the good land that is on the other side of the Jordan, this good mountain and the Lebanon."	**כה.** אֶעְבְּרָה נָּא וְאֶרְאֶה אֶת הָאָרֶץ הַטּוֹבָה אֲשֶׁר בְּעֵבֶר הַיַּרְדֵּן הָהָר הַטּוֹב הַזֶּה וְהַלְּבָנֹן:

But, Moshe request was not granted, as he relates to the Jewish people, "But HaShem became angry with me because of you, and He did not listen to me; HaShem said to me,

27. Go up to the top of the hill and lift up your eyes westward and	כז. עֲלֵה | רֹאשׁ הַפִּסְגָּה וְשָׂא עֵינֶיךָ יָמָּה וְצָפֹנָה

northward and southward and eastward and see with your eyes, for you shall not cross this Jordan.	וְתֵימָנָה וּמִזְרָחָה וּרְאֵה בְעֵינֶיךָ כִּי לֹא תַעֲבֹר אֶת הַיַּרְדֵּן הַזֶּה:

Rav Soloveitchik, in the essay "And From There You Shall Seek" ("V'kashtem Meesham") draws on this final defeat of Moshe's plea as a vehicle to clarify the role of suffering in the redemption of the person. The Rav states:

Judaism has firmly established the halakhic principle that even when man confronts an unchangeable evil degree coming from God, when his rejected prayers are thrown back in his face, he must see God and conjoin with Him in spite of the tragic reality that weighs him down. God reveals Himself through suffering and tragedy, when the individual or the community is in trouble and distress. Moshe pleads with God, but his prayer is not accepted (Devarim:3:23-28). His destined fate turns to a fate without destiny. He sees the chosen land, but he cannot go there. The divine attribute of justice indicts him and seals the gates of heaven before him. Precisely out of the pain and torment, out of the affliction and suffering, the kiss of God suddenly appears, detaching Moshe from this world and bringing him to a world full of goodness and light. Saul at Gilgal, powerless, deprived of his royal future and messianic vision, surrenders to the prophet of rage and bows down before his God. (pages 33-34)

The Rav, explains that the complete surrender to God 's will is only accomplished through the suffering of being broken by God and though it is terrible it reveals within a person a new and deeper dimension of his or her true relationship with the Creator. The Rav continues:

The Inscrutable Will conquers and subdues him. The Revealed Will does not brook any opposition. Man appears as absolutely subordinate, as receiving the commandments and bending under the weight of his burden...."He placed the mountain over them like a barrel and said, "If you accept the Torah, well and good; if not, this will be your grave."(Shabbat 88a). There is no refuge from God; He demands of man absolute submission." (From There You Shall Seek, page 35).

It seems to me the Rav is saying that the essence of man's relationship with God is not one of inquirer, child or student but a completely subjugated will. Only suffering reveals this relationship. But being the true, personal relationship with G… there is a profound sweetness and joy in it. It is a joy to be God's willing servant and to, so to speak know and feel your place in that relationship. This requires of man to accept it. Maimonides, in the "Guide for the Perplexed" clarifies that the story of Iyov (Job) is, at its core is an explanation of how to conceive of the suffering that occurs in life and how to avoid the pitfall of viewing it from the point of view of one who has been mistreated or mishandled by the one in charge. Maimonides' deep and subtle insights here bear close analysis. He explains the revelation to Iyov of the wonders of nature and man's inability to fathom them as a vehicle by which a person can begin to understand his inability to fathom how God rules his world. Maimonides states:

The description of all these things serves to impress on our minds that we are unable to comprehend how these transient creatures come into existence, or to imagine how their natural properties commenced to exist, and that these are not like the things which we are to produce. Much less can we compare the manner in which G… rules and manages His creatures with the manner in which we rule and manage certain beings. We must content ourselves with this and believe that nothing is hidden from God, as Elihu says: :For his eyes are upon the ways of man and he seeth all his goings. There is no darkness nor shadow of death where the workers of iniquity may hide themselves.' But the term "management" when applied to God has not the same meaning which it has when applied to us; and when we say that He rules His creatures we do not mean that He does the same as we do when we rule over other beings….When we know this we shall find everything that may befall us easy to bear; mishap will create no doubts in our hearts concerning God, whether He knows our affairs or not, whether He provides for us or abandons us. On the contrary, our

fate will increase or love of God; as it is said in the end of this prophecy: 'Therefore I abhor myself and repent concerning the dust and ashes' and as our Sages say, 'The pious do everything out of love and rejoice in their own afflictions' (Shabbat 88b)." (Guide for the Perplexed; Book 3, Chap. 23)

The Rambam, with breathtakingly brilliant insight, is identifying and "treating" what he views the major impediment to a person's ability to fathom why "bad things happen to good people". He explains that the intellectual mistake that often occurs is that one views God's management of his world by a human standard and, in doing, view God as abandoning man in his times of suffering. But once one achieves the humility and clarity to realize that God's will does not operate by the same patterns as a human will, a person will not mistakenly conclude God as being indifferent when human being endure or observe suffering. When it states that the righteous rejoiced in their suffering perhaps it means that they understood this suffering to be part of a larger order of things and part of the human being's fortunate state of being ruled over by God, and through this, were more connected to Him through the suffering. Agreed, this would be a very high level of refinement for the human being. Most of us do achieve such a level.

EIKEV

Imitating the Ways of God

In the Parsha Eikev Moshe says to Bnei Yisrael:

12. And now, O Israel, what does the Lord, your God, demand of you? Only to fear the Lord, your God, to walk in all His ways and to love Him, and to worship the Lord, your God, with all your heart and with all your soul,

יב. וְעַתָּה יִשְׂרָאֵל מָה יְהֹוָה אֱלֹהֶיךָ שֹׁאֵל מֵעִמָּךְ כִּי אִם לְיִרְאָה אֶת יְהֹוָה אֱלֹהֶיךָ לָלֶכֶת בְּכָל דְּרָכָיו וּלְאַהֲבָה אֹתוֹ וְלַעֲבֹד אֶת יְהֹוָה אֱלֹהֶיךָ בְּכָל לְבָבְךָ וּבְכָל נַפְשֶׁךָ:

Many have reflected, discussed and written about the meaning of "to go in all His ways" stated in this pasuk. How can one go in the ways of God? God is absolutely unique, without a body or any structure. It seems, therefore, that we cannot understand Him so as to imitate his ways. He is also "One" and would not have "ways", which is a plurality. If God has a "way" it is only <u>one</u> way. The Rambam brings clarity to this most important pillar of Judaism, the imitation of God the Rambam states in the Mishneh Torah:

We are bidden to walk in the middle paths which are the right and proper ways, as it is said, "You shall walk in His Ways". In explanation of the text just quoted, the Sages taught, "Even as God is called gracious, so be you gracious; even as He is called merciful, so be

you merciful; even as He is called holy, so be you holy (see Sotah 14a). Thus too the prophets described the Almighty by all the various attributes "long-suffering and abounding in kindness, righteous and upright, perfect, mighty and powerful," and so forth, to teach us that these qualities are good and right, and that a human being should cultivate them, and thus imitate God as far as he can (MT, Laws of Character Traits 15:6)

It seems to me that the Rambam is explaining that these characterizations of God's ways in the Torah as having specific manners of acting and reacting are certainly not the actual "ways of God". The Creator does not suffer to be "long-suffering" and does not, according to the Rambam, possess emotions such as kindness, as these emotions are a result of a body which God does not possess. God also does not change to have varied states of mind at different times, as expressed in the literal words of the Torah. The Rambam is explaining that the Torah is written to express God's acts in the perspective of human acts and the human emotions that would accompany them. When we provide help for someone who does not truly merit that help, we are being merciful. So when God acts in a way that, externally, takes this form, the Torah states that God is merciful. It seems then that man's imitation of God can be described as man imitating God imitating a righteous human being. The Torah is characterizing God is human terms to help human beings understand how to behave properly. God's acts take the form of the acts of a righteous person and therefore act as a guide for man. But we must know that these human-like characterizations of God's acts in human terms are for our benefit in character development and refinement and are not an actual description of God's "ways". The Rav sees the same pasuk as a more complex and subtle expression of man's ongoing, conflicting desires. On the one hand man longs to come closer to God and cleave to him. To lose himself in God. But the closer he comes to God, the more he senses God's absolute existence and his own absolute nothingness. So man then recoils and runs from God to regain his sense of self and his sense of importance. But then when man is far from God he longs once again to come close and join with God. And so it goes, back and forth, with no resolution. So what does man do? According to the Rav, "walking in the ways of God" is an attempt to address this dilemma. The Rav states in his essay, "Oov'kashtem MeSham" ("And From There You Shall Seek"):

But complete union is impossible, since man begins by coming closer but ends by recoiling. The man of God therefore makes do with imitation, which is intended to compensate, as I pointed out above, for the failure of his aspiration to join together. Imitating the deeds of his Creator and adopting His attributes constitutes-to repeat the point once again-a tendency born out of love and awe together, out of running to and fro, out of the mysterious dialectic of the divine

revelation of a God who is both honored and awesome. "And now, Israel, what does the Lord your God ask of you, if not to revere the Lord your G… and walk in all His ways and love Him." (Devarim;10:12) Walking in His ways is the central link in the chain of awe and love. Imitation is essentially both a revelational (commanded-RB) and a spontaneous (free-RB) phenomenon, directed at once towards total subordination and the achievement of liberation….The imitation of God contains an intense effect to overcome the tragedy involved in these convulsion of the spirit." ("And From There You Shall Seek: Chapter 10, page 78)

The Rav sees the imitation of the ways of God as a compromise between man maintaining his own life mission, but at the same time retaining a sense of connectedness to the Creator. By making the decision to imitate God, man retains his "I" sense of self and of being important. But at the same time, he gives up himself to God by making his life's path one of imitation of that Being who is truly real and truly exists. Whereas the Rambam in Hilchos Deot, views the imitation of God as a method of refining the human being character traits by following the "ways" in which God's interacts with His creation as expressed in the Torah, the Rav sees something sad and even tragic in the imitation of God. It isn't really what man wants to do. He wants to be completely merged with God. This would satisfy his *ahavas HaShem* (love of God). But to do this, man would have to “lose” himself. This he cannot do or will not do. He could also try to walk away from God. But this he cannot do either. Man’s love is too great. So he “pretends” to merge with God by imitating Him, which allows him retain his own independent self.

RE-EH

Blood & the Preciousness of Life

In the parsha of Re-eh, when Moshe relates the situations when a Jew may slaughter and eat meat, he reconfirms the prohibition against consuming the blood of a slaughtered animal. He states:

23. However, be strong not to eat the blood, for the blood is the soul; and you shall not eat the soul with the flesh.	כג. רַק חֲזַק לְבִלְתִּי אֲכֹל הַדָּם כִּי הַדָּם הוּא הַנָּפֶשׁ וְלֹא תֹאכַל הַנֶּפֶשׁ עִם הַבָּשָׂר:
24. You shall not eat it, you shall spill it on the ground, like water.	כד. לֹא תֹּאכְלֶנּוּ עַל הָאָרֶץ תִּשְׁפְּכֶנּוּ כַּמָּיִם:
25. You shall not eat it, in order that it be good for you, and for your children after you, when you do what is proper in the eyes of the Lord.	כה. לֹא תֹּאכְלֶנּוּ לְמַעַן יִיטַב לְךָ וּלְבָנֶיךָ אַחֲרֶיךָ כִּי תַעֲשֶׂה הַיָּשָׁר בְּעֵינֵי יְהֹוָה:

The Rambam explains this prohibition against consuming blood as one which was necessary to distance the Jewish people from idolatrous practice. He states in the "Guide for the Perplexed":

The Law (the Torah), which is perfect in the eyes of those who know it, and seeks to cure mankind of these lasting diseases, forbade the eating of blood, and emphasized the prohibition exactly in the same terms

as it emphasized idolatry: "I will set my face against that soul that eats blood" (VaYikra, 17:10). The same language is employed in reference to him "who gives his seed to Molech"; "then I will set my face against that man" (VaYikra, 20:5). There is, besides idolatry and eating blood, no other sin in reference to which these words are used. For the eating of the blood leads to a kind of idolatry, to the worship of spirits." (Guide, Book 3: Chapter 46).

The Rambam goes on to explain that the Torah utilized blood for a different purpose: for the purification of what it touches. He states:

Our Law declared the blood as pure, and made it the means of purifying other objects by its touch. "And thou shalt take of the blood… and sprinkle it upon Aaron, and upon his garments, and upon his sons, and upon the garments of his sons with him. And he shall be made holy, and his garments and his sons," etc. (Shemot: 24,21). Furthermore, the blood was sprinkled upon the altar, and in the whole service it was insisted upon pouring it out, and not upon collecting it. "And he shall pour out all the blood at the bottom of the altar. (VaYikra 4,18); And the blood of your sacrifices shall be poured out upon the altar of the Lord your G…" (Devarim: 12:27). Also the blood of those beasts that were killed for common use, and not for sacrifices, must be poured out, "You will pour it upon the earth

as water" (Devarim: 12:24). We are not allowed to gather and have a meal round the blood, "You shall not eat round the blood" (YaYikra 19:26). And the Israelites were inclined to continue their rebellious conduct, to follow the doctrines in which they had been brought up, and which were then general, and to assemble round the blood in order to eat there and to meet the spirits. God forbade the Israelites to eat ordinary meat during their stay in the wilderness; they could only partake of the meat of the peace-offering. The reason of this precept is distinctly stated, regarding that the blood shall be poured out upon the altar and the people do not assemble round about." (Guide: Book 3: Chapter 46).

The Rambam is focusing here on the utility of the mitzvah of refraining from consuming blood as a preventive measure against a form of idolatry that utilized blood as a part of spirit worship. By not consuming it and pouring it out on the ground, the blood would not be collected for gathering around as part of this idolatrous ritual. One could ask how this explanation addresses the statement in the Torah that the blood is the "*nefesh*" or life and therefore, should not be consumed. Is the Rambam's explanation addressing this aspect of the blood as the "life" or is he explaining the prohibition only regarding its usefulness in avoiding idolatrous error?

"The Rav" (Rabbi Joseph B. Soloveitchik) in his essay "The Emergence of Ethical Man", presents, as the concept behind the prohibition of eating the animal's blood, an expression of the fundamental principal of refraining from taking any life, animal or human. The restriction on consuming blood results from a Torah principal that to take any life is unjust and outside of the realm of man's rights as an ethical being. He too, like the Rambam, notes the fact that the unique wording of the warning by G…stating, "I will set my face against that person" is only mentioned twice in the Torah: once for the consuming of blood and a second time for the person who gives their child to Molech. The Rav states:

Obviously, the Torah looks upon blood-eating with so much horror and abomination that it is almost placed on a par with the worship of Molech. What is the reason for such an attitude?...Because the blood is the very essence of life and as such it must be consecrated as a sacrificial offering to God. That is why I enjoined the Israelites from eating blood." The Torah's expression in Leviticus is unique, and truly remarkable: "Whoever…kills an ox, or lamb, or goat… and bring it not to the door of the Tent of Meeting to offer an offering…blood shall be imputed to that man, he has shed blood, and that man shall be cut off from among his people." (VaYikra 17:3-4). The implication is clear; whoever kills an animal for non-sacramental purposes is guilty of bloodshed, of murder; the term

shefkhut damim **applies equally to the slaughter of man and animal. Under a certain aspect, the life of the animal has been placed on an equal plane with that of man. Why?" ("The Rise of Ethical Man" :Chapter 2, page 41).**

There is a lengthy and subtle development in the Rav's essay at this point in the text. I will only be able to state a portion of the conclusions here. The Rav concludes:

Hence, a new concept evolves. ***All*** **life in considered by Judaism as belonging to God. He has absolute ownership rights to all living creatures, to everything that has been redeemed from lifelessness and dead matter, and raised to the plane of life….Each life must be surrendered to God; this is the only way life shall be terminated. Destroying life because of selfish motives is forbidden. This applies to man and animal alike. ..Only after the people entered the Land of Israel did the Torah make concession and begin to tolerate the slaughtering of animals for non-sacral purposes. To this compromise, however many conditions were attached that make the slaughtering of the animal and its consumption the most complicated process. But even as the Torah came to terms with the lusty sensual human being concerning the meat, it retained full possession and dominion over the blood. Blood is life, and as such can never become the object of man's desire or lust- hence the many prohibitions against**

blood consumption. ("The Rise of Ethical Man": Chapter 2: 42-44)

SHOFTIM

God Belongs to Man

It states in the parsha Shoftim that **"The Kohanim and the entire tribe of Levi shall not have a portion or an inheritance with Israel"** (Devarim, 18:1). The Sifrei comments that the tribe of Levi is precluded not only from taking a portion in Eretz Yisrael, but also from accepting the kingship. The phrase "to lengthen the days of his and the days of his sons' kingdom" does not apply to Shevet Levi. In Aaron Ziegler's book, "Halachic Position of Rabbi Joseph B. Soloveitchik, Volume 3", he writes:

Rav Soloveitchik explained the significance of this restriction in the following manner. The Rambam writes (Hilchot Melachim 1:8) that although we prefer to bestow the Malchut (kingship-RB) upon Shevet Yehuda, the appointment of a king by a Navi from any Shevet is valid. The notable exception is Shevet Levi. Levi is never to occupy the Machut. This is because every king required a spiritual guide to serve as his mentor. During the period of the first Bet Hamikdash, each king had a Navi who served in this capacity. Shaul has Shmuel, Dovid had Natan, Chizkiyahu had Yeshayahu, and even Yeravam had Achiah Hashiloni. During the second Bet Hamikdash, Nevauah (prophecy) ceased to exist. The spiritual mentors were then the Kohanim and the Leviim. Consequently,

Shevat Levi could never occupy the Malchut. It was this merger of Malchut and spiritual guidance that eventually led to the downfall of the empire (Source: Rabbi Yosef Adler, Teaneck, NY). (page 168-169).

There is a relevant discussion in the text "Hararey Kedem". In this sefer, Rabbi Michal Sirkin has compiled summaries of Rav Soloveitchik's lectures related to the *moadim* (holidays). In one of these *shiurim* on Hanukah, the Rav discusses the difference of opinion between the Rambam and the Ramban on the Hasmonian Dynasty that ruled Israel after the overthrow of the Selucid Greek Empire of Antiochus. The question is whether in this case, due to the Hasmonyim being Kohanim, they had sinned in becoming the kings. The Ramban holds that they did sin and were worthy of punishment. The Rav, it seems, reads the Rambam as disagreeing with this position. The Rav interprets the Rambam as seeing the case of the Hasmonayim as acceptable due to the factors that : 1) It was a temporary kingdom and 2) it was required since there was a need to re-establish the sanctity of the Beit HaMikdash after this sanctity had been violated by the Greeks and their Jewish collaborators. Since the Kohanim were charged with the protection of the sanctity of the Beit HaMikdash, the Hasmonian Kingship was a temporary, emergency measure needed to assure this sanctity. The Hasmonians, therefore, were not in violation.

The parsha of Shoftim states: **"Righteousness, righteousness you shall pursue (*tzedek, tzedek*) so that you will live and possess (*vayarashta*) the land that the Lord your God has given to you."** (Devarim: 17, 20). The Rav in his first of five lectures given to the Convention of the Mizrachi Religious Zionist Movement during the period of 1962-67 brings an amazing and unexpected idea about the possession of the land of Israel described in this pasuk. He states at the opening of the first of these lectures:

It is impossible to acquire ownership in the land of Israel if one has not at the same time acquired something else of extreme importance. The act of possessing the land of Israel has effect not only on the physical earth, but also on something else. What is it? What is included in the act of acquisition of the land? The Lord of the land! (Nachmanides explains the Biblical phrase "Lord of the land" (Beresheit: 24,3) to mean "The Lord of the land of Israel"). The Rav continues: "Judaism has a unique outlook on the Man-God relationship. Not only does man belong to the Creator of the universe-"The soul is Yours and the body Yours" (Slichot); not only is man God's possession, "the earth is the Lord's and all it contains, the world and those who dwell in it" (Tehillim 24:1); God also belongs to man. He, so to speak, is the possession of man!

The Rav utilizes this insight to explain a perplexing statement in the Talmud. He continues:

This mysterious relationship between God and the creations of His hands, between the Lord of Israel and the community of Israel, comes to expression in an extraordinary statement by the Sages of the Talmud (Berachot 6B): "those phylacteries (tefillin) of the Master of the world, what is written in them? 'and who is like Your people Israel, a unique nation on the earth.' We, in our tefillin, affirm the belonging to God of the children of Israel (Hear O Israel, the Lord our God, the Lord is One), and in the tefillin of the Eternal One, as it were, is expressed the possessory rights we have in Him." "I am my beloved's and my beloved is mine." (Song of Songs: 6:3) How does one acquire rights in God? Which formal possessory act relates to Him who owns all? How does one express acquisition of the Eternal One? The Torah reveals to us the manner: "and you shall seek-when you will search with all your heart and all your soul" (Deveraim 4:29). Through this one process the Jew may acquire "rights" in the Master of all worlds-by seeking and searching with all his heart and all his soul. We all know the exposition of R.Akiva regarding "with all your soul" (Devarim: 6,5): 'even if He takes back your soul" (death). One can acquire God with blood-with affliction, with obstinate self-sacrifice-"despite all this "we are to God and our eyes to God". One possesses

God by bringing sacrifice.' (The Rav Speaks: Five Addresses by Rabbi Joseph B. Soloveitchik, pages 14-17).

The Rav, in many of his writings, describes this concept of whole-hearted, complete devotion. In the essays of "Lonely Man of Faith" and "Halakhic Man" this complete devotion is described from different perspectives. However these writings and many others of the Rav express the idea that a devotion to God and the search for God through study of his Torah, must occupy a unique place in a person's value structure in order for it to be fruitful. It is not enough that this seeking of God is important to the person. It is also not enough that the seeking of God is the primary interest of the person. It is necessary that this seeking of God is the sole motivation of a person's life. Perhaps the expression in the Torah of God as a "jealous God" can be seen as not only relating to idols, but to anything at all that shares the "value space" with God in a person life.

KI TZEITZE

Maimonides and the Love of God

In the parsha of Ki Seitzei there is a directive restricting the Ammonite or Moabite from becoming part of the Jewish people as well as the reasons for this restriction. The pasha states:

4. An Ammonite or Moabite shall not enter the assembly of the Lord; even the tenth generation shall never enter the assembly of the Lord.	**ד.** לֹא יָבֹא עַמּוֹנִי וּמוֹאָבִי בִּקְהַל יְהֹוָה גַּם דּוֹר עֲשִׂירִי לֹא יָבֹא לָהֶם בִּקְהַל יְהֹוָה עַד עוֹלָם:
5. Because they did not greet you with bread and water on the way, when you left Egypt, and because he [the people of Moab] hired Balaam the son of Beor from Pethor in Aram Naharaim against you, to curse you.	**ה.** עַל דְּבַר אֲשֶׁר לֹא קִדְּמוּ אֶתְכֶם בַּלֶּחֶם וּבַמַּיִם בַּדֶּרֶךְ בְּצֵאתְכֶם מִמִּצְרָיִם וַאֲשֶׁר שָׂכַר עָלֶיךָ אֶת בִּלְעָם בֶּן בְּעוֹר מִפְּתוֹר אֲרַם נַהֲרַיִם לְקַלְלֶךָּ:
6. But the Lord, your God, did not want to listen to Balaam. So the Lord, your God, transformed the curse into a blessing for you, because the Lord, your God, loves you.	**ו.** וְלֹא אָבָה יְהֹוָה אֱלֹהֶיךָ לִשְׁמֹעַ אֶל בִּלְעָם וַיַּהֲפֹךְ יְהֹוָה אֱלֹהֶיךָ לְּךָ אֶת הַקְּלָלָה לִבְרָכָה כִּי אֲהֵבְךָ יְהֹוָה אֱלֹהֶיךָ:

7. You shall not ever seek out their welfare or their good, all your days.	ז. לֹא תִדְרֹשׁ שְׁלֹמָם וְטֹבָתָם כָּל יָמֶיךָ לְעוֹלָם:

"The Rav" (Rabbi Joseph B. Soloveitchik), in his essay "And From There You Shall Seek" focuses on the part of these verses where it states "because HaShem your God, loved you..." ("*key ahaavchah Hashem Elokechah*") and strives to dispel the idea that this statement is completely metaphorical. The Rav states:

I would like to call the reader's attention to one thing in order to prevent misunderstanding on the part of those who study our master's (Maimonides') teachings in depth. Love in Aristotelian philosophy is one-way: the world yearns for the Prime Mover, without experiencing reciprocal love. The Prime Mover is aloof from the world and does not long for it. His relationship to the world is that of a teleological and necessary cause, without desire or intention. Since there is no directed providence in Aristotle's view, the love of the Prime Mover for the world is abolished. Moveover, the world's love for the pure form is not an intentional act but an immanent function that sets the cosmic process in motion. The Torah, which bases all of Judaism on the principle of the chosenness of the Jewish people, introduced into the center of our world the concept of loving kindness and of love as a reciprocal process. The creation of the world is the embodiment of God's grace. God's providence over

His creatures in general, and His choice of the congregation of Israel in particular, is a manifestation of infinite love. Anyone who says that Judaism commands the individual to love God but does not promise him reciprocal love is a heretic. How unfortunate it is that many scholars pursued folly and suspected that Maimonides, Heaven forbid, agreed with the teachings of Aristotelian philosophy that the yearnings of the world for God are one way, without any reciprocal yearnings." ("And From There You Shall Seek , pages 153-154)

The Rav anticipates the objection of those who would quote the following Rambam, stating:

Maimonides does indeed say the following in the *Guide of the Perplexed*:

We have already made it clear to you that that intellect which overflowed from Him, may He be exalted, toward us is the bond between us and Him. You have the choice: if you wish to strengthen and fortify this bond, you can do so; If, however, you wish gradually to make it weaker and feebler until you cut it, you can also do that. (Guide of the Perplexed, Book III, Chapter 51)

Although, this statement may imply that God is a "neutral party" in the relationship, the Rav dispels this idea stating:

As a result (of this statement in the Guide of the Perplexed), many scholars claimed that God does not care about maintaining a love relationship between Himself and His creatures. But such an interpretation is wrong, and locating the error does not require deep investigation. The principle of free will makes it necessary for many to have the ability to loosen his ontic link with God. If people can sin, why can't they abolish God's love for them? But there is not even the slightest hint here (in the Rambam's statement) of a lack of divine love." ("And From There You Shall Seek", page 154).

The Rav goes into great depth to examine this concept of love of God but within this brief presentation I will conclude with the Rav's show of evidence that the Rambam agrees that God loves the Jewish People. The Rav states:

Maimonides himself mentions the attribute of love in many places in his code of Jewish Law (Mishneh Torah-)"...because God loves us and is keeping his vow to our Father Abraham' (Laws of Idolatry 1:3); "God Himself loves *gerim* (converts to Judaism), as it is written, '*And He loves the ger*' (Laws of Character Traits 6:4); "Great is repentance, for it brings one near to the Shekhinah... Yesterday he was hated by the Deity, abhorred and distanced from Him, and today he is beloved, desirable and a close friend... Moreover, they (penitents) are eagerly desired" (Laws of

Repentance 7:6-7). Maimonides call the second book of his code "The Book of Love." It is unimaginable that Maimonides, the pillar of Halakhah, was influenced in a fundamental issue like this by Arabic philosophical inquiry, which was somewhat affected by Aristotle's view. ("And From There You Shall Seek", page 155).

This clarification of how closely aligned the Rambam's philosophy is to Aristotle reaches down to the deepest core issues of the Maimonidean thought and is a frequent topic in the Rav's writings.

KI TAVO

The Two Torahs & the Mishneh Torah

There is a distinction between the blessings and curses given in the parsha of Bechukosai and those given in Ki Tavo. Those in Bechukosai were given from God ("from the mouth of Hashem") and relayed through Moshe speaking in the name of God.

If you pursue the study of My laws in order to guard My commandments and observe them....(Bechukosai 26:3). But those given in Ki Tavo are stated directly by Moshe as his own words, **What will happen to you if you do not listen to God, your God to be careful to observe all the laws and statutes I command you this day, then the following curses will come upon you and curse you." (Ki Tavo 28:15).** In the Gemorah Megillah 31b the sages of the Talmud explain that the admonishments of Bechukosai were given *mi pi Hagevurah* (from the mouth of the Almighty) but the admonishments of Ki Tavo were given *mi pi atzmo* (from Moshe himself) *be-ruach Hakodesh*-through Divine inspiration.

Rabbi Saul Weiss, in his book "Insights of Rabbi Joseph B. Soloveitchik: Discourses on Fundamental Theological Issues in Judaism" brings an explanation of this difference that reveals a fundamental change that took place in the transmission of the Torah between these two admonitions. He states:

The Rav explained in the name of his great-grandfather, the Beis HaLevi, that prior to the breaking of the first tablets, *Torah she-ba'al peh* (Oral Law) was not in fact Oral Law; everything was written down. It was intended that there be one *Torah-she-bichsav*, one Written Law. After the breaking of the *luchoth* (the tablets), God ordained that Moshe transmit the "Oral Law" via the *Mesorah* (God to Moshe to Israel). Hence, said the Rav, Moshe's role was changed after he broke the *luchoth.* In Bechukosai, where everything was to be included as part of the corpus of the Written Law, Moshe's role was simply that of a messenger. He was not yet Moshe Rebbeinu, the teacher of Israel. God alone adjured the Israelites "*mi pi Hegevurah* "(in His own words). However, when the second *luchuth* were given, the Oral Law was transmitted exclusively to Moshe who then became "*Rabban shel Yisrael*", the teacher of all Israel. Hence Moshe proclaimed the "blessings and curses" from himself because it was he who now adjured the Israelites to follow the Oral Law as well as the Written Law. Moshe only became Moshe Rabbeinu, the *Adon Haneviim*, the greatest of all prophets, with the transmission of the second *luchoth* (notes of Dr Israel Rivkin and Joshua Rapps, Parshas Bechukosai, May 25,1976). (pages 36-37)

The Rambam, does not, to my knowledge, comment on this transition of Moshe between the receiving of the first *luchos* and the second *luchos*. The Rambam's introduction to the Mishnah describes the precise method by which God gave Moshe the Oral Torah corresponding to the Written Torah. He states:

Know that every commandment which the Holy One Blessed Be He" gave to Moses our Teacher, may he rest in peace, was given with its clarification. First He told him the commandment, then he expounded on its explanation and its content, including all that which is included in the Torah. The manner of its transmission to Israel occurred as stated in the Gemara: Moshe entered into the Tent, and first Aaron entered unto him. Moshe then stated to him a single time the commandment he had received, and taught him its explanation, (following which) Aaron retreated to the right of Moses, our teacher. Thereupon Elazar and Ithamar, Aaron's sons entered and Moses told them what he had told Aaron, and then they stepped back. One sat on the left of Moses, our teacher, and the other on the right of Aaron. Then the seventy elders arrived and Moses taught them, just as he had taught Aaron and his sons. Following this came the masses of the people and everyone seeking God and he (Moses) placed before them that commandment until all had heard it from his mouth. (pages 41-42)

The Rambam continues to explain, in precise detail how Aaron, his son and the elders repeated the Torah, preceding their leaving, and how the people were to write the Torah onto scrolls, writing the precepts of the Torah and learning by heart the oral Torah. The Rambam states here:

Thus our Sages, of Blessed Memory, said in the Braitha (Torath Kohanim): And the Lord spoke to Moses at Mount Sinai" (VaYikra, 25:1) 'Why does the teaching specifically state 'at Mount Sinai'? Was not the entire Torah given at Mount Sinai? But this lesson is to tell us that just as the law of Shmita was stated with all its generalities, specifics and fine details at Mount Sinai. So too all the commandments were stated with all their generalities, specifics and fine details at Mount Sinai. (Maimonides Commentary on the Mishnah, translated by Dr. Fred Rosner. (page 42).

The Rambam does not indicate here, anything about a process of transmission without the Oral Torah as the Rav stated in the name of his grandfather the Beis Levi. What would this "first" Written Torah have resembled? One could only wonder regarding the Rambam's view on this issue. However the historic statement of the Rambam that one only needs the Chumash and his Mishneh Torah, to obtain full knowledge of the *mesora*, may provide some insight about how he might conceive of such a Torah. Maimonides states in his introduction to the Mishneh Torah:

To summarize (the intent of this text is) that a person will not need another text at all with regard to any

Jewish law. Rather, this text will be a compilation of the entire Oral Law, including also the ordinances, customs and decrees that were enacted from the time of Moses, our teacher until the completion of the Talmud, as were explained by the Geonim in the texts they composed after the Talmud. Therefore I have called this text, "Mishneh Torah" ("second to the Torah"), with the intent that a person should first study the Written Law, and then study this text and comprehend the entire Oral Law from it, without having to study any other text between the two. What Maimonides meant precisely by this statement is greatly debated. Was it meant as a prescription for the "average man" with the scholars still having to study the Mishnah and Talmud? Was it meant with regard to knowing how to fulfill the mitzvot, but that Torah scholarship (achieving the "crown of Torah") required additional texts? Certainly Maimonides who speaks often of man's "small, dark, mind" aside God's infinite wisdom did not think that the Mishneh Torah and the Written Torah were completely exhaustive as would be the first Torah that the Rav speaks of as given to Moshe and which he destroyed. One can speculate, but with the awareness that these are areas of great depth and requiring profound knowledge of the *mesora* and the relationship between the Written Torah and the Oral Torah.

NITZAVIM

Isolation, Participation & Israel

The parsha of Nitzavim states (Devarim 30:11-14):

11. For this commandment which I command you this day, is not concealed from you, nor is it far away.	יא. כִּי הַמִּצְוָה הַזֹּאת אֲשֶׁר אָנֹכִי מְצַוְּךָ הַיּוֹם לֹא נִפְלֵאת הִוא מִמְּךָ וְלֹא רְחֹקָה הִוא:
12. It is not in heaven, that you should say, "Who will go up to heaven for us and fetch it for us, to tell [it] to us, so that we can fulfill it?"	יב. לֹא בַשָּׁמַיִם הִוא לֵאמֹר מִי יַעֲלֶה לָּנוּ הַשָּׁמַיְמָה וְיִקָּחֶהָ לָּנוּ וְיַשְׁמִעֵנוּ אֹתָהּ וְנַעֲשֶׂנָּה:
13. Nor is it beyond the sea, that you should say, "Who will cross to the other side of the sea for us and fetch it for us, to tell [it] to us, so that we can fulfill it?"	יג. וְלֹא מֵעֵבֶר לַיָּם הִוא לֵאמֹר מִי יַעֲבָר לָנוּ אֶל עֵבֶר הַיָּם וְיִקָּחֶהָ לָּנוּ וְיַשְׁמִעֵנוּ אֹתָהּ וְנַעֲשֶׂנָּה:
14. Rather,[this] thing is very close to you; it is in your mouth and in your heart, so that you can fulfill it.	יד. כִּי קָרוֹב אֵלֶיךָ הַדָּבָר מְאֹד בְּפִיךָ וּבִלְבָבְךָ לַעֲשֹׂתוֹ:

Rabbi Joseph B. Soloveitchik ("the Rav") stated in his address to the Mizrachi movement:

The second fundamental principal upon which our movement is based is expressed in the fourteenth "*Ani Mamin*"-I believe. What does this "*ani maamin*" say? By straightforward declaration it state: 'I believe with perfect heart that the Torah is given to observed, realized and fully carried out in every place and at all times, within every social, economic and cultural framework; in every technological circumstance and every political condition.' The Torah was given for realization in the simple society and homogeneous economy of the ghetto where Jews "ate manna", as it were, and the environment was saturated with Judaism, the street being an extension of the home; and in the modern, developed society with its scientifically planned technological economy in which the Jew is an integral part of his environment which has no connection with his private domain. The Torah is given for realization in the galuth, where it relates to the private life of the individual, and in the Jewish State where it must embrace new problems and embrace forms of Jewish life. This *"ani maamin"* was formulated by Moses, our teacher during his last days on earth when he parted from the Children of Israel who were about to pass from the nomadic, desert existence into State life in Eretz Yisrael.....this *"ani maamin"'* of "for the world is nigh to you", rejects a further theory, that separation from the world is the only way to observe Torah. In other words, those who uphold this theory of complete isolation admit by their

silence the position of the reformers to the effect that within the modern cultural, historical constellation of the observance of mitzvoth and the study of Torah are almost impossible. In their heart of hearts they also lack the recognition that Torah, as the eternal Torah, was given for practice within all social changes and meanderings to which a dynamic society, that is constantly on the move like a might stream is subject. (The Rav Speaks-Five Addresses Delivered to Conventions of the Mizrachi Religious Zionist Movement 1962-1967)

Maimonides ("The Rambam") in his great philosophical treatise "The Guide for the Perplexed" provides a wonderful insight into the varying assessments people make of how difficult it is to observe the Torah. The Rambam attributes the reason why those who view Torah as a particularly onerous system to their own unrestrained and raw character, while those who are more developed find the Torah to be a pleasant and perfect system of life. He states:

The statutes of the Law do not impose burdens or excesses as are implied in the service of a hermit or pilgrim, and the like; but, on the other hand, they are not so deficient as to lead to gluttony or lewdness, or to prevent, as the religious laws of the heathen nations do, the development of man's moral and intellectual faculties.... "The Law of God is perfect, refreshing the heart" (Ps.xix, 8). There are persons who believe that

the law commands much exertion and great pain, but due consideration will show them to be in error. Later I will show how easy it is for the perfect to obey the Law...But this applies only to the noble ones, while the wicked, violent, and pugnacious persons find it most injurious and hard that there should be any divine authority tending to subdue their passion. To low-minded, wanton and passionate persons, it appears most cruel that there should be an obstacle in the way to satisfy their carnal appetite, or that a punishment should be inflicted for their doings. Similarly, every godless person imagines that it is too hard to abstain from the evil he has chosen in accordance with his inclination. We should not consider the Law, easy or hard according as it appears to any wicked, low-minded and immoral person, but as it appears to the judgment of the most perfect, who according to the law, are fit examples for all mankind.

The Rambam in the Mishneh Torah (Hilchot Deot) writes in detail about the issue of living in a place where "the norms of behavior are evil and the inhabitants do not follow the straight path". He states:

It is natural for a man's character and actions to be influenced by his friends and associates and for him to follow the local norms of behavior. Therefore, he should associate with the righteous and be constantly in the company of the wise, so as to learn from their

deeds. Conversely, he should keep away from the wicked who walk in darkness, so as not to learn from their deeds. (Mishneh Torah, Hilchot Deot: 6:1)

Here the Rambam states clearly that it is normal to be influenced by friends and associates and the choosing of these must be done with care, separating from the "wicked who walk in darkness". The Rambam states that person should move if he finds the neighborhood to be one where these undesirable associates live. He continues in the same halacha:

A person who lives in a place where the norms of behavior are evil and the inhabitants do not follow the straight path should move to a place where the people are righteous and follow the ways of the good.

If there is no such place that the person can go to due to distance or some other impediment, then the person must live in seclusion. The Rambam continues:

If all the places with which he is familiar and of which he hears reports follow improper paths, as in our times, or if he is unable to move to a place where the patterns of behavior are proper, because of [the presence of] bands of raiding troops, or for health reasons, he should remain alone in seclusion as [Eichah 3:28] states: "Let him sit alone and be silent."

In the worst scenario, where the righteous person is not permitted to live in seclusion, but is coerced into some level of participation in the evil ways of the inhabitants, then the person must attempt the drastic step of living outside of society. The Rambam continues:

If they are wicked and sinful and do not allow him to reside there unless he mingle with them and follow their evil behavior, he should go out to caves, thickets, and deserts [rather than] follow the paths of sinners as [Jeremiah 9:1] states: "Who will give me a lodging place for wayfarers, in the desert.

Do the Rav's words, quoted above, show a divergent position from the Rambam? At first reading, it seems to be so, since the Rav is promoting the participation in the affairs of state in the Modern State of Israel which is not a religious community, as such. This was even more the case at the time of the Rav's speech to Mizrachi. But a closer review of the Rav's words show that he is describing a very special case. The situation is not simply whether one should live among the non-believers and non-observant or whether one should cloister oneself among one's religious brethren. The Rav is addressing the issue of forming the Jewish State- The State of Israel. To withdraw in this case and not participate in the affairs of state, along with the "reformers" as he calls them, would be to disparage Torah as a relevant system of governance in modern times. The Rav held that the establishment of the State of Israel was a miraculous occurrence that reflected God's providence. As such, the observant Jew must participate in the formation and shaping of that state so that it will be a kiddush Hashem and provide an opportunity for Torah to grow in Jewish world on an international stage which could have a profound impact on the world and possibly bring about the redemption of mankind. In this situation, where the stakes are so high and the possibilities so lofty, no Jew can retreat into the confines of the *beis medrash* and the kosher home and leave the task to those who are blind to the Torah and without interest in utilizing the State of Israel for the glory of the Creator.

VAYELECH

Hakhel & Torah's Exoteric Nature

Devarim: Chapter 31

10. Then, Moses commanded them, saying, "At the end of [every] seven years, at an appointed time, in the Festival of Succoth, [after] the year of release,

י. וַיְצַו מֹשֶׁה אוֹתָם
לֵאמֹר מִקֵּץ | שֶׁבַע שָׁנִים
בְּמֹעֵד שְׁנַת הַשְּׁמִטָּה בְּחַג
הַסֻּכּוֹת:

11. When all Israel comes to appear before the Lord, your God, in the place He will choose, you shall read this Torah before all Israel, in their ears.

יא. בְּבוֹא כָל יִשְׂרָאֵל
לֵרָאוֹת אֶת פְּנֵי יְהֹוָה
אֱלֹהֶיךָ בַּמָּקוֹם אֲשֶׁר
יִבְחָר תִּקְרָא אֶת הַתּוֹרָה
הַזֹּאת נֶגֶד כָּל יִשְׂרָאֵל
בְּאָזְנֵיהֶם:

12. Assemble the people: the men, the women, and the children, and your stranger in your cities, in order that they hear, and in order that they learn and fear the Lord, your God, and they will observe to do all the words of this Torah.

יב. הַקְהֵל אֶת הָעָם
הָאֲנָשִׁים וְהַנָּשִׁים וְהַטַּף
וְגֵרְךָ אֲשֶׁר בִּשְׁעָרֶיךָ
לְמַעַן יִשְׁמְעוּ וּלְמַעַן
יִלְמְדוּ וְיָרְאוּ אֶת יְהֹוָה
אֱלֹהֵיכֶם וְשָׁמְרוּ לַעֲשׂוֹת
אֶת כָּל דִּבְרֵי הַתּוֹרָה
הַזֹּאת:

13. And their children, who did not know, will hear and learn to fear the Lord, your God, all the days

יג. וּבְנֵיהֶם אֲשֶׁר לֹא
יָדְעוּ יִשְׁמְעוּ וְלָמְדוּ
לְיִרְאָה אֶת יְהֹוָה

that you live on the land, to which you are crossing the Jordan, to possess.	אֱלֹהֵיכֶם כָּל הַיָּמִים אֲשֶׁר אַתֶּם חַיִּים עַל הָאֲדָמָה אֲשֶׁר אַתֶּם עֹבְרִים אֶת הַיַּרְדֵּן שָׁמָּה לְרִשְׁתָּהּ:

Rabbi Soloveitchik ('the Rav") in the text "And From There You Shall Seek" ("ooV'Kashtem Meesham") views the mitzvah of "*hakhel*" (assembling all the people for the public Torah reading by the king) as an expression of what he terms the "exoteric nature" of the Torah system. The Rav, quoting from Rabbi Bahya's great work "Duties of the Heart" explains that there are two levels of the human being's relationship with God. The first level of the relationship is open to all as an intense intuitive desire to serve and approach God which is fulfilled through the performance of the mitzvot. Beyond this there is an analytic, intellectual experience where reason brings one to deeper levels of understanding and a closer connection to the Creator. Rabbi Bahya explains citing the commandment of "*hakhel*" as the expression of this first stage, which is open to all ("exoteric"). Rabbi Bahya states:

It sometimes also happens that a person falls short in some duties and excels in others. The intellectual stimulus varies in different individuals in accordance with their capacity of apprehension. But the urge of the Torah is not subject to variation. Its obligation is the same for the child, the youth, one advanced in

years and the old man, the wise and the foolish...And so Scripture says in regard to the comprehensive character of the instruction of the Torah for all people, "Gather the people together, men and women and children and the stranger that is within your gate, that they may hear and that they may learn and fear the Lord your God" (Devarim: 31:22). Further, it is said, "You shall read this law before all Israel in their hearing (Devarim: 31:11)....the stimulus of the Torah is a preparation for, and introduction to, that of the intellect, the reason being that a man in his youth needs training and guidance...Thus, the instruction of the Torah turns about hope and fear-the poles of its axis. Whoever does not fall short in fulfilling the obligations of this service belongs to the class of the truly pious and is worthy of reward in this world and in the next. But one who rises from this stage to the service of God, induced by reason, reaches the degree of the prophets and the elect of the Supreme – the saints. (Duties of the Heart, Gate of Divine Worship, Chapter 3).

The Rav, commenting on the statements of Rabbi Bahya explains:

The exoteric aspect of the Torah enlightenment, however, refers only to the actual objective action, not the subjective experience. Understanding the actions belongs to the individual.

The Rav expounds on the exoteric nature of the Torah in his essay "Halakhic Man". Here the Rav is focusing on non-elitist aspect of the Torah. One law exists for all Jews regardless or wealth or pedigree and, as opposed to other religions who confined religious scholarship to the priestly class, the "crown of Torah" is open to all. He states:

Halakhic man's religious viewpoint is highly exoteric. His face is turned toward the people. The Torah, whether in terms of study of practice, is the possession of the entire Jewish community. Everyone, from the judges and leaders of the people to the hewers of wood and drawers of water, is obliged to live in accordance with the Torah. "Ye are standing this day, all of you before the Lord your God: your leaders, you tribes, your elders and your officers…from the hewer of thy wood unto the drawer of thy water" (Deut. 29:9-10). The ideal of eternal life is not the private domain of a small spiritual elite or some particularly gifted individuals, but is the public domain of all Israel. 'With three crowns was Israel crowned-with the crown of the Torah, with the crown of the priesthood, and with the crown of royalty. Aaron acquired the crown of priesthood… David acquired the crown of royalty. The crown of the Torah, however, is ready and available for all Israel, for it is written: 'Moses commanded us a law, an inheritance of the congregation of Jacob." (Devarim 33:4)- Whoever desires it may come and take it…. The thrust of

Halakhah is democratic from beginning to end. The Halakhah declares that any religion that confines itself to some remove corner of society, to an elite sect or faction, will give rise to destructive consequences that far outweigh and putative gains. (Halakhic Man, pgs. 42-43).

Maimonides explains the mitzvah of "*hakhel*" is the Mishneh Torah (Hilchos Hagigah:1:1:

It is a positive commandment to gather together the entire Jewish people - men, women, and children - after every Sabbatical year when they ascend for the pilgrimage holiday and to read so that they hear passages from the Torah that encourage them to perform mitzvot and strengthen them in the true faith, as Deuteronomy 31:10-12 states: "At the end of a seven-year period, at the time of the Sabbatical year on the Sukkot holiday when all Israel come to appear... gather the nation, the men, the women, the children, and your stranger in your gates...."

Maimonides states his position on the purpose of this mitzvah here as " encourage them to perform mitzvot and strengthen them in the true faith." This is well-aligned with the stated of Rabbi Bahya, cited by the Rav earlier where the "*hakhel*" is explained as:

"Gather the people together, men and women and children and the stranger that is within your gate, that

they may hear and that they may learn and fear the Lord your God" (Devarim: 31:22). Further, it is said, "You shall read this law before all Israel in their hearing (Devarim: 31:11)…. the stimulus of the Torah is a preparation for, and introduction to, that of the intellect, the reason being that a man in his youth needs training and guidance…Thus, the instruction of the Torah turns about hope and fear-the poles of its axis.

For Maimonides and Rabbi Bahya this assemblage is to create encourage and reinforce the adherence to the Torah in performance of mitzvot as a first stage of development, which some we move beyond to the stage that Rabbi Bahya describes:

But one who rises from this (initial) stage to the service of God, induced by reason, reaches the degree of the prophets and the elect of the Supreme – the saints.

HA-AZENU

Hester Panim- God Hides His Face

In the parsha of Haazinu, Moshe is warning the Jewish people of the horrors that will befall them if they do not keep the Torah. He states:

They would slaughter to demons without power, gods whom they knew not, newcomers recently arrived, whom your ancestors did not dread. HaShem will see and be provoked by the anger of His sons and daughters, and he will say, 'I shall hide My face (*Ahsteerah panaiy mayhem*) and see what their end will be. " (Devarim 32:17-20)

Rabbi Joseph B Soloveitchik ("the Rav") explains the great severity of the punishments that result from "*hester panim*" (God's hiding of his face) as opposed to *middat hadin* (Divine judgment). "Hester panim", he explains was the form of punishment that allowed for the Holocaust. *Hester Panim* is the punishment of God's removal of his protection from the Jewish people. When this occurs, there is no limit to the level of punishment as it is completely in the hands of the enemies of Israel. Even here, though, God will not permit the punishment to annihilate the Jewish people completely or to create a situation where fulfillment of the covenant God has with the Jewish people is abrogated. *Middat hadin*, on the other hand is a divine judgment in which God demands punishment for sin, but carries it out in such a way to facilitate teshuvah, limiting its level of severity. The Rav explains:

There are two levels of Divine punishment, *Middat Hadin* and *Hester Panim.* The former involves measure for measure punishment, commensurate with one's sins. It does not signify God's withdrawal; on the contrary, it reflects His involvement and concern, intended to stimulate *teshuvah* (repentance). *Middat Hadin,* therefore, never inflicts annihilation or total extermination, *kelayah. Hester Panim,* however, is a temporary suspension of God's active surveillance. He turns His back, so to speak, on events and leaves matters to chance. Under such circumstances, the usual vulnerability of the Jew invites the threat of total extermination. This is strikingly conveyed by the words *vehyahale-ekhol,* "they shall be devoured." What ensues is not circumscribed by consideration of measure for measure, and the magnitude and severity can be devastating. Without God's governing control, events may simply go beserk....The *Asarah Haruge Malkhut (*10 martyrs*)* were victims of *Middat Hadin,* not *Hester Panim.* It was a measured *onesh* (punishment)*,* but it indicated God's involvement, *gezarah hi milefanai.* It is related in the *Eleh Ezharah* piyyut of the Yom Kippur Musaph service that, when the angels protested against the torturing to death of the Sages, a heavenly voice replied: 'If I hear further

protest, I will force the world to revert to water. I will reduce the world to *tohu vavohu' (*chaos and disorder*)* God threatened the *tohu vavohu* of *Hester Panim* if the *Middat Hadin* of controlled retribution were not accepted. The Holocaust was *Hester Panim.* We cannot explain the Holocaust but we can, at least, classify it theologically, characterize it, even if we have no answer to the question "why?" The unbounded horrors represented the *tohu vavohu* anarchy of the pre-*yitzirah* state. This is how the world appears when God's moderating surveillance is suspended. The State of Israel, however, reflects God's return to active providence, the termination of *Hester Panim.*" ("Reflections on the Rav"-Abraham Besdin- pages 36-37)

Rabbi Soloveitchik holds that the horrific destruction and torment of the Holocaust was not a punishment planned or structured by God, but instead the result of Hitler and the Nazis operating without God's providential oversight. Amalek has no compassion, but only a sadistic desire to annihilate the Jewish in the most cruel manner possible. When the Jews reach the level of sin where *Hester Panim* occurs, this is when punishment can turn to horror.

Maimonides ("The Rambam") in his philosophical treatise "The Guide for the Perplexed" explains his perspective on God's providence and how the withdrawal of individual protection is related to each person's level of knowledge of and focus on God. He states:

An excellent idea presents itself here to me, which may serve to remove many doubts, and may help to solve many difficult problems in metaphysics. We have already stated in the chapters which treat Divine Providence, that Providence watches over every rational being according to the amount of intellect which that being possesses. Those who are perfect in their perception of God, whose mind is never separated from Him, enjoy always the influence of Providence. But those who, perfect in their knowledge of God, turn their mind sometimes away from God, enjoy the presence of Divine Providence only when they meditate on God; when their thoughts are engaged in other matters, divine Providence departs from them. The absence of Providence is this case is not like its absence in the case of those who do not reflect on God at all it is in this case less intense, because when a person perfect in his knowledge is busy with worldly matters, he has not knowledge in actuality, but only knowledge in potentiality (though ready to be actual).... Hence it appears to me that only in times of such neglect that some of the ordinary evils befall a prophet or a perfect and pious man; and the intensity of the evil is proportional to the duration of those moments, or to the character of the things that thus occupy their mind. ... If a man frees his thoughts

from worldly matters, obtains a knowledge of God in the right way, and rejoices in that knowledge, it is impossible that any kind of evil should befall him while he is with God. When he does not meditate on God, when he is separated from God, then God is also separated from him; then he is exposed to any evil that might befall him; for it is only that intellectual link with God that secures the presence of Providence and protection from evil accidents. Hence it may occur that the perfect man is at times not happy, whilst no evil befall those who are imperfect; in these cases what happens to them is due to chance. This principle I find expressed in the Law: "And I will hide my face from them; so that they will say in that day, 'Are not these evils come upon us, because our God is not among us?' (Devarim:31:17) It is clear that we ourselves are the cause of this hiding of the face, and that the screen that separates us from God is of our own creation. This is the meaning of the words: "And I will surely hide my face in that day, for all the evils which they have wrought' (Devarim: 31:18). There is undoubtedly no difference in this regard between one single person and a whole community. It is now clearly established that the cause of our being exposed to chance, and abandoned to destruction like cattle, is to be found in our separation from God" (Guide for the Perplexed, Book III, Chapter 51)

Maimonides sees individual and communal providence as a function of a person's level of *yedia* (knowledge of God) and the person's state of involvement in reflecting on this knowledge. If one's understanding is distorted or if one is , at a particular moment, uninvolved with the experiencing of the knowledge, then the person loses the protection of God, to varying degrees and is under providence as part of the group (Bnei Yisrael) but not as an individual. As quoted in the "Guide for the Perplexed" above:

If a man frees his thoughts from worldly matters, obtains a knowledge of God in the right way, and rejoices in that knowledge, it is impossible that any kind of evil should befall him while he is with God.

V'ZOS HABRACHAH

The Death of Moshe Rebbenu zt'l

In this, the last parsha of the Torah, V'Zos HaBerachah, Moshe dies. The Torah states:

And Moses, the servant of the Lord, died there, in the land of Moab, by the mouth of the Lord.	ה. וַיָּמָת שָׁם מֹשֶׁה עֶבֶד יְהֹוָה בְּאֶרֶץ מוֹאָב עַל פִּי יְהֹוָה:
6. And He buried him in the valley, in the land of Moab, opposite Beth Pe'or. And no person knows the place of his burial, unto this day.	ו. וַיִּקְבֹּר אֹתוֹ בַגַּי בְּאֶרֶץ מוֹאָב מוּל בֵּית פְּעוֹר וְלֹא יָדַע אִישׁ אֶת קְבֻרָתוֹ עַד הַיּוֹם הַזֶּה:
7. Moses was one hundred and twenty years old when he died. His eye had not dimmed, nor had he lost his [natural] freshness.	ז. וּמֹשֶׁה בֶּן מֵאָה וְעֶשְׂרִים שָׁנָה בְּמֹתוֹ לֹא כָהֲתָה עֵינוֹ וְלֹא נָס לֵחֹה:

The Rambam in "The Guide for the Perplexed" explains that as a person ages and the body weakens he or she becomes more accessible to knowledge. The Rambam states:

The philosophers have already explained how the bodily forces of man in his youth prevent the development of moral principles. In a greater measure, this is the case as regards the purity of thought which man attains through the perfection of those ideas that lead him to an intense love of God. Man can by no means attain this so long as his bodily humours are hot. The more the forces of his body are

weakened, and the fire of passion quenched, in the same measure does man's intellect increase in strength and light; his knowledge becomes purer, and he is happy with his knowledge. When the perfect man is stricken in age and is near death, his knowledge mightily increases, his joy in that knowledge grows greater, and his love for the object of his knowledge more intense, and it is in this great delight that the soul separates from the body.

The Rambam explains that 3 individuals, Moshe, Aaron and Miriam experienced this "perfect death". The Rambam continues here:

To this state our Sages referred, when in reference to the death of Moses, Aaron, and Miriam, they said that death was in these three cases nothing but a kiss. They say thus: We learn from the words, "And Moses the servant of the Lord died there in the land of Moab by the mouth of the Lord". (Devarim, 34:5), that his death was a kiss. The same expression is used of Aaron: "Aaron the priest went up into Mount Hor.... by the mouth of the Lord, and died there" (BaMidbar 33:38). Our sages said that the same was the case with Miriam; but the phrase "by the mouth of the Lord" is not employed, because it was not considered appropriate to use these words in the description of her death as she was a woman. The meaning of this saying is that these three died in the midst of the pleasure derived from the knowledge of God and their great love for Him. When our Sages figuratively call the knowledge of God united with intense love for Him, a kiss, they follow the well-known poetical

diction, "Let him kiss me with the kisses of his mouth (Song of Songs 1:2). This kind of death, which in truth is deliverance from death, has been ascribed by our sages to none but to Moses, Aaron and Miriam. The other prophets are pious men are beneath that degree; but their knowledge of G... is strengthened when death approaches. The intellect of these men remains then constantly in the same condition, since the obstacle is removed that at times has intervened between the intellect and the object of its action; it continues for ever in that great delight, which is not like bodily pleasure. We have explained this in our work, and others have explained it before us. (Book 3: Chapter 51 – Page 390-391 in Friedlander translation)

It seems that the type of knowledge that Moshe, Aaron, Miriam and the prophets possessed did not diminish because it did not reside in the body. The body, which it seems, when vigorous, disturbs the clarity of this type of knowledge. An image that might be helpful would be that of a person gazing into a still pool of water to see the reflection compared to one staring into a pool that of water with some ripples. The reflection in the water would be knowledge. The still water would be the old person with diminished passionate energy and the rippling pool would be the younger person whose passions distort the image.

What is interesting is that the pasuk in this parsha states that Moshe's "eyes were not dim nor his natural force diminished". This seems, on the surface to require an explanation in light of the Rambam's explanation, especially if we equate "natural force" with the youthful strength that the Rambam has explained to be an impediment to the clarity that comes with the perfect death.

Rabbi Soloveitchik in his essay "And From There You Shall Seek" comments on the "kiss" being an example of the sudden, unexpected salvation of God which occurs not in man's times of glory and victory but when he is broken and defeated. He states:

God reveals Himself through suffering and tragedy, when the individual or the community are in trouble and distress. Moses pleads with God, but his prayer is not accepted (Deut.3:23-28). His destined fate turns into a fate without destiny. He sees the chosen land, but he cannot go there. The divine attribute of justice indicts him and seals the gates of heaven before him. Precisely out of the pain and the torment, out of the affliction and suffering the kiss of God suddenly appears, detaching Moses from this world and bringing him to a world full of goodness and light." (page 34).

This seems to be a quite divergent reading of the state of Moshe's mind at the moment of his death when compared with the view of the Rambam. According to the Rambam "the kiss" seems to be an almost natural process of increased insight due to the falling away of the body's strength and distorting effect on the soul. This falling way occurs as one approaches the moment of death. To the Rav, the "divine kiss": seems to be more an act of divine mercy bestowed at a moment when one in a state of loss and despair.

About the Author

Rabbi Richard Borah received smicha in 1991 from Rabbi Yisrael Chait, Rosh Yeshiva of Yeshiva Bnei Torah, located in Far Rockaway, New York. He has taught Torah and science subjects at various education institutions in the New York area. Rabbi Borah recently published "Yad on the Yad: 14 Essays on Maimonides Laws of Repentance" and "Understanding the Lonely Man of Faith", a guide to Rabbi Joseph B. Soloveitchik's essay. Rabbi Borah lives in Hewlett, New York with his wife Andrea and their children.

To receive weekly articles, purchase copies of books or for other inquires please send an email request to Rabbi Borah at: rambamrav@gmail.com.